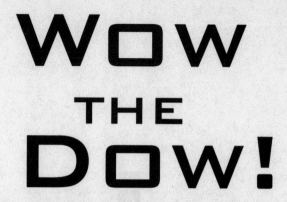

# Wow
## THE
# Dow!

## The Complete Guide to Teaching Your Kids How to Invest in the Stock Market

## Pat Smith and Lynn Roney
### A LARK PRODUCTION

**A FIRESIDE BOOK**
PUBLISHED BY SIMON & SCHUSTER
NEW YORK TORONTO LONDON SYDNEY SINGAPORE

FIRESIDE
Rockefeller Center
1230 Avenue of the Americas
New York, NY 10020

FIRESIDE and colophon are registered trademarks
of Simon & Schuster, Inc.

Designed by Elina Nudelman

Manufactured in the United States of America

1   3   5   7   9   10   8   6   4   2

Library of Congress Cataloging-in-Publication Data
Smith, Pat, date
Wow the Dow! : the complete guide to teaching your kids how to
invest in the stock market / Pat Smith and Lynn Roney.
p.   cm.
1. Stocks—United States.   2. Dow Jones Industrial Average.
3. Investments—United States.   I. Roney, Lynn, date
HG4910.W69  2000
332.63'22—dc21                                    00-041273

ISBN 0-684-87149-1

for Danielle and Shannon

# ACKNOWLEDGMENTS

This book is the book I wanted to read twenty years ago, but it wasn't available then, and it could not have been done now without the help of some very special people. I am especially thankful for the encouragement I received from my husband, Russ Smith; but more than being a supportive spouse, he also taught me everything I know about "numbers," and he taught me that numbers can tell a story as well as words. I am forever grateful for his lessons.

This book could not have been done without the early support of my broker and friend, Greg Bain, who taught me how to execute a stock trade and never made a mistake on my stock trades; his perfection allowed me to excel.

I am eternally grateful to our editors at Simon & Schuster for being the visionaries who believed in this book and knew how to tell the story to the world. I also thank Janet Bodnar at *Kiplinger's* magazine for spotlighting our efforts and telling others about kid investors through her articles.

Thanks must go to the original visionary at the National Association of Investors Corporation (NAIC), Kenneth Janke, who was the first to recognize the increasing importance of investing in a kid's world. He sponsored our first article in *Better Investing,* which was instrumental to the entire kids' investing movement. However, he was following in the footsteps of our earliest mentor, Salvadore Waller, from the Maryland NAIC Council, whose constant banter that "we were doing something special" was inspirational and will never be forgotten.

Our corporate sponsor, Gary Van Dyke, is one of the most special people I have ever known because he believed in what we were doing enough to put his money into our efforts, and my appreciation to him is enormous.

There are many people who encouraged me along the way, but none as much as my very good friend Ellen Findley, who never tired of talking about stocks with me; our friendship is forever. Another favorite stock phone buddy was my friend and fellow investor Jean Croner; my thanks. And, of course, there is my coauthor, Lynn Roney, who took me on a great adventure and continues to expose me to new ideas that expand my mind; she has demonstrated through her actions every day her love for investing and for her granddaughter, Danielle; what a powerful combination!

I also want to thank my mother, Mary Sanders, who was always too busy "living for today" to worry about investing. We are a true study in contrasts, yet she always encouraged me to "do my thing."

Last but not least, three special people at Lark Productions deserve special mention: Lisa DiMona, Karen Watts, and Robin Dellabough. Of these three, the one special person who made this possible above all is Robin. She is such a gifted writer and editor that she would have edited our publicity photos if we had let her! She provided the "glue" for this book and made it happen, and without her guidance, talent, and intellect, all this would not have been possible. I am especially proud of her for taking the plunge into stock picking while working with us. Many happy returns!

—*Pat Smith*

This work is a guidebook, and it is most appropriate to acknowledge all the people who have helped to guide us through this process. It is fitting to start with our agent, Lark Productions, particularly Robin Dellabough, for this book could not have been written without her.

I want to thank my coauthor, Pat Smith, who worked diligently to the end.

I want to thank my husband, Wallace, for his support and encouragement.

Most of all I want to thank my granddaughter, Danielle, for being the "test variable" in my personal experiment: Can kids learn finances at an early age? She is living testimony that children can grow up to be financially responsible.

Finally, I want to thank Simon & Schuster for publishing this book, which has cutting-edge educational information that kids and their parents can use into the next millennium.

*—Lynn Roney*

From Lark Productions: Special thanks to Joel Berry, Lisa DiMona, Melinda Marshall, Pamela Saenger, Caitlin Stern, Karen Watts, and Alice Wolfram, all of whom invested priceless time and effort in this project.

# CONTENTS

# INTRODUCTION

Imagine a world in which kids hang posters in their rooms of the New York Stock Exchange instead of rock stars. They collect trading cards of Bill Gates and Warren Buffett instead of sports figures. They watch the financial news instead of cop shows and play an online stock market game instead of shoot-'em-up video games.

Then imagine families all over the country sitting down at the kitchen table once a week to work on their stock portfolios together—parents and kids of all ages sharing a fun, educational experience that is valuable in more ways than one.

Lastly, imagine that through this investing venture with your kids, you expose them to current events and reinforce ideas from history, math, and social studies. Children will address social issues when investing in companies that operate abroad and studying how companies operate at home.

The idea of children investing and understanding what they are doing is beyond many people's wildest imaginations, but we're here to tell you that it is possible. We know because we've seen it happen with our own children.

We first met at an ice-skating rink outside Bethesda, Maryland, in early 1994—an event that would change our futures and that of our girls, Shannon Yoder and Danielle Flythe. That spring, nine-year-old Shannon and eight-year-old Danielle were training with the same skating coach every Tuesday afternoon. Lynn, Danielle's grandmother, passed the time sitting on a bench outside the rink, reading from a stack of newspapers and *Fortune* and *Money* magazines. Pat had noticed Lynn on several occasions: It was rather unusual to see a woman poring over the stock section of *The Wall Street Journal* with the after-school crowd. But since Pat was interested in finance herself, one afternoon she simply went over to Lynn and blurted, "Do you invest? I've recently purchased stock for my daughter, and I really want to learn more about the market."

Investing in the stock market was immediately a common ground for us. Most women we knew weren't too interested in the market; each of us had been investing for years. We were also largely self-taught, although we both had an undergraduate degree in general business and administration.

Our personal circumstances had given us a similar drive and focus. Lynn was caring for her granddaughter because her daughter had divorced and moved back in with her. As a single, divorced mom, Pat had raised Shannon for three years before she remarried when Shannon was four. We both felt strongly that we wanted to give our girls the tools to manage money long before they had money to manage. We wanted to get them on the road to financial independence before they even knew what it meant to feel dependent. With every financial lesson we learned while investing our own money, we encouraged our girls to learn and profit with us. To our surprise and delight, Shannon and Danielle needed little encouragement. Within a year of our first meeting, these two grade-schoolers knew more about investing than we knew when we were thirty.

In 1996, inspired by the girls' progress and enthusiasm, we decided to form an investment club. We wanted to expand our circle of four to include other parents who felt as we did—that nine-through eleven-year-olds were more than ready to learn about investing. We wanted to include other kids because our own kids thought sharing what they knew and tracking stocks as a group would be more fun. So, almost exactly two years after that serendipitous day at the ice-skating rink, Stock MarKids™ Investment Club was born. There were originally nine members, ranging in age from nine to eleven, plus their parents. We met once a month, and since the members showed such enthusiasm for McDonald's, we monitored that stock first. We also held our first couple of meetings there—firsthand product research!

It was a great educational experience, mostly because the learning was in the doing. We showed the kids how to read stock quotes, track highs and lows, and chart the stock's behavior. Because stock prices were quoted in fractions, they had to practice their math skills, converting fractions into decimals and share prices into dollar value. They learned that it paid to stay tuned to the news because right after we started tracking McDonald's, mad cow disease broke out in Britain and fears of an epidemic drove stock prices down almost daily. From reading the papers for news affecting McDonald's, the kids also learned about foreign cultures. They also learned that the cow is sacred in India because when the company opened a franchise there, mutton burgers were served instead of beef.

Going to club meetings was something our girls looked forward to. "Getting ready for a meeting makes me feel businesslike," Danielle told Lynn one afternoon. Danielle served as the club's first vice president; Shannon was the club secretary and then the treasurer. Age didn't get in the way of empowerment: From the beginning all the kids enjoyed having a full voice in the proceedings and being full partners in the club. The club was such a hit that it gained a corporate sponsor who allowed us the use of his corporate offices and funded a trip to the New York Stock Exchange.

Meanwhile, in addition to building the club portfolio, Shannon and Danielle were building their own portfolios at home—and not just on paper. Money they received as gifts, money they earned from lemonade stands and film projects, and money they obtained by cashing in some savings bonds all went into stock purchases. In other words, they invested on a shoestring: Shannon purchased her first share of McDonald's for $59.84. How much the girls invested and how much money they made didn't matter; what mattered was how much they *learned*.

Our goal was to help them acquire an investing habit while they were young enough to form one for life. We also wanted them to learn the tools they'd need to invest profitably later, when making money *would* matter. We let them learn by doing rather than doing it for them—by allowing them to make decisions that were sometimes less than optimal in terms of making money. We encouraged them to see investment opportunity in every penny they picked up, in every roll of quarters they cashed at the bank, in every envelope of birthday money they were given, in every dollar they earned.

The financial advice we hammered home was very simple: Research companies thoroughly, buy and hold for the long term, don't try to time the market, and keep investing. By following that strategy, Shannon and Danielle have seen their initial one share of stock grow into diversified portfolios capable of financing their college educations or their first business venture or their first down payment on a condominium or house. Today, at fifteen, Shannon controls a $25,000 investment portfolio. Danielle, now fourteen, controls one valued at more than $18,000. And *controls* is the operative word: They do the research, pick the companies, tell us when to place a trade, and track their stocks daily, both through the business sections of local newspapers and by logging on to the internet, specifically Yahoo's finance section. Of course they've received some input from us. They also expand their knowledge of companies through Stock MarKids. But they're in charge, and what that responsibility has given them at such a young age—in terms of global awareness, financial savvy, math skills, discipline, and long-range vision—is worth far more than the dollar amount in their portfolios.

## Benefits (We Call It Earning Extra Interest)

Investing *in* your children by learning to invest *with* them yields so many terrific dividends. It:

✓ strengthens the parent-child bond through sheer time spent together on investing and offers fascinating topics for parent-child conversations beyond "How was school today?"

✓ teaches delayed gratification because kids have to wait for a return on their investments.

✓ empowers children by teaching them how to handle money for lifelong financial confidence.

✓ demystifies the market for both parents and children.

✓ builds self-confidence in children as they gain experience and learn to trust their own research into the stock market.

✓ enables children to accept failure or learn through mistakes (when a stock goes down).

✓ broadens their perspective and helps them look beyond themselves by learning about the global economy.

✓ sharpens math skills when practicing multiplication and dealing with fractions while monitoring stocks.

✓ offers extracurricular exposure to history, social studies, and current events; children address social issues when investing in companies that operate abroad and studying how companies operate at home.

✓ creates opportunities to learn about different professions and career possibilities by expanding a child's exposure to different types of work and services.

When you start teaching children about money and investing from an early age, you ensure financial security for the future generation, but you also enjoy all these benefits along the way. The payback is tremendous. Pat says, "My greatest pleasure is reflect-

ing back on Shannon's progress from financial infancy to blossom-
ing into a confident investor. It has been quite an amazing trans-
formation."

Lynn feels that Danielle has a much stronger, clearer sense of
herself and what's important to her than a lot of her peers who are
worrying only about boys and beauty. "She's going through a
metamorphosis like a butterfly in a cocoon," Lynn says. "I've seen
her grow intellectually and academically through this knowledge
of the stock market and about companies that operate globally. It
has broadened her whole horizon. There's a tremendous difference between her and typical kids. She's fourteen, but she inter-
acts at about a sixteen- or seventeen-year-old level."

Lynn adds that when people call her house, they often say, "I
don't know who that lady was who answered the phone." Lynn answers, "That's no lady. That's my granddaughter."

## How You and Your Child Can Profit
## from Our Experience

Our experience with our girls, not to mention the Stock MarKids,
has convinced us that children are never too young to start grasp-
ing the fundamentals of money management. We've written this
book to pass on that experience. Step by step, we show you the
process by which we taught our girls and helped teach the Stock
MarKids. Throughout the book we use examples drawn from our
experiences teaching Shannon and Danielle and from guiding the
investment club they helped us start.

Whatever the age of your child or whatever the level of your investing experience, investing is about ownership. Even toddlers
understand the concept of "mine!" In fact, it's the idea of owning
something they like that sparks their interest in investing. Rest
assured, you won't turn your child into a little money-grubber by
feeding that interest. Through investing you're going to teach
him more about responsibility, discipline, delayed gratification,
and even ethics than you ever thought possible!

We believe very strongly that for children to learn to act responsibly they must be given responsibility—not too much at first, but more and more as they prove themselves capable. The earlier in childhood they're given some control, the more control they'll demonstrate when they're young adults.

Danielle and Shannon are living proof. We didn't wait until they were teenagers to give them lessons in money management. Lynn gave Danielle part ownership of McDonald's when Danielle was just three years old. Pat encouraged Shannon to sort savings bonds when she was a toddler, and bought her a share of Disney when she was nine. Now that Danielle and Shannon are old enough to start thinking like teenagers—about clothes and cars and travel—you'd think the size of their portfolios would be a big temptation. Not so. When a friend of ours asked them if they wanted to cash out and buy themselves a car or go to Europe, they both said, "No way!" It has taken them years to build up to this sum—years during which they postponed gratification on any number of things, from a blouse to a pair of Doc Martens shoes. These girls absolutely know the value of their dollar because it has been *theirs* for some time. "Buying a fancy new car is totally nuts," Danielle said, "because it loses its value the minute you drive it off the lot." Shannon added, "I know a lot of the things I want might go down in value, but the stocks I pick keep going up, keep splitting, and going up more. If I sold my stock now for $10,000 and found out ten years later that I could have had $100,000, I'd be devastated."

Can you believe these are two teenage girls talking?

We're very proud of them. We're also a little jealous. *Where would we be today,* we ask each other constantly, *if our parents or grandparents had taught us about investing when we were kids?* Our families never gave us this vital preparation for adulthood; they didn't know themselves how to invest, how to get the highest yield, how to compare companies—that is, how the market worked. We had to get this information on our own, mostly later in life when it wasn't anywhere near as much fun as it is for our girls. That process was so painful for Pat, in fact, that she wants to spare others the ordeal.

"Here I was, forty years old, and I couldn't read some of the most popular economics books, such as Peter Lynch's *Beating the Street,* even though they looked very interesting," Pat remembers. "I'd read magazines and cry because I didn't understand what they were saying. I had been in the market for almost twenty years but still didn't know what I was doing or how to get the maximum return on my investments. Age forty was the turning point. I said, 'This is *it.* I'm really going to learn this stuff!' I realized that when I retired, the money wouldn't just appear; I'd have to make it happen. I did learn how, but I'd hate to see anyone else go through what I did."

So we're committed to giving our daughter and granddaughter what we didn't have: all the time in the world. We're helping them learn now so they don't feel rushed or panicked or inadequately prepared when they most need to feel competent. Kids who are taught the fundamentals of investing have time on their side in every respect. They have time to research companies and track stocks; they have time to experiment, to gain critical firsthand experience and judgment; and they have time to sit tight and let their money grow and grow and grow.

Let's say your parents bought 100 shares of McDonald's stock for you. It would have cost $2,500 in 1965, the year the company went public. What would it be worth today?

At today's price, approximately $42 a share, the original 100 shares that grew into 74,358 shares would be worth $3,123,036. Now that's what we call a Big Mac!

We urge you to get your own child started on this learning curve while she's young enough to proceed very gradually, at her own pace, driven by her own level of interest and mastery. No matter what education you've had yourself, no matter where you are on your own investment learning curve, you can give her the tools

## McDonald's Growth Chart

| YEAR | ACTIVITY | NUMBER OF SHARES |
|------|----------|------------------|
| 1965 | Purchase | 100 |
| 1966 | 3-for-2 split | 150 |
| 1967 | 2% stock dividend | 153 |
| 1968 | 2-for-1 split | 306 |
| 1969 | 2-for-1 split | 612 |
| 1971 | 3-for-2 split | 918 |
| 1972 | 2-for-1 split | 1,836 |
| 1982 | 3-for-2 split | 2,754 |
| 1984 | 3-for-2 split | 4,131 |
| 1986 | 3-for-2 split | 6,196.5 |
| 1987 | 3-for-2 split | 9,294.75 |
| 1989 | 2-for-1 split | 18,589.5 |
| 1994 | 2-for-1 split | 37,179 |
| 1999 | 2-for-1 split | 74,358 |

she'll need to invest responsibly and profitably. And it's not going to take huge amounts of time or any special materials. You can integrate investment education into just about everything you do with your child, whether it's shopping for school clothes or deciding where to eat, driving in the car or going to a ball game, watching kids at the mall or watching TV on vacation. Just as you taught your five-year-old how to count and know his colors, you can teach him about the Dow by treating it like a treasure hunt, a game of fun and challenge. The opportunities are endless once you know how to do it; that's what this book will show you.

We include ideas in every chapter while relating how we captured our girls' interest in an unpressured, gradual, and very sociable way until they were the ones initiating the topic. At the end of each chapter we offer a range of activities and games for different age levels; these will improve your child's skills as she plays along. In the appendix you'll find additional activities that are just

for fun. Scattered throughout the text are tidbits such as good answers to stock questions, profiles of young investors, and fascinating facts. CEO "trading cards" introduce the important people
behind the companies to future investors of America. We also provide some blank cards for you and your child to research and fill
out with information on your favorite companies' CEOs.

In other words, you'll become savvy about the market in the
process of teaching your kids to be. And it's going to be fun for you
both!

We've discovered there's no substitute for the easygoing learning that can occur at home, one-on-one, day by day. This kind of
learning can continue as kids grow and are able to grasp more and
more complex concepts related to investing. Instead of being a
one-shot deal that they may outgrow, the stock market offers
years of ongoing parent-child connections.

"I chose to empower Shannon with the ability to control her
own portfolio," Pat explains, "and that means the buy and sell decisions—every last one of them, and every single share of stock! By
talking to her about stocks and companies and products and future scenarios, I am helping her think about the world at large
and about the future. Some of her decisions have been better than
mine, which is a humbling experience. It seems that Wall Street is
a two-way street!"

We hope *Wow the Dow!* will help motivate you to invest time—in
each other. The real rate of return for you and your children is immeasurable.

# 1

## Raising Your Child's Interest Rate

When Danielle was a toddler, she loved to go to McDonald's to eat because French fries were her favorite food. Lynn liked McDonald's, too. Eating there together was a weekly outing. She was also a longtime shareholder.

One Friday afternoon Lynn told Danielle, "I'm glad you like McDonald's so much because I'm a part owner of this restaurant."

"You *are*, Nana?" Danielle's eyes widened. "I want to become a part owner, too!"

So, in October 1988, Lynn purchased her granddaughter's first share of McDonald's stock.

"I purchased the stock just as a fun thing for her," Lynn says. "She owned only 1.1984 shares, and all we had to show for it was a statement with the McDonald's logo. But it didn't matter. Danielle was so happy and proud. When we took one of her friends along to eat with us, she would say, 'Nana, tell Kandyce that I am a part owner of McDonald's!' "

Ownership bestows more than pride. It gives people a reason to care, a reason to take on responsibility. Watch how a child behaves toward a beloved stuffed animal or a bike of her very own.

Lynn realized she didn't need to explain abstract concepts such as share price, dividends, interest, or even what a stock is. All she needed to do was tap into Danielle's powerful desire to own. If she owned even a piece of a company whose product made her happy, then she'd be more likely to take an interest in what happened to her piece—her *share*.

Sure enough, long before she ever understood what a share meant or what it was actually worth, Danielle delighted in having a stake to protect. She wanted to keep track of it. She had watched her grandmother read the newspaper, so before she could even pronounce *business section,* Danielle was asking to see it at the breakfast table. "I need the business sezhion to check my stock," she'd say. Lynn showed her where to look in the newspaper—what section, which exchange, which abbreviation—and pointed out the number to focus on. "I told her that what she wanted to check was the price of her stock share," Lynn recalls. "She didn't understand what a stock price was, but she understood that the higher the number, the happier she should be, so she'd shout, 'Nana, it's 39! Yesterday it was only 37, and today it's 39!' "

As Danielle's interest grew and her loyalty to McDonald's remained, Lynn added additional sums to her account by selling Danielle's U.S. savings bonds. "I wanted to reinforce her learning," Lynn explains, "and I knew that by the time she became an adult, this investment would grow and compound nicely for her, whereas the savings bonds might not even keep pace with inflation."

Not only were savings bonds not saving Danielle money, but they weren't teaching her anything. They didn't involve her. They were too abstract and forgettable. In contrast, *investing* money— giving Danielle ownership of a company whose franchises she could see everywhere and whose product she could experience firsthand and enjoy—was engaging her curiosity. From that initial spark of interest, Lynn knew her young granddaughter would pick up practical skills, and by the time the investment was really worth something, she'd be able to manage it competently.

Eight months after Lynn purchased the additional shares in

Danielle's name, McDonald's announced a stock split. What had been 3.053 shares (including dividends reinvested twice before the split) became 6.106 shares—twice as many. Wow! But even more thrilling was Danielle's response.

"Danielle's excitement grew just from knowing she had twice as much McDonald's stock," says Lynn. "She may not have understood that the dollar value of her holdings remained the same, but in time I knew she'd grasp it. And we had so much time—Danielle was only four!"

Is toddlerhood the perfect time to introduce your child to the world of investing? It was for Danielle, who was three when Lynn used the visit to McDonald's to broaden her granddaughter's financial education.

## Piggy Banks and Lemonade Stands

We started our girls' financial education the way most parents do: We urged them to put their allowance in a piggy bank instead of their pocket. We even encouraged them to pick up pennies off the sidewalk. We helped them open a passbook savings account. We felt that teaching them to save their money was teaching them to manage it responsibly. Saving was such a simple, straightforward concept, after all. It's what our own parents did all their lives, and it's what they taught us to do as children.

Pat remembers how her dad used to give her his loose change at the end of the day. In a few weeks she had enough to roll into paper sleeves. "I always loved doing this," says Pat, "so I taught Shannon how to count money and put it into the stacks before putting it into roller sleeves. We did this at the kitchen table or on a blanket in front of the television." Pat would take the rolls to the bank, with Shannon in tow, and give her the cash. With this incentive, Shannon was rolling money on her own in no time. She spent some and saved some. Even now, years later, coin rolling is Shannon's favorite source of "free" money!

Lynn also used an idea from her youth: She got Danielle to open up a lemonade stand. Every summer until she was about nine,

## Kid Cents

*Children can get money for their
stock purchases in the following ways:*

*Gifts:* Many grandparents are happy to give money to their grand-
children for birthdays and holidays when they know the kids are investing it.

*Chores:* Household chores may be part of the family routine already,
but parents can usually find extra chores that are worth additional
compensation to use for stock money.

*Allowance:* Many families give their children an allowance on a regular basis, thinking it is a good way to introduce money management
skills. It is also a source of money for stocks.

*Neighborhood services:* Baby-sitting, snow shoveling, lawn mowing,
and pet walking are the classic services that a youngster can offer other
families in the neighborhood for pay.

*Part-time jobs:* Older children who want financial independence can
find part-time jobs in their community, and these are a good source of
funds for investing.

Danielle accompanied Lynn to the bank to take out money from
her account to buy supplies and set up shop. After two weeks of
working the stand, she had more than enough to pay herself and
her assistant, and replenish her savings account. "Pay yourself
first, I always told her," says Lynn. "Then put aside something for
later."

Both of us wanted our kids to have some sense of money beyond
what they saw come out of an ATM machine. We wanted Shannon
and Danielle to know the value of a dollar and to get in the habit
of putting money aside.

Our approach was very hands-on from the beginning because
we knew our kids would understand only what they could touch,
see, or play with. Pat let Shannon play with the savings bonds she

had purchased for her since birth. They were stashed in a kitchen drawer—"not the safest place," Pat admits—and every once in a while Pat would get them out and have Shannon sort them into piles according to face value or maturity date. Shannon started playing this game before she could even count or read but quickly mastered it because it taught her a little of both. "It got so she started telling *me* how she wanted them sorted," notes Pat, "and I had to follow her directions to the letter."

Our kids learned best whenever they weren't made aware they were being taught. If they were having fun, if they were in our company, and if we didn't lecture or push, they proved themselves good learners. Lynn got Danielle reading at the age of three. Shannon could count and identify coin values before she was in school.

It wasn't long before we realized that our girls were ready to learn a whole lot more about money management than how to put money into a piggy bank or savings account. Saving was simple but not active or engaging enough to keep their attention, whereas investing wasn't all that complicated when you got right down to it. What child doesn't leap at an opportunity to own something? Presented that way, investing was something our girls could get excited about. And if they were excited, they'd ultimately learn everything they needed to know to invest competently, responsibly, and profitably. Teaching them wouldn't be a chore; it would be an adventure.

## Let the Games Begin

If you're thinking, "I'll wait until my child shows an interest," before you embark on this trip, you could miss the boat entirely. Many forty-year-olds we know have no interest because no one ever introduced it in a creative way. Investing has never been considered the best material for kids' education; it is seldom taught in grade school, high school, or even college. Although there has recently been a push for schools to start teaching kids about the stock market, everyone agrees that children learn best from their parents.

That's where you come in. You don't hesitate to expose your child to music you love or books you enjoy; you do that by listening to your favorite songs or by reading aloud from your favorite book. Your child will want to know more about things that she sees you care about.

Shannon, for example, "had no more interest in the stock market than a rock," according to her mom. But that didn't stop Pat from sharing her own growing interest in investing. "The stock market was simply something I enjoyed," Pat reflects. "So, starting in second grade, when Shannon was seven, I very casually began to show her the stock page and talk to her about it. Every time I read the page, I'd read out loud. 'Oh, I think I'll check my stocks today,' I'd say on Saturday morning while she ate breakfast at the kitchen table. 'Let me check Washington Gas.' I would look at Washington Gas and then point it out to her in the paper. 'Here's the closing price. Here's the name of the company,' I'd say. I did it repetitively, with maybe four stocks. Each time I'd say, 'Here's the one I'm looking at. I'm going to look at what the closing price is.' I'd read the closing price out loud. I didn't try to explain and didn't intend for her to remember. I'd just verbalize whatever was running through my mind."

About a year later Shannon starting asking Pat to give her the newspaper first. "Tell me the stocks you want to look at," Shannon would say, and she'd highlight them for Pat in pink. Then she'd hand the paper back, and Pat would continue babbling out loud whatever she read or thought as she scanned the stock pages.

By nine, Shannon was reading the paper before handing it to her mom. Any headline with "Disney" in it caught her attention because she loved *The Little Mermaid* and couldn't get enough of Disney movies and products. She wouldn't give up the paper until she'd given her mom the information Pat was seeking. "Tell me the stocks you want to know about," she'd say to Pat, "and I will tell you the closing price." When *The Washington Post* ran its year-end summary of stocks, Shannon went through it first, highlighting in pink all the stocks her mom owned and in yellow all the stocks she thought her mom *should* own, based on how much more the stocks had increased in value during the prior year than the ones Pat actually owned.

Shannon's interest was clearly sparked, so as Lynn had done with Danielle, Pat leaped at the opportunity by buying her a share of her favorite company—Disney. And as Lynn had come to realize that savings bonds weren't giving her granddaughter much in the way of returns or education, so, too, did Pat come to see that Shannon's savings account at the bank was a poor lesson in money management.

"We looked at her account, which had been giving her three percent interest," Pat explains. "And Shannon, who's in fifth grade, said to me, 'Boy, we can do much better in stocks!' She understood that the savings account wasn't earning her much and felt much more comfortable with stocks. I'm probably one of the few parents who encouraged her child to *close* a savings account!"

Pat's experience with Shannon, as well as our experience with the Stock MarKids, makes us think that nine- through eleven-year-olds make excellent students of investing. They're old enough to have formed strong opinions about what they like and don't like, but they're not old enough to want to spend all their money on clothes and CDs. They can read. They're learning the relevant math skills, such as converting fractions to decimals. They can draw graphs and assemble information that helps them keep up on their investment. And they're able to compare values and choose the best one.

You'll be able to gauge when your child is ready to take the plunge, just as you probably knew when she was ready to step off the diving board into deep water. There are countless opportunities every day, no matter the age of your child, for you to shift your strategy from "it's important to save" to "it's time to invest."

## Profile of a Young Investor

*Chris Stallman, a fifteen-year-old from Illinois, publishes his own monthly newsletter to teach young adults about investing.*

### What got you started or interested in investing?

When I was fourteen, I had some money in an interest-bearing savings account, but I wanted to see if I could increase that money by the time I went to college. So I started going on the Internet to learn about investing, and my parents helped me get started.

### How did you decide what type of account to open?

I was limited to opening UTMA [Uniform Transfer to Minors] custodial accounts. I learned a little information about them and then decided to open one up with my mom in the Stein Roe Young Investor Fund and then a discount or online broker account with my dad.

### What was your parents' involvement in establishing the accounts and guiding your investment decisions?

Both of my parents had to fill out the forms and applications for me to invest. My father always makes sure my investments are wise before I actually make them. When I find a stock that I like, I ask him for his opinion, and if he agrees with me, I make the purchase.

### Where did you get the money to invest?

My first investment in the Stein Roe Young Investor Fund came from money that I had saved over a few years in my savings account. The money that I use to invest via my online broker came from my life insurance policy, which was being used to save for college. Occasionally my father also puts some extra money in for me to work with.

### What stocks or mutual funds did you invest in?

I started with Merck, Walgreen Co., Dell Computer, and the Stein Roe Young Investor Fund, but my portfolio has since changed. I currently own shares in Merck, Walgreen Co., Qwest Communications, Disney, America Online, and the Stein Roe Young Investor Fund.

**What was it like when you first started checking your portfolio?**

When I first started, it was at the tail end of the 1997 market correction, so I was a little nervous to see my stocks decline. But I kept telling myself that I was in it for the long term.

**What is it like now?**

I always get a thrill when I see that my stocks are up. It gives me a great feeling of succeeding.

**What are your favorite companies, and why?**

My favorite companies are large-capitalization companies that I see each day and that I can relate to. However, I like looking into smaller companies to try to discover which one will be the next Microsoft.

**What were your expectations about investing?**

My expectations were to increase my portfolio slowly until the time I attended college. They were met and exceeded. I had no idea that investing would become one of my passions, and I had no idea that I would start writing about what I know in order to help others.

**Are you a risky or a conservative investor?**

I am in between. I'm more of a moderate investor. I hold volatile stocks from time to time, but there's no need for me to risk my entire portfolio.

**What has been the most challenging thing about investing?**

The most challenging thing is deciding when to sell a stock. Although I have sold only two stocks in the last year, it is sometimes hard to get rid of a good company. Sometimes a great company becomes overvalued, and although you still like the company, you have to persuade yourself to sell it.

**Have you changed as a result of your experience in investing?**

I feel that since I started investing, I'm more willing to volunteer time to help people. Every day I receive e-mails from others who are just getting started and have questions, and because I remember what it was like to get started, I immediately begin answering them. Helping someone else is a great feeling.

(continued on next page)

**Would you teach your kids about investing, or would you leave it up to them or their school?**

I would definitely teach them about investing, and I would get them started early. Many times when you leave it up to a child to learn on his own, he doesn't want to think about it until he is an adult. And getting started early is the secret to becoming financially independent.

**Would you consider a career in the market?**

Yes, I'm very interested in a career in this field. I've been thinking about becoming a financial analyst or a portfolio manager.

**What advice would you give other young investors?**

I'd say not to be discouraged by some obstacles in getting started and to invest for the long term. Don't get caught up in the hype of Internet stocks and day trading because most Internet stocks won't be around in thirty years, and 95 percent of all day traders lose money.

Don't delay because you think your child doesn't yet have the interest. Your interest will become hers.

## Testing the Waters

Okay, so exactly how do you bring up investing in an interest-bearing fashion?

Our field-tested strategy, as we've mentioned, was to zero in on a child's favorite things. Start paying attention, as Lynn did with Danielle, to what your kid is crazy about in the way of products and services, whether it's French fries or lawn mower engines, Tonka trucks or Spice Girl dolls, Discovery Zone or Gymboree, Gap or Levi's. What are her favorite toys? Favorite foods? Favorite places? Favorite activities? Favorite tools or clothes or services?

We bet that she's reciting her favorite things every day, whether you're in the car on the way to soccer practice, sitting on a park bench picking gum off the bottom of her sneaker, eating popcorn in front of the television, or walking around a mall looking for jeans. Kids provide a running commentary; you just need to tune in. Maybe at afternoon snacktime your second grader mentions how much he likes Cheez-Its. Maybe while driving on a long trip your twelve-year-old insists there are more Volkswagen Beetles on the road than Honda Civics. Maybe while you're working together on a tree house your fifth grader chatters about his hammer. Count on it: Your child cares about a surprising variety of goods and services.

Show that you care about this favorite thing, too. You have your reasons, but you're interested in hearing his. You want to know why he likes it so much. Ask a question or two. Listen to his response. Don't accept a "because it's cool" answer; press him for details. Ask him if it's cool because everyone else has it. That may be all it takes to get the conversation going.

Let's say your child has cut her knee and insists on the tattoo plastic strip rather than the plain old bandage. "Just what is it about these tattoo bandages that makes them better?" you can ask. Your questions can help you gauge how strongly your child feels. A heartfelt defense of tattoo bandages, for instance, could be the opening you need to feeling out her interest in ownership. You could say, "Well, if you like these bandages so much, maybe you'd like to own part of the company that makes them."

If she fails to take the bait, say nothing more. You're in no rush. You're waiting for curiosity to compel her to ask what you mean by part ownership, and in time you'll get it. Try the same game on another day with another favorite thing. Try Lynn's approach if you're a shareholder yourself. See if that prompts an I-wanna-be-too response. ("I think Schwinn makes great bikes, too," you could say. "That's why I'm a part owner of that company. Would you like to be a part owner also?")

Let's say your child has been eating the same breakfast cereal for weeks. "Mmm, this is pretty tasty stuff," you could say while trying some. Now start her thinking with a series of questions, being patient to get her answer to each: Do you think lots of people would like it? Do you think lots of people know about it? Do you think the company that makes it will make a lot of money? Then, finally: Did you know you can own a part of that company and share in its profits?

Just as kids provide a running commentary, our experience has taught us that you can integrate investment education into everyday activities, such as:

**EATING OUT.** Talk about the restaurant. It may be operated by a publicly owned company, and kids especially enjoy the hamburgers and French fries from fast-food restaurants such as McDonald's and Wendy's.

**GOING TO THE MOVIES.** Disney makes many family-oriented movies that both children and parents enjoy, so families can have a lot of fun searching for different commercial products, such as the clothing and figurines. Remember, Disney makes money from more than just the movie itself!

**SHOPPING FOR CLOTHING.** Talk about the most popular name brands that your kids and their friends are wearing and who manufactures the product, such as Gymboree for toddler clothing and Tommy Hilfiger for young teen products.

**SHOPPING FOR GROCERIES.** Many grocery stores are publicly owned nowadays, such as Giant Food in the Washington, D.C., area. In addition, the manufacturers of many products are companies that trade shares of stock, including the Campbell Soup Co.

**WHENEVER YOU TURN ON LIGHTS IN YOUR HOME.** Talk about your utility company. Most electricity suppliers and other utility companies are traded on the New York Stock Exchange, and many utility companies are regionally based, such as the Philadelphia Electric Co. in Pennsylvania.

**WHILE ATTENDING AN ATHLETIC OUTING.** Notice the corporate sponsors' logos displayed throughout sports arenas across the country. The current trend is for athletic clothing manufacturers to pay players to wear clothing with their logos. Notice how many major corporations are paying to have facilities bear their names, such as the 3COM Stadium in California, which used to be called Candlestick Park.

**IF YOU PURCHASE A CAR.** The American automobile makers Ford and General Motors are public companies that have been around for a long time, but Volvo, the Swedish firm, is also a public company whose stock trades here in the United States.

**WHILE ON VACATION.** If you stay in a hotel, find out who owns it. Don't be surprised if it is owned by a large public corporation such as Host Marriott Corporation, which owns 125 brand-name hotels throughout the United States and Canada.

**BEFORE YOU TAKE A SIP.** Do you like Coke or Pepsi? Both are made by major corporations that trade on the New York Stock Exchange.

You get the idea. The list is endless once you start thinking about the major corporations behind the products and services you use every day. This is the first step to becoming a savvy investor, and it is fun for you and your kids. If you keep things unpressured, eventually you will get a "What did you mean when you said I could own the company?" response.

From your child's list of favorite things, the two of you can decide on one that your child is willing to support with her own money. Never mind if her own money actually comes from you as an allowance or gift, or from Grandma for Christmas, or from coins you allowed her to roll and then cash for herself. The important thing is that she feels it's her choice of company.

# WARREN EDWARD BUFFETT

Chief Executive Officer, Berkshire Hathaway, Inc.

**COMPANY:** Berkshire Hathaway, Inc., operates companies such as GEICO, a leading auto insurer; Borsheim's, a jewelry company; and Berkshire Hathaway Life Insurance Company of Nebraska.

**$$$:** $31 billion net worth (as of October 1999)

**BIRTH DATE AND LOCATION:** August 30, 1930, in Omaha, Nebraska

**EDUCATION:** B.S. from the University of Nebraska; master's degree from Columbia University

**HOME:** Omaha, Nebraska

**TIDBIT:** Buffett is one of the richest and most famous investors in the United States, and his company has the highest-priced stock on the New York Stock Exchange. He has coauthored books about his investing theories and successes.

**FIRST JOB:** Began with his father's brokerage firm, Buffett-Falk & Company

**QUOTE:** "I will keep working until about five years after I die, and I've given the directors a Ouija so they can keep in touch."

It's not important for you to think that her choice of companies is a potential moneymaker. What happens to the stock you buy for your child in terms of value is almost irrelevant. It's a teaching tool. Even if the cash value increase is less than stellar, it will have been a good buy.

Chances are, however, that your child's investments *will* be moneymakers because kids are very good stock pickers. They know what's hot without even trying. Beanie Babies or Barbie dolls, Pepsi or Coke, Tommy Hilfiger or Nike, grade-schoolers can choose the winner every time. Elementary school students can pick growing companies because they are intensely loyal to the products they use regularly. Teenagers recognize trends just by looking at what their friends are doing or wearing, long before *The Wall Street Journal* reports that snowboarding or Skechers shoes are hot. Peter Lynch calls this kind of investment method "the common knowledge theory"; it's just a way of applying everyday observations to the stock market.

From what we've seen, kids have enough common knowledge to rival a skycraper full of stock market gurus.

## THE PRODUCT CONNECTION

Draw a line from the product to the publicly traded company that produces the product.

**Publicly Traded Products**                    **Company Name**

1. *The Little Mermaid* movie                   Ford Motor Co.

2. French fries                                 Campbell Soup Co.

3. Cars and trucks                              Disney

4. Teen clothing                                PepsiCo

5. Pepsi soft drink                             McDonald's

6. Vegetable soup                               Tommy Hilfiger

7. Baseball hats                                Host Marriott Corporation

8. Electricity                                  Gymboree

9. Toddler clothing                             Philadelphia Electric Co.

10. Hotels                                      Adidas

## Answer key:

10. Host Marriott Corporation
9. Gymboree
8. Philadelphia Electric Co.
7. Adidas
6. Campbell Soup Co.

5. PepsiCo
4. Tommy Hilfiger
3. Ford Motor Co.
2. McDonald's
1. Disney

## PLAYING FAVORITES: PARENT-CHILD GAMES

✓ How do we form our opinions about "favorites"? What factors make us feel a service or product is a good one? Help your child become discerning. Visit a favorite food franchise and have your child evaluate the service, the food, and the overall facility. If the place has cards or pamphlets for customers to fill out with comments or complaints, have your child file his report.

✓ Have your child write a list of her favorite things—what she wears, what she plays with, what she likes to eat, where she likes to visit. If she is very young, list them for her and have her provide illustrations. Let her creativity and interest determine how far you take this project. You may wind up with a very useful encyclopedia of stocks worth looking into!

✓ Who makes what? Point out to your child that Barbie is not the name of the company; Mattel is. Have her take you around the house and identify her toys by their manufacturer.

✓ Who is the parent company? It can be a mystery, but a fun one to solve. Make it a game by giving your child some age-appropriate clues. A beginning reader may be delighted just to be shown the fine print on the side of the box: With an older child, give him the town and state, and see if he can get a telephone number. Or hand him the phone and the Customer Satisfaction number, and have him practice his phone and courtesy techniques.

✓ Public or private? Go around your house and list products that you think are made by publicly owned companies. Have your child try to verify your findings (see page 51). Or both of you make lists and verify each other's items; the person who has the most correct wins.

✓ Show your child the stock section of the paper and point out that companies are listed alphabetically under each exchange. It is not important at this point to explain what an exchange is. See if she can find her company listing. (The game doesn't end if she can't. Either the company is privately held or she needs to figure out what parent company or conglomerate owns it.)

## 2

## Jumping In

"**A** boy at school asked me where he could go to buy stock," Danielle told Lynn one afternoon. "He wanted to know what market sells them—Kmart or the supermarket?"

Many adults would find investing a lot easier if they could march into their favorite food chain and pick up a couple of shares of Microsoft along with a gallon of milk—or, better yet, walk into a Kmart or Wal-Mart to buy those companies' shares in bulk and enjoy a volume discount!

Buying stock in a company is a little more complicated than that. There is a stock market, but it isn't one place like a grocery store. Shares of stock, or pieces of part ownership, are bought and sold on exchanges. There are three major exchanges, all located in New York's financial district, known as Wall Street: the New York Stock Exchange (abbreviated NYSE), the National Association of Securities Dealers Automatic Quotations (NASDAQ), and the American Stock Exchange (AMEX), which is now owned by the National Association of Securities Dealers. You can visit them, but you can't go in and just buy stocks. Because millions of people participate in a market where hundreds of thousands of shares trade hands every day, you have to rely on a middleman called a stockbroker to get a stock purchased or sold for you. To get your deal done, stockbrokers, in turn, rely on traders, the people who work on the floor of the exchange.

The fact that you can't just buy or sell without involving a third party (who will charge for his services) is what keeps many beginners, both young and old, from becoming active investors. There is also the fact that children under eighteen aren't allowed to buy stock; adults must purchase it for them through a custodial arrangement. Some parents are reluctant to buy stock in a child's name because it becomes "theirs" when they reach the age of majority. They fear that the kids will just blow the money, but this has not been our experience. Still other parents hesitate buying their children that first share because finding a broker and setting up a custodial account seems too complicated.

But it doesn't have to be. You can buy that first share of stock in your child's name with minimal hassle and minimal expense right now. At some point you might want to spend a little more time researching brokerage houses and finding a broker you like. (In Chapter 5 we give you all the information you need to choose what's right for you, whether it's a full-service broker, a discount broker, or an online brokerage site, in addition to ideas for other shortcut buying methods.) But until you know more about the market and until your child gets a chance to test the waters himself, it doesn't make sense to get bogged down in the *process* of buying stock. The important thing is to get your child into the market.

One of the quickest and cheapest ways to put a child on the fast track so that you can buy those first few shares right away and without a lot of hassle is through the National Association of Investors Corporation (NAIC). It has been around since 1951 and is essentially an umbrella service organization for investment clubs, but it also offers membership benefits to individuals. Chief among those benefits is access to their stock purchase programs that charge minimal transaction fees and allow members to invest very

# MICHAEL D. EISNER

Chief Executive Officer, Walt Disney Co.

**COMPANY:** Walt Disney Co. is best known for its TV and movie production and theme parks. It also owns the Mighty Ducks hockey team of Anaheim, California, and the Anaheim Angels.

**$$$:** $680 million net worth (as of October 1999)

**BIRTH DATE AND LOCATION:** March 7, 1942, Mount Kisco, New York. He grew up on Park Avenue in New York City.

**EDUCATION:** B.A. from Denison University, Granville, Ohio, 1964

**HOME:** Los Angeles, California

**TIDBIT:** As a child, Eisner's parents allowed him to watch only an hour of television a day.

**FIRST JOB:** Federal Communications Commission logging clerk at NBC-TV

**QUOTE:** "Succeeding is not really a life experience that does much good. Failing is a much more sobering and enlightening experience."

small amounts in high-quality stocks, including many of the companies that a young person wants to buy. That makes these programs perfect for beginners and for investors with very little capital to commit. In other words, NAIC is perfect for getting kids into the market.

When Pat went to purchase Shannon's first share of Disney, for example, she called a discount brokerage firm that she had used for her own stock purchases. "I was surprised to learn that they would charge me the same commission for one share of Disney as for 100 shares because there was a minimum commission of $49. The stock itself was going to cost only $42.25! I finally convinced a broker at another firm to sell me one share of Disney for the bargain commission of $6.58, which was still more than 15 percent but looked like a bargain at the time. I could not afford to pay a steep commission on future shares, but I was willing to pay it this one time."

But then Pat met Lynn and learned about NAIC. When she went to buy Shannon a share of McDonald's, she followed Lynn's suggestion. "I thought it was only for clubby types," Pat recalls, "and I didn't have time for that. But after Lynn explained how she purchased a few shares of McDonald's for her granddaughter without paying a lot in fees, I joined immediately."

Pat sent NAIC a check for $75, of which $70 went toward the purchase of McDonald's stock and $5 went toward the one-time setup fee. (Note: NAIC has subsequently increased this fee to $7.) At $59.84 per share on the day the purchase was made, Shannon's $70 bought her 1.1697 shares, registered in her name, with her mom listed as custodian. NAIC acted as broker, confirming the transaction and its registration in Shannon's name. NAIC also set up Pat's custodial account with the First Chicago Trust Company of New York, the company handling McDonald's investment. In a letter to Pat, NAIC explained how and when she would receive a dividend and statement from First Chicago, and how she could contact them to make future investments for a small fee.

## Price of a Stock

*The price of a stock is determined by two factors:*

1. Buyer's price—the amount of money a purchaser (or a person who wants to be an investor) is willing to pay for the stock
2. Seller's price—the amount the current owner of the stock (an investor) wants to receive for his shares in the company

When the two factors come together, that determines the price of the stock. (Note: In the world of classical economics, this is known as the point at which the supply [seller] and demand [buyer] curves intersect.)

Example: If I want to purchase America Online at 85 but the stock is currently selling at 95, then it is highly unlikely that I will be able to buy the stock because the "price" that sellers want to receive for the stock is higher than I am willing to pay. On the other hand, if I decide that I want to buy America Online at 95 and my broker tells me that it is currently being offered for sale at 95, then there is a high likelihood I will buy the stock at 95. This is because I, the buyer and wanna-be investor, am willing to pay the price that the sellers and current investors want to receive for their shares.

Buyers and sellers think about many considerations when they set a price for shares of a company.

These are some of the things a seller might consider:

✓ How much he paid for the stock when originally purchased
✓ What the future potential is for this stock
✓ Whether he can make more money from other investments

These are some of the things a buyer might consider:

✓ How much money she has to invest at the present time
✓ What she knows about the company's earnings and future possibilities
✓ How the stock has performed in the past in terms of increasing price
✓ Whether or not the stock pays dividends (some buyers want dividends, but others do not)

"It couldn't have been easier," says Pat. "I liked having all that assistance in filling out purchase order forms, setting up an account, and taking care of the registration in Shannon's name."

## The NAIC Stock Service

Through NAIC's Stock Service Program Pat discovered that with as little as $10 a month (plus fees) investors can begin purchasing shares of stock in over 240 companies. This is a relatively new service for NAIC. It is a vast improvement over what was available just five years ago and represents a trend toward making more companies accessible to more people. Pat says that it's a good thing it wasn't available when she first started buying stocks for Shannon because she probably would have bought at least 20 different companies in her zeal to introduce Shannon to the investing world!

The program includes such kid-friendly companies as:

Campbell Soup Co.
Caterpillar Inc.
Coca-Cola Co.
Deere & Co.
Harley-Davidson, Inc.
Hershey Foods Corporation
H. J. Heinz Co.
Johnson & Johnson
Kellogg Co.
Mattel, Inc.
McDonald's
Nike, Inc.
Pep Boys—Manny, Moe, and Jack
PepsiCo, Inc.
Sara Lee Corporation
Starbucks Corporation
Toys "R" Us, Inc.
Wal-Mart Stores, Inc.
Walt Disney Co.
Wm. Wrigley Jr. Co.

Lynn has used the NAIC stock service for two years for her own personal investing and likes it so much that she is opening a new account for Danielle in custodian form. Danielle received $200 for her fourteenth birthday and wanted to buy Netegrity stock with the money. Danielle says the company's product, e-commerce software, is hot and that she must have it while the company is young and growing just like her.

Netegrity is not one of the 240 stocks offered in the program, but the service will purchase out-of-program stock for an extra $25, which is what we did. The NAIC stock service also allows investors to transfer stock certificates into their NAIC stock account once it is established. To apply for the stock service, call (888) 780-8400. You may join NAIC at the same time. An NAIC account can be registered in the following categories:

✓  individual

✓  IRA

✓  joint tenants

✓  investment club

✓  custodial account (Uniform Gifts to Minors Act/Uniform Transfer to Minors Act)

✓  partnership

✓  corporate account

Of all the ways to give money or stocks to a child under the age of eighteen, the best is to set up a custodial account. Every state has its own form of registration for minors under either the Uniform Transfer to Minors Act (UTMA) or Uniform Gifts to Minors Act (UGMA).

Stocks may be registered in a child's name using the child's Social Security number. As custodian you can manage or spend the money as you see fit until your child comes of age (reaches the age of majority). Whenever you buy stock for a child or establish an account with a broker for a child, you simply write the words "Cus-

## UNIFORM GIFTS TO MINORS ACT AND
## UNIFORM TRANSFER TO MINORS ACT

Every state has its own form of registration for minors. The Uniform Gifts to Minors Act registration is recognized in the following states:

| | | |
|---|---|---|
| Arkansas | Mississippi | Tennessee |
| Connecticut | Nebraska | Texas |
| Delaware | New York | Utah |
| Georgia | Pennsylvania | Vermont |
| Michigan | South Carolina | Washington |

The Uniform Transfer to Minors Act is recognized in the following states:

| | | |
|---|---|---|
| Alabama | Kansas | New Mexico |
| Alaska | Kentucky | North Carolina |
| Arizona | Louisiana | North Dakota |
| California | Maine | Ohio |
| Colorado | Maryland | Oklahoma |
| District of Columbia | Massachusetts | Oregon |
| Florida | Minnesota | Rhode Island |
| Hawaii | Missouri | South Dakota |
| Idaho | Montana | Virginia |
| Illinois | Nevada | West Virginia |
| Indiana | New Hampshire | Wisconsin |
| Iowa | New Jersey | Wyoming |

todian for" after your name and enter the child's name. This allows you to authorize all transactions and sign proxies, but your child should be involved in all decisions because, after all, that's why you're investing together.

When you call the stock service administrators, you'll also be asked to choose from three types of membership: Silver, Gold, and Platinum; these are based on your anticipated level of usage. If you plan to buy and sell a nominal number of shares, then the Silver plan should be fine; if you think you'll be trading pretty actively, the Platinum plan may be more economical. Annual service

## ----------------------------------------
## AGE OF MAJORITY
## ----------------------------------------

A parent may act as custodian for a child's stocks until the child reaches the age of majority, making all the decisions regarding stock purchases and sales. The stocks automatically belong to the child once the age of majority is reached (which depends on the state of residence). To make the changeover official on the accounts, however, the child has to write a letter to the broker informing her of the change and including a copy of his birth certificate.

Once the child reaches the age of majority, the stocks are transferred into the child's name directly, and the child assumes responsibility for all buy and sell decisions. The age of majority varies by state.

The age at which majority is attained is eighteen in the following states:

| | | |
|---|---|---|
| Arizona | Kentucky | Oklahoma |
| Arkansas | Louisiana | Tennessee |
| California | Maine | Texas |
| Connecticut | Michigan | Rhode Island |
| Delaware | Nevada | Vermont |
| District of Columbia | New York | Virginia |

The age at which majority is attained is nineteen in Nebraska.

The age at which majority is attained is twenty-one in the following states:

| | | |
|---|---|---|
| Alabama | Maryland | Oregon |
| Alaska | Massachusetts | Pennsylvania |
| Colorado | Mississippi | South Carolina |
| Florida | Missouri | South Dakota |
| Georgia | Montana | Utah |
| Hawaii | New Hampshire | Washington |
| Idaho | New Jersey | West Virginia |
| Illinois | New Mexico | Wisconsin |
| Indiana | North Carolina | Wyoming |
| Iowa | North Dakota | |
| Kansas | Ohio | |

fees range from $36 for the Silver and $60 for the Gold to $200 for the Platinum; additionally, there is a cost for each share traded, which ranges from zero to $8 depending on your membership and the number of shares you're trading. Fractional shares of stock and odd lots of less than 100 shares can be traded without a penalty.

Once you have membership in the stock service, you and your child can start purchasing stocks. An interest-bearing money market account is automatically set up for you as a holding account for any funds you've sent that are not yet invested. It can also serve as a savings account for your child, a place to deposit regular allowance money or gift checks—that is, a way to build up sums that are earmarked specifically for investments. In addition, as a member of the stock service, you'll receive monthly statements showing asset summary, income summary, activity summary, and activity details.

One of the biggest advantages of the stock service programs is that parents who already own stock can transfer shares to their minor child in custodian form at no cost. Here's how Lynn transferred shares of General Electric to Danielle:

> When our stock investment club started to study General Electric and Danielle became the stock monitor for it, I decided to give her shares as a Christmas present in 1996 to add to her learning experience. I contacted the investor relations department of GE and requested a transfer of two shares from my name to Danielle's name in the custodian form. Within a few weeks Danielle became a part owner of GE. She still holds the certificate for the two shares at home so that anytime she wants to look at it or study it, it is there.

In the end, what matters most is that you get your child into the market in a way that gets her involved. If she is crazy about Barbies, she may soon feel equally affectionate toward a share of Mattel. Decide whether you have a piece of a company that your child will take pride in owning—enough pride to be interested in learning how to protect it.

## Getting Ready to Take the Plunge

Your child's choice of company in which to invest must meet only
one basic criterion: It must be publicly traded. This means that
anyone can buy shares of it at any time. These days it seems as
though every company has either gone public or is announcing an
IPO, an initial public offering. This means that what was once privately held is now available for individuals to invest in. It is a good
bet that what attracts your child is manufactured by a publicly
held company.

You can figure this out together. First, you have to find out
whether the company that manufactures the product or provides
the service your child likes is the *parent,* or holding, company. It is
not unusual for the parent company to bear little or no resem-
blance to its holdings. Sara Lee, for example, whose cakes "nobody
doesn't like," owns both the Playtex and the Hanes underwear
companies.

Start by looking up the manufacturer in the stock section of the
newspaper. Companies are listed alphabetically under the different trading exchanges, such as New York Stock Exchange, American Stock Exchange, and NASDAQ. If it is listed, then you have
your answer: The stock is publicly traded. If you find no listing,
then you have to do some research to determine the parent company. If you get your child involved in this detective work, he can
hone his research skills without even realizing it. Kids are always
more interested in answers they arrive at themselves than those
that are handed to them, especially when getting those answers is
like a treasure hunt. When you don't know something—or even
when you do—make it a problem for your child to help solve.

"You know, I can't find this breakfast cereal company listed in
the newspaper," you might say. "Are you sure Cinnamon Oat
Crunch is made by Mother's? Or could it be that Mother's is
owned by a bigger company? Does it say anything on the box?"
Sure enough, the answer (Quaker Oats) is as close at hand as the
cereal box.

Sometimes it isn't quite that easy, but teaching your child about investing is also teaching him how to gather information. Try a few of the following strategies if you get stumped:

✓   Sometimes the easiest course of action is the least technical: Have him ask someone at the store that sells the good or provides the service.

✓   Call company headquarters toll-free either by using the customer satisfaction number (usually printed on the packaging or instructions or warranty) or by calling toll-free directory assistance at 1-800-555-1212 or 1-888-555-1212. The toll-free customer satisfaction numbers will also put him in touch with people knowledgeable about the company. Show your child how to call 411 and use the address to get a phone number.

✓   See if the company is listed in the stock pages of your newspaper.

✓   You might try a field trip: going to the public library to look up the company in a book called *Value Line,* which can be found in the reference section.

✓   Search the Internet. If your child has online access, suggest he try to find the company's website by bracketing its name with "www." and ".com." If you are checking on Quaker Oats, you'd key in www.quakeroats.com to discover if it is correct! If this doesn't work, try using a search engine to find the company's name or product. Pat used Yahoo to look for any matches for Pepperidge Farm, Inc. The search produced six hits, or matches. She selected http://dir.yahoo.com/Business and Economy/Companies/Food/Brand Names/Campbell Soup Company/Products and Services and, sure enough, discovered that Campbell Soup is the parent company of Pepperidge Farm, Inc., products. (A closer look at a box of croutons revealed the Campbell Soup logo next to the UPC code!) Once you know the parent company, you can go to http://quote.yahoo.com and do a search on its name. When Pat looked up Campbell's, for instance, the Yahoo site yielded such stock information as the company symbol, the exchanges it trades on, and current and historical stock prices.

One tip we picked up while using online search engines: Enter in the brand name rather than the product. When Lynn entered "magic markers," for instance, she didn't get anywhere, but as

## Profile of a Young Investor

*Joel Berry, a sixteen-year-old from Westchester, New York,
describes how he first started investing.*

After I had decided to open up a brokerage account and cleared the idea
with my parents, the first choice I had to make was where to open my account. One of the top factors that influenced my decision was commissions. Like most kids, I did not have a ton of money. Opening an account
at one of the full-service brokerage firms, which charge $150 per trade
even on the low end, would quickly drain what money I had.

Luckily, a new kind of brokerage had sprouted up in the past few years.
These were online firms that skip the step of an actual stockbroker and
instead carry out trades automatically through the Internet. I had first
learned of these companies through friends who had been investing their
parents' money and were making huge profits in the booming markets of
the 1990s. "Why aren't I doing the same thing?" I asked myself. Then
some of the online brokerages' flashy advertisements caught my eye, de-
picting billionaire truck drivers, grandmothers rich enough to bail out
Middle Eastern countries, and kids whose helicopters picked them up in
their backyards, all a result of their electronically created wealth. I realized, of course, that this was an exaggeration. My economics class had
taught me the values of earning money slowly over time through compound interest and doing thorough research of companies rather than the
crazed "day trading" so popular with online brokerages.

Choosing a particular company was pretty easy, given that all I had to
do was surf over their websites. Charles Schwab seemed like a great site,
but the $29.99 commission was still a bit too high for me. I had $4,000 to
invest, and I figured I'd be making around twenty trades per year. That
would have been almost $600 right there for commissions. E*trade
looked very good; they had a lot of features, and the price was only $15
per trade. I decided to go with Ameritrade, a slightly smaller company
with basement-level prices of $8 for market orders and $13 for limit orders. The next decision was what type of account to open.

Being a minor, I couldn't open an account in my own name. In the end
we decided on a UGMA/UTMA custodial account in which the money
was legally controlled by my parents but was set up so I could place the

trades. We mailed the check to officially open the account, and I began to make more exciting decisions. What companies would I buy stock in?

I had already set up and tracked a mock portfolio as an economics class project. We analyzed the P/E ratio, past stock performance, expected earnings growth, and market share of companies, among other statistics, in order to choose the best ones to invest in. Here are a few of my favorite research sites:

Yahoo Finance: http://quote.yahoo.com
E*trade: http://www.etrade.com
CBS Market Research: http://cbs.marketresearch.com
The Motley Fool: http://www.fool.com

The best thing for a beginner to do at these sites is read any tutorials available, such as the "Fool School" at The Motley Fool site. After this, look for research, profiles, and charts to evaluate stocks. Other great tools are the Bloomberg financial television station, if that is available, *Wall Street Week* and the *Nightly Business Report* on public television, and *The Wall Street Journal*. Even after you're invested, you should always watch out for news on the companies you own, and even companies you don't.

In picking my stocks, I didn't want to miss out on the huge gains that technology stocks had been producing. However, I knew that these companies were very risky. In the event of a downturn in the economy, these stocks that have a high valuation with regard to earnings or very low earnings per share would be hit very badly. I chose to have about 60 percent of my portfolio in technology stocks, with the rest in safer blue-chip companies and cyclical stocks. Among the technology stocks I chose were America Online (AOL), Cisco Systems (CSCO), CMG Information (CMGI), and RealNetworks (RNWK). AOL and Cisco seemed like the safest of the bunch, given that they are very large companies and possess the majority of their respective market shares. CMGI is a sort of publicly traded venture capital fund that holds only Internet-related companies. Its stock price had risen more than tenfold, and possibly it would continue those gains. RealNetworks is a new company that makes software that enables live broadcasts of music and video over the Internet, called streaming media. I had used its RealPlayer software to listen to radio broadcasts of baseball games that weren't available in my area except

(continued on next page)

over the Internet, and to hear clips of songs I didn't yet own. I'd found it to be quite useful and a lot of fun. RealNetworks owned more than 80 percent of this market, although it had yet to prove its profitability. All of these stocks were quite risky. I knew that I had to choose some safer companies to offset potential losses and to stabilize my portfolio.

After considering the P/E values and dividends of several large blue-chip Dow stocks, I settled on Eastman Kodak, Goodyear, and Sears. These high-dividend, low-valuation stocks were recommended on a website I had been using, The Motley Fool. It illustrated an investing approach that looked low risk and profitable: choosing four of the five stocks on the Dow with the lowest valuation but the highest dividend. After settling on these seven initial companies, I divided up my money and bought roughly equal amounts of both. Initially I placed market orders instead of limits, noting the lower price. A market order directs a company to buy a stock at whatever price it is at, while a limit order specifies a price you choose ahead of time. I quickly learned that placing market orders was a mistake: I placed an order for CMGI, and the stock went up $5 per share between the quote I chose to buy it at and the price at which the market order was filled. The good thing about limits, I realized, was that you can choose a price ahead of time—say a stock is at 50, and you would rather buy it at 45. The market regularly fluctuates, so you can place a limit to buy at 45, and when the stock goes down to 45, it will automatically be placed. If the stock goes back up to 60, then you've earned 15 per share instead of only 10. You can see how the same thing would work with selling. You can specify a price you want to sell at and make sure you don't sell until the stock gets that high.

Checking my portfolio every day and watching the ups and downs of the market was exciting. One day I'd be up $100, the next day I'd lose

soon as she tried "Crayola," Yahoo furnished her with a bunch of website references. At the end of the listings it said: "Sponsored by Binney & Smith, maker of Crayola products." Bingo! Lynn had her holding company. She took that piece of information and logged on to the quote.yahoo.com site for stock information but found no listing. It's a privately held company. She confirmed this by sending an e-mail request for parent company information to

$300, and the next I'd earn $400. Looking at the lists of the highest percentage gainers each day, I was tempted to make more trades, to take advantage of the daily and weekly fluctuations to make loads of money. With Internet stocks changing in value by 10 percent to 20 percent on normal days, and when all you need to do to make a trade is hit a few keys on a computer, it seems like a very easy thing to do. "Hmmm," I thought, "why do I need these blue-chip companies that will give me only 10 percent gains in a good year when I can sell them and buy more Internet stocks and double my money?" I must say it seemed like a good idea at the time to a beginner like me, so I followed the ill-advised lead of the many people who take part in "day trading." I soon learned that at a certain point it becomes more like gambling than investing. I sold my shares in Goodyear and Sears, and bought more CMGI and a small, very volatile software IPO called Silknet. Soon after I made this choice, investors began to worry about rising interest rates and inflation, and Internet stocks took a tumble, some losing up to half their value. I lost about 20 percent of my money in a matter of days. My stocks did rise again, and I had been prepared for losses like that, but the experience taught me that the best strategy is to invest for the long term, keeping trading down to a minimum. You'll be better off if you find a great company and stick with it for at least a year unless something terrible happens to the company.

The other lesson I came away with from this downturn is that it can be a great idea to buy after a dip in the market. I considered keeping some of my money in cash at first, waiting for a low point to buy in, but I decided against it. When the market did dip and stocks were at bargain prices, my money was already tied up. If I'd kept a little in cash, I could've made a lot as the markets went back up after the dip.

www.crayola.com: Most companies with websites furnish both their 800 number and an e-mail service whereby you can e-mail them for more information. A day later, Lynn received a message from the company's webmistress confirming that Crayola is privately owned and, interestingly, that it is part of the Hallmark (as in cards) family. So much for investing in crayons!

Your child will be amazed and really proud of himself at the

> ### A Good Answer to a Stock Question
>
> **Why would I give a company money for just a piece of paper?**
> **What do I get for being a part owner?**
>
> The piece of paper, otherwise known as a stock certificate, is basi-
> cally a promise. It says that if the company gets richer, then it has to
> share its money with you because you're an owner. For the company
> to get richer, it first has to grow. Maybe it has to build a factory so it can
> make more Coke. If it bottles more soda, finds more stores to carry it,
> and sells more Coca-Cola, or if it comes up with new sodas or juices or
> products people like, then it will probably earn bigger profits. But
> that's why the company sold you a piece of itself. It's going to use your
> money to make itself bigger so it can make itself and its shareholders
> richer.

mysteries he can solve himself, all the while getting more confident and competent on the phone, in person, and online. Pat
couldn't believe how quickly Shannon's friend Doug, who at eighteen has his own lawn-cutting business, took to the research end
of the investing process. Shannon got him to list the companies
whose products he uses every day—everything from Home Depot
and Kohler to Makita and Wm. Wrigley Jr. Company (makers of
Winterfresh gum, which Doug swears is the best)—and then get
information on them by going online. Doug couldn't get enough!
He surfed the web for hours and couldn't wait to get started buying stocks.

Like Doug, once you have your key information on a company—
who owns it and whether it's public or private—all you need to do
is buy a share of it in your child's name. You're ready to take the
plunge, to make your child a part owner. Buying this first share is
like buying an instruction manual for $70. Think of the thousands
you could spend sending your child to some institution for her financial education! The way we see it, this first stock, this first

share or partial share, no matter what it costs or how it performs over time, is going to give your child an immeasurable return in experience.

## Instant Gratification

Congratulations! Your child is in the market: He's an actual investor now, a part owner, a voice in the company with the single vote his single share nets him. You can't wait to present him with the evidence: an actual stock certificate or enrollment certificate or other documentation that he's a shareholder.

One word of advice: Stock shares are not dolls or baseball cards. They don't have the power to satisfy childish urges. Holding stock is a way of teaching your child how to *defer* gratification. That's one of the great lessons that investing teaches, and it's a lesson your child will learn in time. Until he has had the experience of ownership—of choosing a stock, of putting his own money on the line to purchase shares, of tracking the progress of his investment—he's likely to see this piece of stock paper as nothing more than a piece of paper. However, with more knowledge and experience, your child will become more attached to that piece of paper than to dolls and baseball cards.

Pat learned this the hard way—when she tried to give Shannon her very first share of stock as a Christmas present. She had gone to the trouble of getting one share of Disney in her daughter's name in time for Christmas morning. She managed to close the transaction on December 22, but that meant the stock certificate wouldn't arrive in time for Pat to present it as a gift. So she took a blank piece of paper, drew her own version of a certificate, and penned in, "This piece of paper entitles Shannon Yoder to one share of Walt Disney Stock." For extra impact Pat put the certificate in a box, along with an ink stamp pad and two stampers, one Mickey Mouse and one Minnie Mouse. She wrapped it and put it under the tree, quite proud of her impromptu creativity.

On Christmas morning Shannon opened the box, looked at the

stampers and stamp pad, and said, "What's this?" Pat started to
explain how the actual stock certificate would arrive in a couple of
weeks with Shannon's name on it, but Shannon was unimpressed.
"Do you have something else for me?" she asked her mother.

"I'm not sure if her reaction would have been as extreme if I
had enclosed the actual certificate," muses Pat, "but I do know
that it was *not* the reaction I expected!"

Now, of course, that first share of Walt Disney stock is the one
Shannon says she will never sell. Over the years it has come to
symbolize her introduction to the stock market, and as she matured—as she began to take an interest in its ownership, as she
learned to track its progress, and as she came to understand its
power to earn—she began to feel that this *was* a special piece of
paper. It was, after all, a real present.

## Circle one:

*1. Some principles of investing are:*

    (a)  invest regularly
    (b)  start investing early
    (c)  invest in growth companies
    (d)  diversify your investments
    (e)  all of the above

*2. When we invest in the stock market, we may:*

    (a)  make a lot of money
    (b)  lose some or most of our money
    (c)  both of the above

*3. You may invest small amounts of money on a regular basis with:*

    (a)  McDirect
    (b)  a full-service broker
    (c)  a discount broker
    (d)  an online broker

*4. When you purchase shares in a company, you are:*

    (a)  part owner of a company
    (b)  a shareholder
    (c)  entitled to vote on issues through a proxy statement
    (d)  all of the above
    (e)  none of the above

*5. When you diversify your investments, you:*

    (a)  buy stocks in different types of companies
    (b)  decrease your risk of losing all your money if one industry fails
    (c)  sleep better at night
    (d)  all of the above

## Answer key:

3. a

2. c       5. d

1. e       4. d

## MATCH THEM UP

Match the parent company with the subsidiary companies that it owns. There may be more than one subsidiary for a company.

| Parent Company and Subsidiaries | Whom Do I Belong To? |
| --- | --- |
| General Electric | Bath and Body Works |
| | Exxon Chemical Company |
| Microsoft | Frito-Lay, Inc. |
| | GE Capital Finance Services |
| Berkshire Hathaway | GEICO Insurance |
| | General Electric Appliance |
| Tricon Global Restaurant | Henri Bendel |
| | Kentucky Fried Chicken |
| The Limited | Lerner New York |
| | MSN.com |
| Exxon Oil Co. | NBC Television |
| | Penske Truck Leasing |
| PepsiCo, Inc. | Pepperidge Farm Inc. |
| | Pizza Hut |
| Campbell Soup Co. | Sam's Club Warehouse |
| | Taco Bell |
| Wal-Mart | |

## WHO MAKES WHAT?

Draw lines between the products on the left and the company that produces them on the right:

Touchstone Films                        Coca-Cola Co.

Frostee                                 Ford Motor Co.

Mercury Taurus                          Danone International

Minute Maid orange juice                Campbell Soup Co.

Dannon spring water                     Wendy's

Healthy Choice soup                     Walt Disney Co.

Gatorade                                Quaker Oats, Inc.

# 3

## Families Who Invest Together

$A$t first your child's interest in stock ownership may ebb and flow. And like Shannon, your child may not be overwhelmed by her first stock certificate. Luckily, there's more than one train to Topeka (or Wall Street). Six months or so after her initial disappointment upon receiving the Disney stock for Christmas, Shannon received a colorful package of "welcome" materials for investing in McDonald's. The McDonald's package included a folder with notepaper designed to look like French fries in a French-fry packet. Shannon immediately forgot she was owner of a major U.S. corporation; what thrilled her was owning this cool-looking packet of French-fry paper!

So look for opportunities (and, yes, even fun and games) to trigger your child's interest. Every time she drinks a soda, have her check the fine print to see if it's "made by the company you own." Every time you go into a deli or a fast-food franchise or a supermarket where soda is sold, have her pay attention to how many people are buying products "from her company." Every time you go to the movies, have her check to see what soda the concession stand is selling. Every time she sees an ad for Coke on TV, ask for her opinion: Does she think her company is doing a good job advertising its product? Have her note what brand of soda vending machines carry; maybe her company has a better product, but maybe the competition is getting more soda to its customers. Who is the competition? Ask her to survey what her friends drink. Show her how what appear to be non-Coke products are made by the Coca-Cola Company. (Minute Maid is a Coca-Cola product, for instance.) See how many she can find or name. You'll be opening her eyes not only to the product but to the company and the industry. The more aware she is, the more she'll want to know about this stock she owns and how to protect or manage her investment.

## Wall Street on *Your* Street

As we've said before, everyday errands and outings offer opportunities to discuss investment ideas, share investor news, and make abstract concepts concrete.

Whenever we eat out at a fast-food franchise, we seem to wind up reviewing our investments and news that affects them. Take our excursions to Kentucky Fried Chicken, which was for a while the only fast-food outlet for chicken in Olney, Maryland. When Taco Bell eventually moved in, Pat got to tell Shannon why: Both franchises were owned by Pepsi. That piece of news explained why they couldn't order a Coke at either restaurant, and Shannon and Pat reviewed the topic of parent companies and how even a parent company seeks to diversify its holdings.

Pepsi ultimately decided to spin off its fast-food franchises into a separate company called Tricon Global Restaurants in order to refocus its business in beverages. Danielle picked up on this piece of news because her grandmother Lynn is a shareholder. But it was going out to eat at KFC that gave Lynn the opportunity to explain all about Pepsi's consolidation and subsequent transfer of stock in Tricon to Pepsi shareholders.

Even something as simple as ordering a soda becomes an opportunity to review what your kids are learning as investors—or to introduce concepts they need to be learning.

Going shopping for clothes is another great way to garner first-hand information on a company your child owns or is considering buying. Danielle found The Limited to be a very investor-friendly company, in addition to being one that sells her favorite clothes. She has an account that allows her to make $30 incremental investments—right in line with her income these days. The more shares she owns, the more she likes to shop there, and the more she shops there, the better she feels about being a part owner of the company.

As a part owner in The Limited, Danielle has come to understand she also owns stock in Bath & Body Works, Lerner New York, Limited Too, Structure, and Henri Bendel. This understanding has changed her buying habits. Whenever she goes to the mall, she consciously chooses to support companies she owns. (Her bathroom is full of supplies from Bath & Body Works!) Recently her company spun off Limited Too, giving stockholders a share in the new company for every 7 shares they owned of The Limited. Danielle, with only 6.063 shares, didn't qualify (she got a check instead), but now that she knows about stock transfers, she's making regular contributions to her stock accounts in addition to supporting her companies at the mall.

Chances are that everywhere you go with your child—to the movies, to the supermarket, to a ball game, to a restaurant, to the mall—you're going to sample the products or tour the facilities of a publicly traded company, possibly one your child owns. Take advantage of this and use these outings to tie in news events about the companies or repeat explanations about such things as stock transfers and parent companies. At the very least, remind your child that it pays to spend his money on products and services whose parent companies he supports. He is part of the market, and nothing brings that home better than being out in the marketplace!

## How to Read a Stock Quote

During this discovery process you can make reading the newspaper stock section a family activity. The newspaper can't be beat as a convenient source of stock information. Newspapers are very kitchen table friendly; they're something you can hold, spread out, tear things out of, mark up, pass back and forth, discuss over a meal, and carry around. With a topic as abstract as the stock market, the more concrete you can make your child's learning experience, the more comfortably and quickly he'll learn.

It is also something your child may have already seen you do on a regular basis. As Pat has described, her poring over the stock pages and babbling her thoughts aloud got Shannon intrigued enough to ask for the paper and find the quotes herself, highlighting them for her mom. And Danielle, having seen Lynn work through a pile of newspapers over breakfast every morning, was quick to imitate her, asking for the business section when she wasn't even old enough to pronounce it correctly.

"Let's see how Coca-Cola is doing today" could be your opener, addressed to no one in particular. Open the newspaper to the stock section, explaining as you do it how you found the right page in the newspaper's index or how you just turned to the end of the business section. You can give hints. "Stocks are listed alphabetically by exchange," you might say. "I know Coke is traded on the New York Stock Exchange, so it should be here under C."

You can ask your child for help in reading the fine print: "Read me the one that is second to last, to the left of the plus or minus sign, because that's the closing price. That will tell us what a share of Coca-Cola was worth at the end of yesterday."

Next, point out the last number in the row, the change for the day. A stock's daily movement is another good concept to learn along with the daily closing price. Walk him through each of these numbers in this way, but not all at once. Let him get the hang of zeroing in on the company and the closing price before you introduce him to the other figures in the quote. Be patient enough to

## A Good Answer to a Stock Question

**What about the $50 you invested for me in Coca-Cola? Can I get it back?**

Yes. But understand that you probably won't get back exactly what we spent on your share. You might, for example, get more. If the company has gotten bigger and richer, then the actual worth of your share has gone up, too. You can tell how much your share is worth every single day by looking in the newspaper. Today your $50 share is worth $53¹⁄₁₆, or $53.06. If the company keeps growing and making money, you might want to leave your money where it is because if you take back your $53.06 today, you'll no longer be a part owner, and your $53.06 won't make you any more money—unless you invest in another company, that is!

let him ask you rather telling him what each one means—even if it takes days. The amount of time is unimportant because it's all going toward a lifelong goal of learning to read the stock page.

If he is reading *The Wall Street Journal,* he is bound to notice that in addition to being listed by name, companies are identified by symbol. Other newspapers may use only the company name or only the symbol. Acquaint your child with his stock's trading or ticker symbol; for example, MCD is McDonald's, GE is General Electric, and MSFT is Microsoft. Stock symbols are a kind of shorthand left over from the days of ticker tape. They help traders and brokers on the exchange floor identify a company quickly, while making it impossible for investors to confuse companies with similar names when they read the listings. A few companies have one-letter symbols, such as T for AT&T, and S for Sears, Roebuck, because they were assigned symbols way back when the market was young and very few companies were publicly traded.

In response to questions such as "What does P/E mean?" don't be too quick to provide an answer. Instead, point out to your child

## Stock Symbols

Every stock has an abbreviation, called a symbol, that is a shorthand way of locating the stock. The symbols also indicate whether the stock is on the New York Stock Exchange or the NASDAQ. The symbols for all stocks on the NYSE are three letters or less, while those on the NASDAQ are four or more.

Example: The stock symbol for Disney is DIS, while the stock symbol for Microsoft is MSFT, which tells us automatically that Disney shares trade on the NYSE while Microsoft shares trade on the NASDAQ.

the "key" or explanatory notes in every stock section that explains what the abbreviations mean, along with footnotes on various symbols. We've included a chart that explains what the numbers and symbols in each column tell you.

See what your child can learn on his own. Some of the concepts, such as dividend, yield, and price-earnings ratio, are complicated, so your child doesn't need to know them in the beginning. Have him focus on prices for starters, and be on hand to explain what he can't figure out for himself.

Stock prices are never quoted in dollars and cents. The price of a share appears instead in whole numbers and fractions, with each whole number being a dollar amount and each fraction translating into cents. To convert a fraction into cents, have your child practice a little fifth-grade math by dividing the top number by the bottom number. For example, 51⅝ converts to $51.63 when you divide the 8 into the 5 in ⅝. And $51.63 is the price you must pay for every share of stock you wish to purchase.

See if your child notices the duplicate hi/lo columns. The fact that there are two sets of **Hi** and **Lo** figures can be confusing. The first set, or those in the left-most columns, shows the highest and lowest prices that have been paid for a share of that stock over the last fifty-two weeks. A stock that at one point in the last year dou-

## How to Read a Newspaper Stock Listing

### McDonald's stock price on August 12, 1999

| 1 | 2 | 3 | 4 | 5 | 6 | 7 | 8 | 9 | 10 | 11 |
|---|---|---|---|---|---|---|---|---|---|---|
| 52 Week | | | | | | | | | | |
| Hi | Lo | Stock | Div | Yld | P/E | 100s | Hi | Lo | Close | Chg |
| s47⅜ | 26¾ | McDonalds | .20 | .5 | 31 | 33900 | 40⅛ | 39⅛ | 39⅜ | −⅜ |

1–2. **52 Week Hi/Lo:** Hi/Lo numbers show that McDonald's stock hit this price sometime between August 12, 1998, and August 12, 1999. The small "s" indicates that a stock split occurred.

3. **Stock:** Stocks are listed alphabetically by the company's name. Company names that are made up of letters (such as IBM) appear at the beginning of the letter's list.

4. **Div:** Current annual dividend rate paid on McDonald's stock.

5. **Yld:** Current annual dividend rate divided by the closing price of the stock, expressed as a percentage. If a stock does not pay a dividend, no yield is shown.

6. **P/E:** Closing price of stock divided by the company's earnings per share for the latest 12-month period. When you see three periods ( . . . ), it usually means the P/E cannot be calculated.

7. **Sales 100s:** Day's volume in hundreds of shares. McDonald's volume for the day was 3,390,000.

bled its share price is having quite a year—either a pretty rocky one (meaning it is down by half of what it was valued at some time during the year) or an explosive growth one (it has doubled during the year). By comparing a share's closing price to its fifty-two-week high and low prices, an investor can get some idea of where the stock stands in terms of how much the stock price has bounced around in the past year. The second set of Hi/Lo figures shows the very least and the very most traders were willing to pay for a share

8–9. Hi/Lo: Highest and lowest of McDonald's stock price fluctuation for the day.

10. Close: The price at which McDonald's stock was trading when the exchange closed for the day.

11. Chg: The loss or gain for the day, compared with the previous session's closing price. McDonald's had a loss for the day. No change at the close is indicated by three dots ( . . . ).

## FOOTNOTE ABBREVIATIONS:

Have you ever noticed the little letters or symbols next to a stock listing? Newspapers call them footnote abbreviations. Why don't you grab the newspaper now and find a stock that has a small letter or symbol next to it while you are reading this paragraph so that it will make more sense to you when you look at it later. Listed below are some of the most commonly used footnote abbreviations that will prove helpful as you learn.

d: New 52-week low
n: Newly issued in the past 52 weeks
p: Initial dividend, annual rate unknown; yield not shown
s: Stock split or stock dividend of 25 percent or more in the past 52 weeks
u: New 52-week high

in the course of just one day. A big spread between low and high indicates a lot of activity for this particular stock—or a lot of *volatility*, we say—either because traders are scurrying to buy it, driving up the price of each share, or they're frantic to unload it, driving down the price of each share.

Point out to your child that he doesn't have to worry too much about the **Div** and **Yld** columns. These numbers are important only to investors looking to get a steady income out of their stocks, whereas your child is looking for long-term growth in the company—meaning growth in the value of his share, not his dividend. What the company pays out to its shareholders in a year might be quite small; when a company doesn't pay out any dividend at all, the Div column has three dots. But that's not bad. It means the company is taking all its profits and putting them back into itself, to grow even more. A high dividend number could signal that the company is paying out too much to shareholders, leaving itself too little to grow on. A growing company needs to take its earnings and plow them back into the company for things like equipment, factories, and new products.

Yield (as shown in the column labeled Yld) is simply a calculation for the year based on the dividend. Divide the dividend figure by the closing price, and you'll get the stock's annual yield, expressed as a percentage. Again, for long-term investors, what a stock yields in a year in the way of payouts, or the dividend checks sent to investors, is not important.

Ditto for the P/E, or price-earnings ratio. It will be important to your young investor when he compares one stock with another to find out which is the best buy. Some investors say that P/E is helpful in getting a read on whether a company is undervalued (meaning its share price is a good buy) or overvalued (meaning you're probably paying too much for its stock). But until your child starts researching, investing, and managing his own portfolio, it is premature to discuss the P/E ratio.

What you want to direct his attention to is the **volume** number (sometimes labeled **sales**), measured in 100s (33900 equals 3,390,000). Volume shows just how many shares of this stock were traded yesterday. It is another measure of activity, volatility, or just plain interest on the part of investors in this particular stock. Have your child regularly check the Most Active list, which appears in the newspaper among the summary data before the stock exchange listings. The Most Active list, a compilation of stocks whose trade volume exceeded that of all other stocks being traded for the day, is a good way to size up what stocks are hot right now—again, not because they're necessarily going up in value but because some news is affecting their price, and everyone is trying to profit from it.

The **plus** and **minus** signs need the least explanation: A plus means the stock is up in price for the day; a minus means the share price has gone down for the day. The number that follows tells you by how much the stock is up or down. If there is no number but only three dots, it means there was no change in the share price at market close from the day before. The number in the right-most column labeled **Chg** is given in fractions that you need to convert to decimal form to discover the actual dollar amount that each share of the company's stock increased or decreased.

## How to Track and Chart a Stock

Once your child is checking her stock quote and closing price in the daily newspaper pretty regularly, it's time to help her see how that quote, tracked over time, can give her a clearer picture of the company's performance. It is time to teach her how to *monitor* her stock, one of the key ways investors gather important information about a company. Stock monitoring is a tool even the most sophisticated Wall Street analyst puts into practice every day. In an exercise we developed for the Stock MarKids, weekly stock monitoring is also one of the simplest of tools.

Monitoring begins with the Weekly Tracking Form (see Danielle's example). It lets you record a stock's high, low, and closing price along with space for notations about daily volume levels and places where news clippings can be attached. The idea is for your child to gather data about a favorite stock for a week at a time; summarizing all the information will show her the price trends and events that affect her stock. Because there is nothing quite so dramatic as a picture of a stock's progress, we've also devised a tracking chart, basically a graph, where your child can plot all those closing prices on a line. Each day's closing price gets

## Danielle's Weekly Stock-Tracking Form

### Week of March 18–22

#### McDONALD'S

**Monday**

Date: 3/18/96

Closing Price: 52 1/8

Daily High: 52 1/4

Daily Low: 51 5/8

change: 3/8

**Tuesday**

Date: 3/19/96

Closing Price: 50 3/8

Daily High: 52 1/2

Daily Low: 50

change 1 1/4

**Wednesday**

Date: 3/20/96

Closing Price: 50 7/8

Daily High: 51 1/4

Daily Low: 50 1/2

change 1/2

**Thursday**

Date: 3/21/96

Closing Price: 50 1/8

Daily High: 51 1/8

Daily Low: 50 1/8

change 3/4

**Friday**

Date: 3/22/96

Closing Price: 50 3/4

Daily High: 51

Daily Low: 50 3/4

change 5/8

**WEEKLY NEWS:**

Made the most active list on March 26, 1996 (they lost!)

**WEEKLY STOCK SUMMARY**

WEEKLY Closing Price: 50 3/4

WEEKLY High: 51

WEEKLY Low: 50 3/4

marked with a dot at the appropriate coordinate on our graph. Connect the dots day by day, and in a week your child will have a line showing the stock's ups and downs. Connect four weeks' worth of graph sheets, with all the dots connected, and she'll have a complete picture of that company's performance for a month.

After absorbing all those technical words—yield, dividend, P/E ratio—your child will find the tracking chart a refreshingly concrete approach to investing.

The logical first stock for your child to track is the one you bought her. The fact that she owns it will keep her motivated enough to keep filling out the forms. She'll see how much the forms show about a company. Soon she will realize how useful they are as a tool to learn about a new stock she thinks she wants to buy.

We introduced stock monitoring to our kids in the club *before* they bought their first club stock. We wanted them to see how this tool could help them determine whether the stock they wanted to buy was a good bet. The kids wanted to buy McDonald's as their first club stock (Danielle and Shannon already owned shares as individuals), and so we set them up with stock-monitoring forms and tracking charts for a monthlong study of the company.

Of course, these young investors already had "common knowledge" of the company, having eaten there for years. We held our club meetings at the restaurant so they could size up not only the company's product but how it was marketed and distributed—another important piece of research. But tracking McDonald's share price on a day-to-day basis for four weeks opened their eyes to information they simply could not have come by any other way.

This little exercise with our forms got the kids so practiced at reading a stock quote, they could fill out the monitoring form, plot the closing price, and connect the dot from the day before on the tracking form in about five to ten minutes. We had them check not just highs, lows, and closing prices but also the volume of stock activity each day. Stocks with the heaviest trading volume made the Most Active list, a fact they also recorded.

The kids also learned that the prices quoted in the newspaper are from the day before and that even though the market is open on Monday, there are no stock prices in Monday's newspaper. It took some of them, a while to realize that the prices in Saturday's

74

Wow the Dow!

Danielle's McDonald's Graph

March 18 - 29 1996

# McDONALD'S

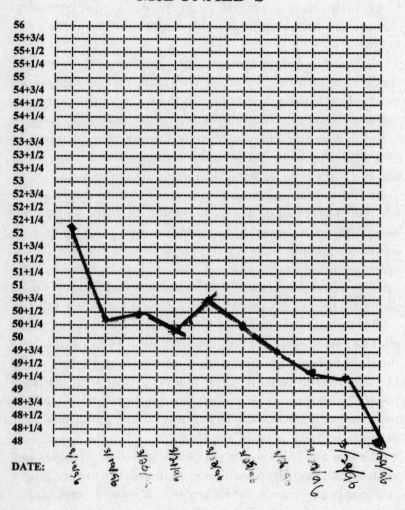

DATE:

paper were those from Friday. The Sunday summary quotes were probably the most interesting because the kids got to compare their weekly information with the newspaper's summaries, and they knew exactly which day the stock hit a new high or a new low or made the headlines. They had more information at their fingertips than the newspapers they were reading.

In no time they could see for themselves the relationship between heavy volume and daily price fluctuations. When we prepared the forms for the month, we customized the prices along the side of the graph to match each stock's recent price trading range. Anytime their graph ran off the top or bottom of the page, it turned out to be a high-volume week for that particular stock; it took lots of investors frantically buying and selling to drive a price way up or down. We asked them to think about what could affect a stock so much in a day that it could make the Most Active list. We helped them formulate the question: *What news so affected the marketplace that every investor rushed to unload or load up on the stock?*

Scrambling to find the key to this puzzle, they stumbled on the incredible importance of staying attuned to the news as investors. They had to read the paper, listen to the radio, or tune in to CNN every day, and they had to listen very carefully because the link between world news and their company's performance wasn't always spelled out for them. We provided a place on the forms so they could write in the answer or attach a newspaper clipping that explained the volume number or the spiking or dipping share price.

As it turned out, we couldn't have chosen a better company at a better time for them to track. While they were charting McDonald's, mad cow disease broke out in Britain. Nearly every day the news reported on the problem and its implications for U.S. consumers, and nearly every day McDonald's stock price reflected the news. The kids' graphs ran off the bottom of the page, well below what we had estimated would be the lowest possible price for the stock during that month. Brother, were we wrong! Suddenly they saw how the marketplace determined, through supply and demand, the value of a share: People were no longer eating at McDonald's. Investors, seeing a trend, unloaded their shares. And, *boom,* down went the share price. Sort of a Cow the Dow! situation.

It was, in effect, a crash course for the kids. It gave them a profile of the fast-food industry, of McDonald's as a company, and of the global economy we live in. Just like investors and analysts in top-ranked Wall Street firms, the Stock MarKids that month were poring over their graph lines and chart statistics to see where their company was going, where the industry as a whole was headed, and how the global marketplace might have a say in the matter. The whole exercise gave them an understanding of the interconnectedness among world events, the fate of a particular company in our economy, and their own habits as consumers and investors.

Eventually we modified the forms so that the kids could track several different companies at a time. No matter what the stock was, monitoring it taught them something. While monitoring General Electric, Danielle and Shannon learned what a conglomerate was—a parent company whose holdings are so diverse that its fate is no longer tied to the fate of one particular company or industry. They learned that GE, a firm that started out as an electrical appliance company, owns NBC, the television broadcast giant. They learned that record viewership of the 1996 Olympics boosted GE's bottom line and share price.

Studying stocks helped the children look beyond themselves. Every day they had to give themselves a news briefing, not just on their school or area or country, but on the world. They gained an understanding of how events abroad could affect their own behavior at home. They acquired a newshound's habit that lingered long after they stopped monitoring McDonald's. The monitoring and charting exercises gave them insights we couldn't have given them. Best of all, they didn't think of what they were learning as doing homework; they thought of it as recreational.

### A Good Answer to a Stock Question

**Will I always make money on my stock?**

There's no guarantee that your stock will go up in value. Sometimes companies that issue stock don't use the money they raise wisely. They don't grow. They don't make money, or unexpected things happen to the company. A few years ago some bottles of Coca-Cola got contaminated with bacteria, and the people who drank them got sick. That scared others away from buying Coke, and sales dropped. That caused share prices to drop in value. So if you'd sold your Coca-Cola stock during that period, you probably would have gotten back less than what you spent on it.

The kids loved to compare their graphs, especially when a price ran off the top of the page into uncharted territory, past the top number we had anticipated. They had to pencil in the actual share prices. Shannon liked to use different-colored pencils for her charts. Each day she picked another color so that at the end of the week she had a rainbow of lines. Other kids used sparkling markers or adhesive dots to mark the closing prices. We encouraged all this because we wanted the activity to be an appealing project, not a tedious chore.

On the other hand, we noticed that teenagers needed no gimmicks to keep them tracking. Shannon's after-school baby-sitter, Tracy Holt, who was eighteen years old at the time and a freshman in college, actually asked if she could have charts to do herself along with Shannon every afternoon. She'd never had any exposure to the market or to investing, but as a result of Shannon's stock monitoring, Tracy started reading the business section of the newspaper every day. What she saw on those graphs and forms of ours made her want to learn all she could.

The charting activities seemed to have that effect on everybody. The Stock MarKids wanted to learn all they could, even beyond

# ROBERT E. "TED" TURNER

### Vice Chairman, Time Warner, Inc.

**COMPANY:** Time Warner, Inc., is one of the world's leading media companies, operating cable networks such as CNN and Cartoon Network, Warner Music Group, publishing, films and music and cable systems.

**$$$:** $6.9 billion net worth (as of October 1999)

**BIRTH DATE AND LOCATION:** 1938, Cincinnati, Ohio

**EDUCATION:** Bachelor's degree from Brown University

**HOME:** Roswell, Georgia

**TIDBIT:** Turner is an active environmentalist and donated $1 billion to the United Nations. He owns the largest bison herd in the country on his ranch in Montana. He enjoys yachting, having won world sailing titles, including successfully defending the coveted America's Cup in 1977.

**FIRST JOB:** At an Atlanta UHF TV station in 1970

**QUOTE:** "I've been through a lot. I've already got the mileage of a 150-year-old man. I'm like a New York City taxicab that has three drivers, driving twenty-four hours a day, seven days a week."

what we had taught them with the newspaper. They discovered it was not the only tool available to check stock prices, obtain stock quotes, or tune into current events. Those with Internet access quickly found a number of sites to log on to for the information they needed to fill out the forms (see our favorite sites on pages 208–210). Shannon and Danielle began using NAIC's *Better Investing* monthly magazine, which they received at home, for investment advice. On their own initiative they began to read a host of other financial materials and to pick up financial information from all kinds of sources.

A sixth-grader, Danielle began taking Lynn's *Wall Street Journal* on the way out the door. She read the money and investing section while Lynn drove her to school. She would not only check the stocks she owned but those Lynn owned and the club's holdings— all before school.

Lynn, taking the cue, started leaving financial magazines all over the house, particularly on the reading rack in the bathroom. One day, when she was in eighth grade, on the drive to school Danielle piped up from the backseat, "Nana, I am so glad I own some of the ten best companies out there." Sure enough, Danielle had leafed through an issue of *Kiplinger's* she had found in the bathroom and read the article "Top Ten Stocks of the Decade." "It said EMC and Cisco were companies I'd be glad I owned and to hold on to them for the next ten years," Danielle told Lynn.

## Stocks and Bonding

When kids own stocks, they naturally behave like owners. They try to arm themselves with the tools they need to keep tabs on their investment. They don't need to be pressured into it. Or, as Pat says, "I don't sit here every day and say, 'You must come home and get online and check your stocks.' In fact, there are plenty of days when Shannon comes home and says, 'Mom, when are you going to get off the computer so I can check my stocks? This is *important!*' "

The more you are involved in the market yourself, the more

## Profile of a Young Investor

*Jay Liebowitz, a Californian, is an entrepreneur as well as an online columnist. At seventeen he has already developed his own investment website.*

### What got you started or interested in investing?

I got myself involved. When I was thirteen, I didn't know that you could passively put money into something and expect it to grow. When I first learned this, I was thrilled. After that, I became even more interested in how people did this—and did it successfully.

### Did you have a role model?

No, but eventually I developed a role model in Warren Buffett. If there is an investor who is successful, it's Buffett. Virtually every investment he has made in the last thirty years has been successful, and he has one of the most astute analytical minds that business has ever seen. What is more, he's proof that you can be ethical on Wall Street.

### How did you decide what type of account to open?

I opened an Internet brokerage account. I was pretty hip and knew about the Internet, so even in 1995–96, when the Internet was beginning to gather steam, I saw it as the clear alternative to investing through an expensive brokerage firm.

### Where did you get the money to invest?

I earned about $30,000 from the sale of a software business I owned. It wasn't a business in the traditional sense. I would program software, upload it onto CompuServe, and then ask a fee if the person wanted a full version. I had a successful operation going. At times I earned up to $500 per week gross. Eventually, someone spotted the software and bought all of my programs, inventory, manuals, and so forth.

### What stocks or mutual funds did you invest in?

I made many foolish investments when I got started. In one week I lost $2,000 day trading. After several months of agonizing over the day-to-day fluctuations of my stocks, I decided that there had to be a better way. One of the first long-term stocks I chose was Microsoft, then Cisco, then a number of others I've suggested on my website.

## Where did you research your investments?

Virtually all the research I do is via the Internet. One of the ways I judge the pulse of the market is through my screening of stocks. During high times, like the last few years, there have been fewer and fewer technology companies, for example, selling at reasonable prices. After screening I choose quality companies with good numbers.

## What were your expectations about investing?

I expected to make a lot of money very quickly. I thought that it was more important to earn incredible rates of return so that you could make a living from the stock market. Not every stock I owned rose as quickly as I wished. I eventually abandoned all those ideas and began looking for returns that were still excellent but not unsustainable.

## What is your favorite part of investing?

I love investing. My favorite part is the treasure hunt. I like to look through company reports and be an expert about the company. I like the confidence of being an informed investor.

## Did you make or lose money?

I began with about $30,000, and I own about $150,000 in stock now. I manage about the same amount of my parents' money.

## What is the most important thing you have learned?

Of course, I have learned about business. Investing is a gateway to understanding the business world. Investors are just spectators who risk money for businessmen. I'd like to be on the other end and be a businessman.

## What has been the most challenging thing about investing?

Selecting good companies among the several thousand companies that exist. This has been made infinitely easier by the Internet since I can do financial screening—that is, inputting criteria for a company such as earnings, debt, etc., and receiving a result list of companies.

(continued on next page)

**What advice would you give to other young investors?**

Start early. Time is a golden advantage. Learn the fundamentals of business, how the stock market works, and how to invest with long-term goals. You'll be on your way to success in no time.

**What is the product you make, and how do you make it? What does it do?**

I make a product called the annual report crib sheet, a guide available for over five hundred publicly traded companies. It is a simplified booklet to help young and/or novice investors understand the complex financials and products of a company. It took years to develop it, and I charge $9 per copy per stock.

**When and why did you decide to start your own business?**

I initially began to make money, but then I learned an aspect of what I consider compassionate business. That means helping people as best you can and letting that be your reward. Whether or not I make money, I'm happy with what I do.

likely your child's interest will grow. An interest stays new and vital if it is one that others share, especially other people your child loves to spend time with—like you! The more interest you take in your own learning curve, in your own investments, in your own stock quotes, the better you can keep a dialogue going with your child, one that is bound to teach you both something about the market, the world, and each other.

There are days, Lynn says, where the only dialogue she has with Danielle about investing lasts about thirty seconds. (Lynn: "How's your stock doing?" Danielle: "Fine.") But she never pushes it. On other occasions a headline in the news, an article she left lying on the coffee table, or a news brief on the car radio will provoke a full-blown discussion. "Hey, did you see what your company's up to? They're investing over in Europe," Danielle will say over dinner, hauling out *The Wall Street Journal* for Lynn.

**What would you like to do or be?**
I probably will end up as an investment banker or a Wall Street lawyer.

**Are you a risky or conservative investor?**
Conservative, no question.

**What was it like when you first started checking your portfolio?**
Painful.

**What is it like now?**
Painful. I don't like to worry about short-term fluctuations. I have a stake in a company that I thoroughly researched and decided would be a quality company for the next several years. In fact, if the company can continue to grow, I'd love to own it for as long as possible.

One night, as Lynn was about ready to fall asleep, Danielle came and plopped down in bed beside her with an issue of *Worth* magazine. "I just want to read you this article about Bill Gates," she said. She started reading an excerpt from a major story on the fifty best CEOs until Lynn fell asleep. Quite a bedtime story for a child to read to her grandmother!

But make no mistake: Getting your child to track her stock isn't about transforming her into a budding capitalist. In fact, it can be a powerful consciousness-raising tool. For example, when Danielle and Shannon discovered that Nike used child labor to make their sneakers, they really felt bad about it. They stopped considering Nike as a possible buy and felt good that they were not adding to the burden of the children making the shoes. This raised their social consciousness about business practices in other countries.

So investing is about giving kids a window on the world, on the events and people that make it turn. That window increases the possibilities for conversation, for activity, and for sharing between you. It has been our experience that with investing as a common interest, you and your child will establish rapport that not even adolescence can derail. And it can begin with an act as simple as sharing the newspaper each day.

## TRUE OR FALSE

1. A young investor who purchases stocks becomes a part owner of the company.    ____T    ____F
2. Capital gains is extra money a young investor may earn by purchasing stocks.    ____T    ____F
3. It is guaranteed that you will get more money back when you invest in a stock.    ____T    ____F
4. An investor can look at trends to find new companies to invest in.    ____T    ____F
5. A company cannot exist until it is sold to the public.    ____T    ____F
6. Stock purchases take place at supermarkets and Kmart.    ____T    ____F
7. Once an initial public offering takes place, the company controls the stock price.    ____T    ____F
8. A ticker symbol is used to identify a company's stock.    ____T    ____F
9. Most companies' symbols are one letter.    ____T    ____F
10. Finding investing ideas is as easy as reading, watching, and listening to what goes on around you.    ____T    ____F
11. Stock quotes are printed in the newspaper every other day.    ____T    ____F
12. On each and every stock trading day stocks may reach a new high or new low.    ____T    ____F
13. The change in a stock price from the previous session's closing price reflects either a loss or gain for the day.    ____T    ____F
14. Stocks are listed alphabetically by the company's name.    ____T    ____F
15. Stock monitoring is a simple way for kids to learn about stocks.    ____T    ____F
16. When kids monitor stocks, they learn other things about a company and the industry it operates in.    ____T    ____F
17. A conglomerate is a parent company whose holdings are so diverse, its fate is no longer tied to the fate of one particular company or industry.    ____T    ____F

18. Stock quotes can be found only in newspapers. \_\_\_\_T \_\_\_\_F
19. Investors will receive dividends if a company pays them.
    \_\_\_\_T \_\_\_\_F
20. If kids invest a portion of their money in good-quality stocks, it will compound quite a bit by the time they are twenty-five years old.
    \_\_\_\_T \_\_\_\_F

## Answer key:

| | |
|---|---|
| 1. T | 11. F |
| 2. T | 12. T |
| 3. F | 13. T |
| 4. T | 14. T |
| 5. F | 15. T |
| 6. F | 16. T |
| 7. F | 17. T |
| 8. T | 18. F |
| 9. F | 19. T |
| 10. T | 20. T |

## STOCK-MONITORING WEEKLY TRACKING FORM

Use the newspaper to track McDonald's stock.

# McDONALD'S

Date: _____ + Date: _____

Closing Price: _____ + Closing Price: _____

Daily High: _____ + Daily High: _____

Daily Low: _____ + Daily Low: _____

+++++++++++++++++++++++++++++++++++++++++++++

Date: _____ + Date: _____

Closing Price: _____ + Closing Price: _____

Daily High: _____ + Daily High: _____

Daily Low: _____ + Daily Low: _____

+++++++++++++++++++++++++++++++++++++++++++++

Date: _____ + Weekly News: _____

Closing Price: _____ + _____

Daily High: _____ + _____

Daily Low: _____ + _____

+++++++++++++++++++++++++++++++++++++++++++++

**Weekly Stock Summary**

Closing Price: _____

Daily High: _____

Daily Low: _____

+++++++++++++++++++++++++++++++++++++++++++++

## STOCK-MONITORING TRACKING CHART

Plot the price of McDonald's stock for one week.

## McDONALD'S

Price:

_____ |-----|-----|-----|-----|-----|-----|-----|-----|-----|-----|-----|-----|-----|-----|-----|-----|
_____ |-----|-----|-----|-----|-----|-----|-----|-----|-----|-----|-----|-----|-----|-----|-----|-----|
_____ |-----|-----|-----|-----|-----|-----|-----|-----|-----|-----|-----|-----|-----|-----|-----|-----|
_____ |-----|-----|-----|-----|-----|-----|-----|-----|-----|-----|-----|-----|-----|-----|-----|-----|
_____ |-----|-----|-----|-----|-----|-----|-----|-----|-----|-----|-----|-----|-----|-----|-----|-----|
_____ |-----|-----|-----|-----|-----|-----|-----|-----|-----|-----|-----|-----|-----|-----|-----|-----|
_____ |-----|-----|-----|-----|-----|-----|-----|-----|-----|-----|-----|-----|-----|-----|-----|-----|
_____ |-----|-----|-----|-----|-----|-----|-----|-----|-----|-----|-----|-----|-----|-----|-----|-----|
_____ |-----|-----|-----|-----|-----|-----|-----|-----|-----|-----|-----|-----|-----|-----|-----|-----|
_____ |-----|-----|-----|-----|-----|-----|-----|-----|-----|-----|-----|-----|-----|-----|-----|-----|
_____ |-----|-----|-----|-----|-----|-----|-----|-----|-----|-----|-----|-----|-----|-----|-----|-----|
_____ |-----|-----|-----|-----|-----|-----|-----|-----|-----|-----|-----|-----|-----|-----|-----|-----|
_____ |-----|-----|-----|-----|-----|-----|-----|-----|-----|-----|-----|-----|-----|-----|-----|-----|
_____ |-----|-----|-----|-----|-----|-----|-----|-----|-----|-----|-----|-----|-----|-----|-----|-----|
_____ |-----|-----|-----|-----|-----|-----|-----|-----|-----|-----|-----|-----|-----|-----|-----|-----|
_____ |-----|-----|-----|-----|-----|-----|-----|-----|-----|-----|-----|-----|-----|-----|-----|-----|
_____ |-----|-----|-----|-----|-----|-----|-----|-----|-----|-----|-----|-----|-----|-----|-----|-----|
_____ |-----|-----|-----|-----|-----|-----|-----|-----|-----|-----|-----|-----|-----|-----|-----|-----|
_____ |-----|-----|-----|-----|-----|-----|-----|-----|-----|-----|-----|-----|-----|-----|-----|-----|
_____ |-----|-----|-----|-----|-----|-----|-----|-----|-----|-----|-----|-----|-----|-----|-----|-----|
_____ |-----|-----|-----|-----|-----|-----|-----|-----|-----|-----|-----|-----|-----|-----|-----|-----|
_____ |-----|-----|-----|-----|-----|-----|-----|-----|-----|-----|-----|-----|-----|-----|-----|-----|
_____ |-----|-----|-----|-----|-----|-----|-----|-----|-----|-----|-----|-----|-----|-----|-----|-----|
_____ |-----|-----|-----|-----|-----|-----|-----|-----|-----|-----|-----|-----|-----|-----|-----|-----|
_____ |-----|-----|-----|-----|-----|-----|-----|-----|-----|-----|-----|-----|-----|-----|-----|-----|
_____ |-----|-----|-----|-----|-----|-----|-----|-----|-----|-----|-----|-----|-----|-----|-----|-----|
_____ |-----|-----|-----|-----|-----|-----|-----|-----|-----|-----|-----|-----|-----|-----|-----|-----|
_____ |-----|-----|-----|-----|-----|-----|-----|-----|-----|-----|-----|-----|-----|-----|-----|-----|
_____ |-----|-----|-----|-----|-----|-----|-----|-----|-----|-----|-----|-----|-----|-----|-----|-----|
_____ |-----|-----|-----|-----|-----|-----|-----|-----|-----|-----|-----|-----|-----|-----|-----|-----|
_____ |-----|-----|-----|-----|-----|-----|-----|-----|-----|-----|-----|-----|-----|-----|-----|-----|

Date:

## STOCK-MONITORING WEEKLY TRACKING FORM

Use the newspaper to track your favorite stock.

## Stock Name: _____

Date: _____ + Date: _____
                          +
                          +
Closing Price:_____ + Closing Price:_____
                          +
Daily High: _____ + Daily High: _____
                          +
Daily Low: _____ + Daily Low: _____
+++++++++++++++++++++++++++++++++++++++++++++++++
Date: _____ + Date: _____
                          +
Closing Price:_____ + Closing Price:_____
                          +
Daily High: _____ + Daily High: _____
                          +
Daily Low: _____ + Daily Low: _____
+++++++++++++++++++++++++++++++++++++++++++++++++
Date: _____ + Weekly News: _____
                          +
Closing Price:_____ + _____
                          +
Daily High: _____ + _____
                          +
Daily Low: _____ + _____
+++++++++++++++++++++++++++++++++++++++++++++++++

### Weekly Stock Summary

Weekly Price: _____

Weekly High: _____

Weekly Low: _____
+++++++++++++++++++++++++++++++++++++++++++++++++

## STOCK-MONITORING TRACKING CHART

Plot the price of your stock for one week.

### Stock Name: _____

**Price:**

_____  |-----|-----|-----|-----|-----|-----|-----|-----|-----|-----|-----|-----|-----|-----|-----|
_____  |-----|-----|-----|-----|-----|-----|-----|-----|-----|-----|-----|-----|-----|-----|-----|
_____  |-----|-----|-----|-----|-----|-----|-----|-----|-----|-----|-----|-----|-----|-----|-----|
_____  |-----|-----|-----|-----|-----|-----|-----|-----|-----|-----|-----|-----|-----|-----|-----|
_____  |-----|-----|-----|-----|-----|-----|-----|-----|-----|-----|-----|-----|-----|-----|-----|
_____  |-----|-----|-----|-----|-----|-----|-----|-----|-----|-----|-----|-----|-----|-----|-----|
_____  |-----|-----|-----|-----|-----|-----|-----|-----|-----|-----|-----|-----|-----|-----|-----|
_____  |-----|-----|-----|-----|-----|-----|-----|-----|-----|-----|-----|-----|-----|-----|-----|
_____  |-----|-----|-----|-----|-----|-----|-----|-----|-----|-----|-----|-----|-----|-----|-----|
_____  |-----|-----|-----|-----|-----|-----|-----|-----|-----|-----|-----|-----|-----|-----|-----|
_____  |-----|-----|-----|-----|-----|-----|-----|-----|-----|-----|-----|-----|-----|-----|-----|
_____  |-----|-----|-----|-----|-----|-----|-----|-----|-----|-----|-----|-----|-----|-----|-----|
_____  |-----|-----|-----|-----|-----|-----|-----|-----|-----|-----|-----|-----|-----|-----|-----|
_____  |-----|-----|-----|-----|-----|-----|-----|-----|-----|-----|-----|-----|-----|-----|-----|
_____  |-----|-----|-----|-----|-----|-----|-----|-----|-----|-----|-----|-----|-----|-----|-----|
_____  |-----|-----|-----|-----|-----|-----|-----|-----|-----|-----|-----|-----|-----|-----|-----|
_____  |-----|-----|-----|-----|-----|-----|-----|-----|-----|-----|-----|-----|-----|-----|-----|
_____  |-----|-----|-----|-----|-----|-----|-----|-----|-----|-----|-----|-----|-----|-----|-----|
_____  |-----|-----|-----|-----|-----|-----|-----|-----|-----|-----|-----|-----|-----|-----|-----|
_____  |-----|-----|-----|-----|-----|-----|-----|-----|-----|-----|-----|-----|-----|-----|-----|
_____  |-----|-----|-----|-----|-----|-----|-----|-----|-----|-----|-----|-----|-----|-----|-----|
_____  |-----|-----|-----|-----|-----|-----|-----|-----|-----|-----|-----|-----|-----|-----|-----|
_____  |-----|-----|-----|-----|-----|-----|-----|-----|-----|-----|-----|-----|-----|-----|-----|
_____  |-----|-----|-----|-----|-----|-----|-----|-----|-----|-----|-----|-----|-----|-----|-----|
_____  |-----|-----|-----|-----|-----|-----|-----|-----|-----|-----|-----|-----|-----|-----|-----|
_____  |-----|-----|-----|-----|-----|-----|-----|-----|-----|-----|-----|-----|-----|-----|-----|
_____  |-----|-----|-----|-----|-----|-----|-----|-----|-----|-----|-----|-----|-----|-----|-----|
_____  |-----|-----|-----|-----|-----|-----|-----|-----|-----|-----|-----|-----|-----|-----|-----|
_____  |-----|-----|-----|-----|-----|-----|-----|-----|-----|-----|-----|-----|-----|-----|-----|
_____  |-----|-----|-----|-----|-----|-----|-----|-----|-----|-----|-----|-----|-----|-----|-----|

**Date:**

# 4

## How Now the Dow?

Your kids and ours are bull market babies.

Since their birth the stock market has experienced the most explosive growth in its history—8,000 points in the last eight years alone. That number is even more impressive when you consider that it took the market seventy-six years to break through 1,000, in 1972. Not until 1988 did it pass the 2,000 mark. But then the momentum began to build: By 1991 the market was at 3,000; by 1995 it was over 4,000; and that same year—in nine months' time—the market hit 5,000. The biggest, fastest jump occurred in 1999, when the market leaped from 10,000 to 11,000 in five breathtaking weeks—an event watched and reported like the dropping of the New Year's Eve ball in Times Square.

Of course, if you call your child a bull market baby without explaining what that means, he is sure to look at you as though you've lost it. So say something like " 'Bull market' is how we describe the stock market when prices keep going up and up over time—just the way they have been doing for the last few years and ever since you were born."

How else can you help your child put this astounding growth into context? We've come up with another one of our handy visual aids that helps to personalize the Dow for your child. By taking the Dow Jones Industrial Average (DJIA) for each of her birthdays and plotting these numbers to form a growth curve, you can see how the Dow grows along with your child.

First, log on to the website http://averages.dowjones.com./home.html.

Then click on: Dow Data

Next, click on: Historical Queries

Finally, enter: Month, Day and Year and click on "Submit Date" button to obtain the "DJ Industrial Average" for your special day.

She can look up each of her birthdays and find out what the market's high, low, and closing prices were for those days. Enter the information on the blank form provided at the end of this chapter (page 115). For birthdays that fell on a weekend there won't be any index figures because the market is closed on Saturdays and Sundays. Take a look at Shannon's Dow Growth stats. You can see when her birthday fell on a weekend. Pat was disappointed that Shannon couldn't record the index in 1998 and 1999 because those were the years with the most amazing gains in the index. But the birthday chart does show how much the Dow has grown during Shannon's lifetime: from 1,156.51 on the day she was born to a current high of just under 11,000 now that she's a teenager.

Once your child has made a list of the Dow averages for each of her birthdays, she can transfer them to a graph. When she has plotted the points, have her connect the dots. The line she draws—a steadily ascending hill with a growth spurt at the end—will look a lot like the line her pediatrician has been drawing for her height and weight since her birth. She and the Dow have grown up together!

## All About the Dow

These days when business reporters comment that "the market was up" or "the market barely moved," more and more people

## DOW GROWTH CHART, PART A

------------------------------------------------------------

### SHANNON YODER, BORN APRIL 18, 1984
------------------------------------------------------------

| Age: Year | Dow High | Dow Low | Dow Close |
|---|---|---|---|
| Birth / 1984 | 1,167.71 | 1,151.07 | 1,156.51 |
| 1: 1985 | 1,281.91 | 1,260.82 | 1,265.13 |
| 2: 1986 | 1,870.16 | 1,830.98 | 1,840.40 |
| 3: 1987 | Saturday, market closed | | |
| 4: 1988 | 2,023.04 | 1,985.74 | 2,008.12 |
| 5: 1989 | 2,386.00 | 2,351.36 | 2,379.40 |
| 6: 1990 | 2,775.68 | 2,722.75 | 2,732.88 |
| 7: 1991 | 3,027.72 | 2,976.24 | 2,999.26 |
| 8: 1992 | Saturday, market closed | | |
| 9: 1993 | Sunday, market closed | | |
| 10: 1994 | 3,679.61 | 3,593.35 | 3,620.42 |
| 11: 1995 | 4,205.07 | 4,169.10 | 4,179.13 |
| 12: 1996 | 5,564.38 | 5,522.83 | 5,551.74 |
| 13: 1997 | 6,711.98 | 6,657.40 | 6,703.55 |
| 14: 1998 | Saturday, market closed | | |
| 15: 1999 | Sunday, market closed | | |
| 16: 2000 | | | |
| 17: 2001 | | | |
| 18: 2002 | | | |

Notice that we plotted only the closing price of the Dow to create this chart.

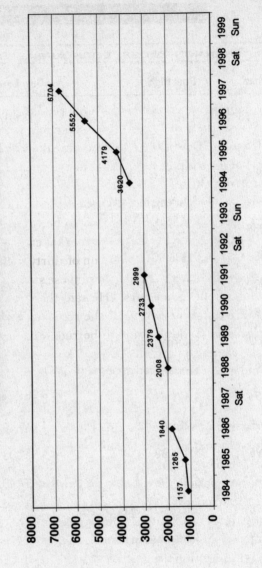

## DOW GROWTH CHART: PART 2

### Shannon Yoder's Dow Growth Chart

tune in because more ordinary people are investing in stocks or mutual funds. Kids, too, can't help but be aware of the stock market. They've grown up hearing the word *Dow* as we grew up hearing the words *women's liberation*. The market boom has been the defining news of their generation just as the women's movement was the defining news of their parents' generation.

People use the word *Dow* interchangeably with *the market* and also refer to the Dow as a number. Where does that number come from? What does it measure? What does it mean?

If you're not entirely sure of the answers, you're not alone. One day Shannon came home from school and reported to Pat that her teacher had lectured about the Dow to her ninth-grade class because they were studying the stock market crash of 1929. He told the class that the Dow was made up of thirty stocks and that the people at *The Wall Street Journal* chose these stocks every day. Shannon couldn't believe her ears. "He said the stocks that make up the Dow are different *every day!*" she repeated to Pat over her afternoon snack. "I didn't want to be rude and say anything, but they *don't* change every day. Even I know that!" Shannon was clearly indignant that everyone did not know this simple fact.

Kids who own stock are going to start listening intently when this mysterious Dow is mentioned on the nightly news. Eventually they are going to ask, *What exactly is the Dow?* You can confidently tell your child that the Dow is a list of thirty stocks chosen by Dow Jones & Company, the people who publish *The Wall Street Journal*. They are not picked every day; they hardly ever change. The list includes the strongest companies in the widest number of American industries. For example, Johnson & Johnson and Merck are two companies in the pharmaceutical industry; they make bandages and prescription drugs. Coca-Cola is in the beverage industry, which supplies soft drinks.

Each of the thirty so-called Dow Industrials represents a segment of the U.S. economy. Taken together, they represent the diversity in the U.S. marketplace from aluminum manufacturers to

## HOW NOW CHARLES DOW?

At the end of the nineteenth century, computers and television did not exist. Up-to-the-minute financial news had to be handwritten and rush-delivered by messengers to banks and brokers, and there was no such thing as a daily stock journal with up-to-the-minute stock information. Enter Charles Henry Dow, born in Sterling, Connecticut, on November 6, 1851. Raised on a farm, he moved at eighteen to Springfield, Massachusetts, where he wrote for the *Daily Republican*. He later moved to Providence, Rhode Island, to work on the *Providence Journal*. It was there that he discovered his keen interest in financial affairs. He finally ended up in New York working at the Kiernan News Agency, which sent messengers to deliver handwritten financial information to banks and brokers. In 1882, Dow and his coworker and friend Edward Jones pounced on the opportunity to create a much-needed financial news bulletin, left the Kiernan agency, and began Dow Jones & Company. Along with colleague Charles M. Bergstresser, they gathered financial news and published it in a daily newsletter.

The quotes were published in a two-page newsletter called the *Customer's Afternoon Letter*, renamed *The Wall Street Journal* in 1889, when it became a complete newspaper. This was the only place investors could turn to find financial information concerning publicly traded companies. No other source existed, and until then companies often refused to report their financial records accurately.

Charles Dow also developed the first stock average that could be used to gauge the progress of the whole market. In 1884 the Dow Jones Index consisted of eleven companies, ten of them railroads (which constituted almost all of the large-volume stocks). This average acted as a barometer for the whole market. It was not until 1896 that the Dow Jones Industrial Average was created. Comprising twelve companies, the average allowed investors and brokers to see the status of the market as a whole. Acting as an editor and contributor to *The Wall Street Journal* and adjusting his list of companies in the DJIA, Charles Dow invested all his energies in his company and newsletter until his death in 1902.

## EDWARD JONES

Notorious for his fiery temper and intense personality, Edward Jones was the perfect complement to Charles Dow's calm manner. The two met while working on newspapers in Providence, Rhode Island, and both relocated to work at the Kiernan News Agency in New York. In 1882 they left the agency to begin their own information bulletin. As the partners of Dow Jones & Company and the *Customer's Afternoon Letter (The Wall Street Journal)*, they worked together until 1899, when Jones left to join a brokerage firm.

Dow and Bergstresser, the third partner, often disapproved of Jones's violent verbal outbursts and quick temper, but his dedication to the journal was evident. He edited, wrote, and socialized in financial circles, gleaning hot tips to be included in the newsletter. He died in New York in 1920 at age sixty-five.

## CHARLES BERGSTRESSER

Charles M. Bergstresser was born to a large Dutch family in Lykens Valley, Pennsylvania, in 1859. He graduated from Lafayette College in 1881 and then moved to New York, where he flexed his reporting muscles at the Kiernan News Agency, covering the stock market. He had a talent for procuring valuable inside information, even landing an interview with John Pierpont Morgan, Sr. It was while working at the Kiernan News Agency that he became acquainted with Charles Dow and Edward Jones. When he heard of their plan to leave the agency and start their own company, he persuaded them to let him be a third partner.

He did have something that Jones and Dow did not—funds. He provided the financial backing for their new publishing enterprise. Due to the unwieldy length of his name, his was not included in the title of the company, but his contributions, monetary and otherwise, were integral to its establishment. It was Bergstresser who, in 1889, renamed the letter-cum-newspaper *The Wall Street Journal*.

beverage producers, from telecommunications to travel and finance. We've listed them here in some detail so that you can see why these few stocks are used to take the pulse of the entire marketplace. They may not be the biggest companies out there, but they are the most representative, which is why people use *the market* and *the Dow* interchangeably.

Reporters also use the term *Dow* to refer to a number, as in "The Dow plunged to 10,678 today." This number is the actual measure of the market, computed by averaging the share prices of those thirty industrials. Used as a number, *the Dow* is shorthand for the Dow Jones Industrial Average (DJIA), as in "the Dow Jones Industrial Average plunged to 10,678 today."

You can also explain to your child that, like so much of the stock market, there is a fascinating human face behind these lists and numbers. (You don't have to mention this is a mini–history lesson; that can be our secret.) Charles H. Dow, cofounder of Dow Jones & Company and the first editor of *The Wall Street Journal,* first computed this average in 1896. Back then the market was thought of as a place to gamble, and there was no way for investors to get a consistent sense of how their bets were paying off. Charles Dow thought his index of companies (originally twelve industrials, not thirty) and his average of their share prices could cut through the confusion of daily price fluctuations by giving a reading that was consistent from one day to the next. Investors could then tell if their stocks were gaining, losing, or holding their own in value.

The twelve companies that Charles Dow chose to average were the largest, most recognizable, and most frequently traded stocks in the market. It wasn't the first average he devised, but it was the most representational. Twelve years earlier he had come up with an index of eleven companies, but since most of them were railroad giants, he eventually called this the Transportation Index (which is still in use today, although it now includes airlines as well). When the first Dow Jones Industrial Average was published on May 26, 1896, it was just a piddling 40.94.

The original twelve companies in the Dow expanded to twenty

---

### THE ORIGINAL DOW 12

| Company | What Became of It |
| --- | --- |
| 1. American Cotton Oil | Distant ancestor of Best Foods |
| 2. American Sugar | Evolved into Amstar Holdings |
| 3. American Tobacco | Broken up in a 1911 antitrust action |
| 4. Chicago Gas | Absorbed by People's Gas in 1887 |
| 5. Distilling and Cattle Feeding | Whiskey trust evolved into Millennium Chemical |
| 6. General Electric | Going strong and still in DJIA |
| 7. Laclede Gas | Active but removed in 1899 |
| 8. National Lead | Today's NL Industries; removed from DJIA in 1916 |
| 9. North American | Utility broken up in 1940s |
| 10. Tennessee Coal & Iron | Absorbed by US Steel in 1907 |
| 11. US Leather (Preferred) | Dissolved in 1952 |
| 12. US Rubber | Became Uniroyal, now part of Michelin |

in 1916 and to thirty in 1928. From the original list of twelve you can see that there is only one company—General Electric—that has remained for the more than one hundred years that the Dow index has been in existence. Companies have been added or removed based on how well each represents a segment of the U.S. economy. In 1997, Hewlett-Packard, Johnson & Johnson, Travelers Group (now Citigroup), and Wal-Mart Stores replaced Bethlehem Steel, Texaco, Westinghouse Electric (now CBS Corp.), and Woolworth. The latest change occurred while we were writing this book: Microsoft Corp., Intel Corp., SBC Communications, Inc., and Home Depot, Inc., were added on November 1, 1999, replacing Sears, Roebuck, Goodyear Tire & Rubber, Chevron Corp., and Union Carbide—four companies that joined the DJIA during the Roaring '20s and the Great Depression. This represented one of the most significant changes in the Dow for two reasons: First, three of the new companies (Microsoft, Intel, and SBC Communications) have made their mark in the technology field, and it is the first time the DJIA has been changed to reflect the growing influence of technology on the global economy. Second, two of the new additions (Intel and Microsoft) are on the NASDAQ Exchange, the first time that a company in the Dow has been on an exchange other than the New York Stock Exchange. Interestingly, it has been reported that the NYSE is saving the stock symbols "M" and "I" in case Microsoft and Intel ever move to the NYSE—moves that would also be historic.

## What the Dow Means

Once your child has learned the Dow's past, the next step is to put the Dow into perspective for the present and look toward the future. In other words, why Wow the Dow?

A friend of Pat's checks on the Dow every day, not just once but several times, and he even checks on the share prices of his own stocks. One day Pat asked him why he was so obsessed with the Index. "Well," he replied, "if I see my stocks are up on a day when the Dow is down, then I feel really good because it means my investment choices are better than the best, the ones in the Index. I've 'beaten the Dow'!"

For Pat's friend, beating the Dow is a measure of his personal success in investing. In fact, from Wall Street to Main Street, from brokers to ordinary investors, and from grown-ups to children, the investing world uses the Dow as a gauge of the economy and its own financial health because the Dow Index is the oldest and most recognized indicator of market performance since performance began to be measured. If the Dow is doing well (meaning the DJIA is climbing), then our economic future looks bright nationally as well as globally since many companies in the Dow serve the world as well. If our stocks are doing better than the Dow, then our personal financial future also looks bright.

The Dow Industrials—the thirty stocks in the Index—are considered excellent stocks to hold because of their reputations within each industry. The reason they're in the Dow—"on the Big

Board," we say, referring to their listing on the New York Stock Exchange's actual big board—is that they have consistently shown steady growth, innovation, product development, and marketing and distribution muscle. They're what we call "blue-chip" stocks, a reference to the most valuable chips in a poker game. We are all familiar with their products or services, and they are the backbone of the U.S. economy.

Without further ado, may we present the Dow (courtesy of the Yahoo Finance website):

## The Dow 30

**Alcoa** is an integrated aluminum company. It manufactures and sells semifabricated and finished aluminum products all over the world.

**AT&T** provides voice, data, and video telecommunications services, including cellular telephone and Internet services, to businesses, consumers, and government agencies. It also provides cable TV services to millions of customers throughout the United States.

**American Express** and its subsidiaries provide travel-related services, financial advisory services, and international banking services worldwide.

**Boeing** develops and produces jet transports, military aircraft, and space and missile systems through two industry segments: commercial aircraft and defense and space.

**Caterpillar** designs, manufactures, and markets earthmoving, construction, and materials-handling machinery and heavy-duty engines.

**Citigroup** is a diversified holding company whose businesses provide a range of financial services, including banking, insurance, and investment services, to consumer and corporate customers around the world.

**Coca-Cola** manufactures, markets, and distributes soft-drink concentrates and syrups, other fruit juice products, and ready-to-drink tea and coffee beverages.

**Disney** is a diversified worldwide entertainment company that operates in three segments: creative content, broadcasting, and theme parks and resorts.

**Du Pont** is a global science company specializing in chemical and materials sciences and biological sciences.

**Eastman Kodak** primarily develops, manufactures, and markets consumer and commercial imaging products.

**ExxonMobil** is engaged in the exploration, production, manufacture, transportation, and sale of crude oil, natural gas, and petroleum products. (The company was formed following the November 30, 1999, merger of the Dow component Exxon Corporation and its competitor, Mobil Corporation.)

**General Electric** is a diversified industrial corporation whose merchandise includes appliances, lighting products, aircraft engines, and plastics. It also provides television, cable, Internet, distribution, engineering, and financial services.

**General Motors** designs, manufactures, and markets automobiles, trucks, and related parts; designs and manufactures locomotives and heavy-duty transmissions; and operates a financial services and insurance company.

**Hewlett-Packard Company** designs, manufactures, and services products and systems for measurement, computation, and communications, and offers systems integration, outsourcing, consulting, education, financing, and customer support services.

**Home Depot, Inc.,** is a home improvement retailer that sells building materials and home, lawn, and garden products.

**Honeywell** (formerly AlliedSignal) is a diversified industrial company operating within three major business segments: aerospace, automotive, and engineered materials. Honeywell's broad base of products includes airplane engines, environmental control systems, airborne weather radar systems, wind shear detection systems, traffic collision avoidance radar systems, guidance systems for missiles and spacecraft, air bags, Autolite spark plugs, Prestone antifreeze, as well as a variety of chemicals, fibers, and plastics.

**IBM** provides customer solutions through the use of advanced information technology; these solutions include technologies, systems, products, services, software, and financing.

**Intel Corporation** designs, develops, manufactures, and markets computer components and related products.

**International Paper** is a global forest products, paper, and packaging company that distributes wood pulp, lumber, panels, photosensitive films, chemicals, and nonwoven products.

**Johnson & Johnson** is a manufacturer of health care products serving the consumer, pharmaceutical, and professional markets.

**McDonald's** develops, operates, franchises, and services a worldwide system of restaurants that prepare, assemble, package, and sell a limited menu of value-priced foods.

**Merck** is a pharmaceutical company that discovers, develops, produces, and markets human and animal health products and services. It also provides pharmaceutical benefit services.

**Microsoft Corporation** develops, manufactures, licenses, and supports a wide range of software products for intelligent devices, personal computers, and servers.

**Minnesota Mining and Manufacturing Company** manufactures and markets pressure-sensitive adhesive tapes, abrasives, and specialty chemicals. It also markets electrical and telecommunication products, medical devices, office supplies, and major automotive parts.

**J. P. Morgan** is a holding company for subsidiaries engaged globally in banking, financial advisory, securities underwriting, trading and investment fund management services, and market making.

**Philip Morris** is a holding company whose principal subsidiaries are engaged in the manufacture and sale of various consumer products, including cigarettes, packaged and processed foods, and beverages.

**Procter & Gamble** markets a broad range of consumer products worldwide in five business segments: laundry and cleaning, paper, beauty care, foods and beverages, and health care.

------------------------------------------------------------
## DOW STOCK SYMBOLS
------------------------------------------------------------

| | |
|---|---|
| Alcoa (AA) | Honeywell (HON) |
| American Express (AXP) | IBM (IBM) |
| AT&T (T) | Intel (INTC) |
| Boeing (BA) | International Paper (IP) |
| Caterpillar (CAT) | Johnson & Johnson (JNJ) |
| Citigroup (C) | McDonald's (MCD) |
| Coca-Cola (KO) | Merck (MRK) |
| Disney (DIS) | Microsoft (MSFT) |
| Du Pont (DD) | Minnesota Mining and Manufacturing (MMM) |
| Eastman Kodak (EK) | J. P. Morgan (JPM) |
| ExxonMobil (XOM) | Philip Morris (MO) |
| General Electric (GE) | Procter & Gamble (PG) |
| General Motors (GM) | SBC Communications (SBC) |
| Hewlett-Packard (HWP) | United Technologies (UTX) |
| Home Depot (HD) | Wal-Mart (WMT) |

**SBC Communications** and its subsidiaries and affiliates provide wireline and wireless telecommunications services and equipment, directory advertising, and publishing and cable television services.

**United Technologies'** principal products are Otis elevators and escalators; Carrier heating, ventilating, and air-conditioning systems; Pratt and Whitney engines, parts, and space propulsion; and Sikorsky helicopters, parts, and services.

**Wal-Mart** operates discount department stores (Wal-Mart), warehouse membership clubs (Sam's Clubs), and a combination of full-line supermarket and discount department stores (Wal-Mart Supercenters) in the United States, Puerto Rico, Mexico, Canada, Argentina, Brazil, China, and Indonesia.

## How the Dow Is Computed

The Dow is such a rich (pun intended) resource to mine for kid-friendly, educational fun. We've shown you the historical side; now let's do the math!

Calculating the Dow used to be as simple as adding up all the share prices for each stock in the Dow Jones Industrial Index and then dividing the total by the number of stocks in the Dow. The Dow Jones Industrial Average was exactly that—an average. Over the years, however, this concept has evolved into something more complex, due largely to stock splits.

Instead of dividing the sum of the Dow stock prices by thirty, a smaller number, called a *divisor,* is used. The divisor isn't something you or we can come up with on our own. It's a mathematical accounting of each and every split. Every time one of the Dow industrials announces a stock split, the divisor changes: It gets smaller. Sometimes stocks in the Dow are eliminated or new ones are added, or companies merge or pay out dividends: These changes affect the divisor as well.

Since the divisor reflects all sorts of changes, it can vary almost daily. For example, on May 18, 1999, United Technologies' two-for-one stock split reduced the divisor from 0.21825395 to 0.21190229—and this was a number that had started out as high as 30! In fact, because the divisor is now a fraction, dividing with it has a multiplying effect: the tinier the divisor number, the bigger the Industrial Average gets. And if you think the Dow is Wow! now, imagine this: Some say the Dow would be over the 40,000 mark today if IBM had stayed among the Dow Industrials instead of being removed for forty years. This is because the company experienced numerous stock splits between 1939 (when it was replaced on the Big Board by AT&T) and 1979 (when it was added to the DJIA again).

You and your child may be relieved to know that we don't have to compute the DJIA for ourselves every day. It's done for us—and not just once but throughout the day. But the formula for

## A Good Answer to a Stock Question

### What's a stock split?

Sometimes, after a stock price has gone up a lot, the board of directors of the company decides the stock has become too expensive for people to buy, so they announce a stock split.

Typically, a stock split may be a two for one or three for two or three for one. A two-for-one split means you will receive two shares for every one you own, and the price for each share goes down by half. A three-for-two split means that for every two shares you already own, you own three shares now, and the price for each share goes down by two thirds.

*Example:* Disney stock closed at 111 on July 9, 1998, and the next morning, before the market opened, there was a three-for-one stock split. This means that on July 10, 1998, shareholders had three shares for every one they previously owned, and the stock price adjusted for this split. Disney closed at 38.125 on July 10, 1998.

arriving at the Index isn't that complicated once you know the divisor, and you can find out what it is for the day by looking in the money and investing section of *The Wall Street Journal* or going online at http://averages.dowjones.com.

1. Click on Dow Jones Averages; then
2. Click on Dow Data; then
3. Click on Divisors; then
4. Click on Dow Jones Industrial Average Divisor

There you will find at the top of the list the "Current DJIA Divisor" for the entire thirty Dow stocks that you will use to compute the closing numbers of the DJIA for the day. Actually, any ten-year-old can compute the Index, and it's great for kids to know how to do just that, which is why we had the Stock MarKids try it (and why we've included a worksheet on page 118 so your child can try his hand at it).

---
## DAY OF THE DOW
---

Here's how the Dow added up to 10,000 for the first time, on March 29, 1999:

| Company Name and Symbol | Stock Closing Price |
|---|---|
| Alcoa (AA) | 41.8125 |
| Allied Signal (ALD) | 50.75 |
| American Express (AXP) | 123.3125 |
| AT&T (T) | 81.69 |
| Boeing (BA) | 34.75 |
| Caterpillar (CAT) | 47.25 |
| Chevron (CHV) | 89.625 |
| Citigroup (C) | 64.1875 |
| Coca-Cola (KO) | 67.1875 |
| Disney (DIS) | 33.0625 |
| Du Pont (DD) | 57.25 |
| Eastman Kodak (EK) | 65.625 |
| Exxon (XON) | 72.9375 |
| General Electric (GE) | 111.9375 |
| General Motors (GM) | 87.25 |
| Goodyear Tire (GT) | 50.0625 |
| Hewlett-Packard (HWP) | 69.625 |
| IBM (IBM) | 177.5625 |
| International Paper (IP) | 44.1875 |
| Johnson & Johnson (JNJ) | 93.9375 |
| McDonald's (MCD) | 45.625 |
| Merck (MRK) | 81.875 |
| Minnesota Mining and Manufacturing (MMM) | 71.3125 |
| J. P. Morgan (JPM) | 125.8125 |
| Philip Morris (MO) | 41.1875 |
| Procter & Gamble (PG) | 101.125 |
| Sears (S) | 46.75 |
| Union Carbide (UK) | 46.375 |
| United Technologies (UTX) | 134.4375 |
| Wal-Mart (WMT) | 95.25 |
| **Daily total:** | **2,253.75** |

The prices totaled 2,253.75. A look at *The Wall Street Journal* tells us the divisor was 0.22522230 on March 29, 1999. Here's the math:

$$\frac{2{,}253.75}{0.22522230} = 10{,}006.78$$

And there you have it: the Dow Jones Industrial Average. You can tell your child that it comes out to more than 10,000 because dividing by such a tiny fraction has an enormous multiplying effect on the share price total—like multiplying 2,253.75 by 4.44.

We take for granted that it's possible to check on the Index at any time, but that's because we have computers to crunch the numbers every minute—for the DJIA as well as for all the other indexes you'll find in newspaper business sections. (We'll discuss these indexes next.) Pat believes it was our demand for constant indexing that spurred the invention of the computer. No wonder Charles Dow computed only *one* index *once* at the end of the trading day!

## The Major Stock Exchanges

Before the latest changes in November 1999, all thirty of the Dow Industrials used to be traded on the New York Stock Exchange. Don't assume your child will understand that this is an actual physical location, especially after he has been reading the paper and thinking of it more as a list. Explain that the NYSE, located on Wall Street in New York City's financial district, is like an actual marketplace, not a farmer's market but a stock market.

There are more than three thousand companies listed on it. Keeping track of this many stocks requires some very sophisticated tools and systems. One of them, called Stock Watch, is a computerized system that automatically flags unusual volume or price changes in any listed stock. It helps the Securities and Exchange Commission (SEC), the federal watchdog agency charged with protecting the stock markets, guard against manipulation of stock prices. Any unexplained large volume or trading price change may trigger an investigation by either the NYSE, the SEC, or both.

In addition to this orderliness, the NYSE is the most popular exchange for investors for one other big reason: Securities can be bought and sold immediately and easily because for every seller there is usually an eager buyer.

With the boom in technology stocks, another exchange has caught the public's trading attention. It's called the NASDAQ, and it was started by the National Association of Securities Dealers, Inc. (NASD), in 1971. In the last twenty years it has become the fastest-growing and second largest stock market in the world. Companies such as Microsoft and Intel are among the best-known technology stocks listed on the NASDAQ. Companies like these have attracted millions of investors to watch the NASDAQ for the next technology IPO. (You may recall that we said the addition of these two particular companies to the Dow was historical because it showed that the major players on Wall Street now recognize the importance of technology companies in the global marketplace.)

NASDAQ has become so powerful that it recently merged with the American Stock Exchange to form the NASDAQ-AMEX exchange. The actual lists of stocks have remained separate, however; the stocks trading on the AMEX tend to be smaller and lesser-known companies. Originally, the AMEX was an outdoor market in New York; traders got fresh air with their stock. Then in 1921 the exchange moved indoors, and it has remained in its present space near Wall Street ever since. The NASDAQ-AMEX Market Group provides a live webcast of the American Stock Exchange trading floor. Check it out anytime from Monday through Friday, between 9:15 A.M. EST and 4:35 P.M. EST, at www.nasdaq-amexwebcast.com.

The oldest and perhaps most colorful of all the exchanges is the Philadelphia Stock Exchange (PHLX), established in 1790. New York was the first to receive news from the ships that arrived from

Europe, and then the news traveled via pounding hooves and lurching coaches over the dirt highways between New York and Philadelphia. Later, construction of the Erie Canal allowed New York to take the lead from Philadelphia in the commercial life of the nation, and the NYSE officially started in 1817 with a constitution that was almost an exact copy of the charter of the Philadelphia exchange.

Now for the best part: You can use the Philadelphia story as a teachable moment for manners! Its charter was accompanied by a code of civility and common decency. It isn't much in evidence on a trading floor today, but back in the nineteenth century the code was so important that much of the PHLX revenues came from fines levied on members who broke it. Offenses were spelled out in detail, along with their fines. For example, addressing the chair with one's mouth full was an offense. Profane language called for a fine of a dollar. Members who uttered the word *devil* had to pay a dollar, too. Winding the clock without the permission of the president was more serious: a $5 fine. Fines were issued for putting feet on chairs, whistling, and being absent from morning roll call. The introduction of the telegraph, and in 1884 the ticker, made many of these rules obsolete.

What sets the Philadelphia exchange apart other than its rich history is its trading hours. In September 1987 Philadelphia was the first securities exchange in the United States to introduce an evening trading session. In January 1989 the exchange responded to growing European demands by adding an early morning session. Finally, in September 1990, Philadelphia became the first exchange in the world to offer round-the-clock trading by bridging the gap between the night session and the early morning hours. The exchange subsequently scaled back its trading hours; currently, the PHLX is open from 2:30 A.M. to 2:30 P.M. EST. Now that the PHLX has agreed to merge with the American Stock Exchange and become a charter member of the proposed NASDAQ-AMEX family, further changes in its trading hours are probably afoot in response to the public's online trading hunger. In fact, we wouldn't be surprised to see other exchanges, adding additional trading hours in the not-too-distant future.

The NYSE, NASDAQ, AMEX, and PHLX are the best-known of the U.S. exchanges, but there are several others. To learn more about them, World Stock Exchanges Links maintains a list. Visit their website at www.fundlinks.com/global-f.html.

## Other Stock Indexes

The DJIA is the most famous of all of the stock market indexes, but there are others. Let your child look at all the stocks in the newspaper on all the exchanges and then ask her if she thinks thirty stocks can accurately represent the entire stock market. If she doesn't think so, you can explain that others agree. There is room for other indexes to offer an alternative to investors who feel the DJIA presents only part of the picture. The best-known of these others are the Standard & Poor's 500 Index (the S&P 500), the NASDAQ Index, the NYSE Composite Index, the American Stock Exchange Index, the Russell 5000, and the Wilshire Index.

Standard & Poor's actually has many indexes, but the S&P 500 is the one we hear about most often. In 1926 the S&P index consisted of 223 companies; now there are 500, most of them in the United States. Technologies, utilities, banks, retail, health care, transportation, and industrials—the Dow 30—are also included. The S&P 500 index is calculated by using what is called a base-weighted aggregate method, which is probably impossible to try to explain to a child. We know many adults who don't really understand it. But for your information, the total market value is determined by multiplying the price of its stocks by the number of shares outstanding. This means that if a stock price surges, its "weight" in the S&P 500 will climb, whereas if the stock price tumbles, its influence on the aggregate declines. Almost every newspaper reports on the S&P 500 daily; no index, aside from the Dow, is more widely used to take the pulse of the marketplace. Some analysts even prefer to use the S&P 500 as a measure of the U.S. economy because the Dow's performance often lags behind it. You and your child can visit the S&P website at www.spglobal.com.

For an even broader representation, many people turn to the NASDAQ Composite Index, which measures all NASDAQ domestics and non-U.S.-based common stocks listed on the NASDAQ, a total of more than five thousand companies. Every company assigned to the NASDAQ Composite Index is also assigned to one of the eight NASDAQ subindexes (bank, biotechnology, computer, industrial, insurance, other finance, telecommunications, and transportation). All of the NASDAQ indexes are market-value weighted, which means that each security affects the index in proportion to its market value. Visit the NASDAQ website at www.nasdaq.com.

The most comprehensive of all indexes is the NYSE Composite Index, which is simply an overall average of all the stocks listed on the NYSE, including the Dow Industrials. The Dow Industrials, although somewhat varied, is more of a niche index than anything else, which is why it is included in bigger composites like the NYSE and the S&P 500. Other niche indexes that measure stock performance in specific areas are the Dow Jones Transportation Index and the Dow Jones Utility Index, which is composed of fifteen utility stocks.

One of the newest niche offerings is the Dow Internet Index, a response to the booming interest in Internet stocks. Just like the stock exchanges, the number of indexes keeps increasing to meet investor interest.

Learning about the Dow and other indexes is like laying another brick in the path you and your child can stroll on as you head toward choosing successful companies and building a winning portfolio. In the next chapter we'll explain the full spectrum of stock-buying methods and other aspects of portfolio management.

HOW NOW THE DOW! QUIZ

## Circle one:

*1. How many stocks are in the Dow?*

   (a)  5

   (b)  25

   (c)  30

   (d)  none of the above

*2. Which of the following companies were added to the Dow in 1999?*

   (a)  Home Depot

   (b)  Microsoft

   (c)  Intel

   (d)  SBC Communications

   (e)  all of the above

*3. Some of the Dow stocks are:*

   (a)  Walt Disney

   (b)  McDonald's

   (c)  Coca-Cola

   (d)  Wal-Mart Stores

   (e)  all of the above

*4. The stock exchange that has the most technology stocks and initial public offerings is:*

   (a)  NYSE

   (b)  NASDAQ

   (c)  American Stock Exchange

   (d)  all of the above

   (e)  none of the above

5. *The only original stock left in the Dow is:*

   (a) General Electric

   (b) Microsoft

   (c) IBM

   (d) Johnson & Johnson

## True or False:

6. *The Dow contains randomly chosen stocks that indicate the market's performance each day.*

     \_\_\_T   \_\_\_F

7. *Charles Dow created the Dow Jones Industrial Average in 1896 as a way of cutting through the daily fluctuations in the market.*

     \_\_\_T   \_\_\_F

8. *The companies in the Dow change regularly.*

     \_\_\_T   \_\_\_F

9. *The Dow is the most watched index of the stock market.*

     \_\_\_T   \_\_\_F

10. *Only the New York Stock Exchange has good-quality stocks.*

     \_\_\_T   \_\_\_F

## Answer key:

| | |
|---|---|
| 5. a | 10. F |
| 4. b | 9. T |
| 3. e | 8. F |
| 2. e | 7. T |
| 1. c | 6. F |

## DOW GROWTH CHART

Track the Dow on the day you were born and on all your birth-days (using the Dow website: http://averages.dowjones.com/historical queries).

**CHILD'S NAME:**

| Dates | Dow High | Dow Low | Dow Close |
|---|---|---|---|
| Date Born: | | | |
| 1 Year: | | | |
| 2 Years: | | | |
| 3 Years: | | | |
| 4 Years: | | | |
| 5 Years: | | | |
| 6 Years: | | | |
| 7 Years: | | | |
| 8 Years: | | | |
| 9 Years: | | | |
| 10 Years: | | | |
| 11 Years: | | | |
| 12 Years: | | | |
| 13 Years: | | | |
| 14 Years: | | | |
| 15 Years: | | | |
| 16 Years: | | | |
| 17 Years: | | | |
| 18 Years: | | | |

Identify the industry, rank, and number of competitors for each stock in the Dow 30 using information published annually in August by *Fortune* magazine.

**COMPUTE THE DOW JONES INDUSTRIAL AVERAGE**

| Dow Component | Industry | Rank Within Industry | Number of Competitors |
|---|---|---|---|
| Alcoa | | | |
| American Express | | | |
| AT&T | | | |
| Boeing | | | |
| Caterpillar | | | |
| Citigroup | | | |
| Coca-Cola | | | |
| Disney | | | |
| Du Pont | | | |
| Eastman Kodak | | | |
| ExxonMobil | | | |
| General Electric | | | |
| General Motors | | | |
| Hewlett-Packard | | | |
| Home Depot, Inc. | | | |
| Honeywell | | | |
| IBM | | | |
| Intel Corp. | | | |
| International Paper | | | |
| Johnson & Johnson | | | |
| McDonald's | | | |
| Merck | | | |
| Microsoft Corp. | | | |
| Minnesota Mining and Manufacturing | | | |
| J. P. Morgan | | | |
| Philip Morris | | | |
| Procter & Gamble | | | |
| SBC Communications | | | |
| United Technologies | | | |
| Wal-Mart | | | |

# Step 1

| Dow 30 Company Name and Symbol | Stock Closing Price on: |
|---|---|
| Alcoa (AA) | |
| American Express (AXP) | |
| AT&T (T) | |
| Boeing (BA) | |
| Caterpillar (CAT) | |
| Citigroup (C) | |
| Coca-Cola (KO) | |
| Disney (DIS) | |
| Du Pont (DD) | |
| Eastman Kodak (EK) | |
| ExxonMobil (XOM) | |
| General Electric (GE) | |
| General Motors (GM) | |
| Hewlett-Packard (HWP) | |
| Home Depot, Inc. (HD) | |
| Honeywell (HON) | |
| IBM (IBM) | |
| Intel Corp. (INTC) | |
| International Paper (IP) | |
| Johnson & Johnson (JNJ) | |
| McDonald's (MCD) | |
| Merck (MRK) | |
| Microsoft Corp. (MSFT) | |
| Minnesota Mining and Manufacturing (MMM) | |
| J. P. Morgan (JPM) | |
| Philip Morris (MO) | |
| Procter & Gamble (PG) | |
| SBC Communications (SBC) | |
| United Technologies (UTX) | |
| Wal-Mart (WMT) | |
| **Daily Total:** | |

Enter divisor here:
The daily total divided by the divisor results in the DJIA.

## Step 2

A.  Enter the date for which you are computing the Dow: _____

B.  Enter the sum of all the stock closing prices on that day: _____

C.  Enter the divisor (taken from *The Wall Street Journal*): _____

D.  Compute the Dow Jones Industrial Average: _____

         Enter total here:  _____

**Congratulations! You have just computed the Dow Jones Industrial Average for the day!**

## MONITOR THE DOW

Identify the yearly high, low, and current stock price for each stock in the Dow 30. Use the daily newspaper or online sources for information.

**STOCK PRICES AS OF:** / /

| Dow Component | Yearly High | Yearly Low | Current Price |
|---|---|---|---|
| Alcoa | | | |
| American Express | | | |
| AT&T | | | |
| Boeing | | | |
| Caterpillar | | | |
| Citigroup | | | |
| Coca-Cola | | | |
| Disney | | | |
| Du Pont | | | |
| Eastman Kodak | | | |
| ExxonMobil | | | |
| General Electric | | | |
| General Motors | | | |
| Hewlett-Packard | | | |
| Home Depot | | | |
| Honeywell | | | |
| IBM | | | |
| Intel | | | |
| International Paper | | | |
| Johnson & Johnson | | | |
| McDonald's | | | |
| Merck | | | |
| Microsoft | | | |
| Minnesota Mining and Manufacturing | | | |
| J. P. Morgan | | | |
| Philip Morris | | | |
| Procter & Gamble | | | |
| SBC Communications | | | |
| United Technologies | | | |
| Wal-Mart | | | |

## 5

## Friendly Takeover: When Your Child Is Ready to Invest

There is a subtle but important difference between parents buying stock for their kids, which is what we led you through in chapter 2, and kids using their own money. When your child is ready to put her own money behind a company of her choosing, with an eye to building her own portfolio, you are witnessing a major milestone in her development. It is a little like watching her ride a two-wheeled bike for the first time without training wheels or your steadying grip: She may be a little wobbly, but she's upright, she's moving forward, and with every yard she covers, she's that much more in control. Watching your child launch herself—whether she's riding a bike or buying her first stock—is an experience both of you will remember for the rest of your lives.

When she feels strongly enough to back a company with her own money, no matter how much she has to invest, she is ready to buy stock for herself.

Let her do it even if you think she doesn't quite know enough. The whole point of getting children into the market at an early age is to allow them to experiment, to learn firsthand how the market works by having a direct say in the buying decisions. While this might strike you as foolhardy or even downright irresponsible of you, look at it this way: You can afford to let your child make a not-so-great buying decision because her portfolio is young enough to recover from any losses. Impulse purchases in the investment world are self-correcting. Your child will learn soon enough whether her instincts are to be trusted or whether she should put her choices to more rigorous tests.

Pat admits that she still struggles with letting Shannon control her own portfolio. "The hardest part has been resisting the urge to force Shannon to pick other stocks, ones that would deliver higher returns," she says. "I have to keep reminding myself that this is *her* portfolio, not mine, and that the first objective is her education and second is returns on her portfolio."

This is not to say that you cannot offer your child guidance. By all means give her your two cents' worth of advice. If you find yourself strongly disagreeing with one of your child's stock choices, then try to find a compromise. There are so many stocks to choose from that you should be able to find one that will please you both. For instance, Pat talked Shannon into buying EMC, a stock Shannon liked because she had bought it with the Stock MarKids and followed it regularly. It was a top-quality stock, Pat argued, and it would give her portfolio some high-tech diversity. When Shannon finally agreed to buy some shares, Pat felt a wave of relief. "As long as we had at least one really good stock that would give her high returns, I could accept some of her other investment choices even if they would not have been mine."

Keep in mind, too, that as a child matures, so will her receptivity to your advice. Teenagers are able to grasp more abstract concepts and are less insistent on having firsthand knowledge of a product. It took Pat years to persuade Shannon to invest in one share of Intel because a computer chip was not something she was ready to appreciate or understand. But eventually Shannon could grasp that this unseeable, unknowable product was nonetheless a driving force in the American economy.

Chances are, the first stock your child decides to back with her

# CARLETON S. "CARLY" FIORINA

### Chief Executive Officer, Hewlett-Packard

**COMPANY:** Hewlett-Packard provides computer software, home PCs, ink-jet technology, and Internet and intranet services and communications products, and is the largest public company ever headed by a woman.

**EMPLOYEES:** 124,600

**BIRTH DATE AND LOCATION:** 1954, Austin, Texas

**EDUCATION:** B.A. in medieval history and philosophy from Stanford University; M.B.A. in marketing from the University of Maryland; M.S. from the Sloan School at the Massachusetts Institute of Technology.

**HOME:** Palo Alto, California

**TIDBIT:** She wanted to make her father proud by following in his footsteps and going into the legal profession, but she didn't like law school. Dropping out of law school seemed like the ultimate personal failure. She says she and her father both laugh about that now, especially since she was rated the "Most Powerful Woman in American Business" by *Fortune* magazine for two years in a row, 1998 and 1999.

**FIRST JOB:** Account executive for AT&T long lines

**QUOTE:** "Don't think of yourself as a woman in business. I've never thought in terms of 'men do this' and 'women do that.' "

own money will be in a company whose product she *does* know from firsthand experience. A child who is emotionally attached to the stocks in her portfolio is that much more likely to buy for the long term. She won't be tempted to unload what she loves at the first downward turn of the market. For example, soon after Shannon bought shares of America Online for herself, AOL began to tank. Pat was alarmed, and if it had been her decision, she probably would have sold the stock. But Shannon wasn't fazed a bit. She had chosen AOL because she and her friends used its Instant Messenger feature. Also, AOL carried her favorite Yahoo site. The more she worked with it, the more she felt its market share would continue to grow as the Internet grew. "It'll rebound eventually," she told her mom calmly.

## You Can Help Your Child Pick a Winner

While you want your child to be the judge of what makes a winner, you can give her tools to use in addition to her own instincts. Watching our girls muddle over buy decisions, we came up with a list of attributes that tend to characterize winning stocks—a checklist they could use just to be sure their instincts were on target. When your child has decided on a stock for purchase, ask her if it has these characteristics:

✓ The company makes products she enjoys using.

✓ The company makes products her family and friends enjoy using.

✓ More and more of her friends are starting to enjoy using this company's products.

✓ No other company makes a product as good as this company's.

✓ There is a trend for more and more people to use this company's products.

✓ The company provides goods or services that will always be needed (such as food, clothing, or shelter).

Danielle's and Shannon's first stocks held up very well to this test. Both owned shares in McDonald's. Shannon continued to buy into McDonald's even when it was her own money because she felt certain that eating at fast-food franchises was a growing trend, as more mothers found themselves working and often too rushed to get a meal on the table at home every night. The fact that McDonald's provided an essential product—food—assured her that it would be around for a long time. Shannon also felt this company was a winner because it produced something no other franchise did: a Happy Meal. "I've always liked the food," she says. "But as a kid if I was given a choice of Taco Bell, Burger King, Wendy's, or McDonald's, I would have picked McDonald's because of the Happy Meals."

The point of this exercise—asking your child to test her choice against the list—is to prompt a discussion between you. What does she think of this company? Why has she chosen it over others? What makes it a winner in her estimation? Spend some time discussing the checklist and how each of her stock candidates measures up against it. The idea is not to talk her out of her choices but to encourage her to use her critical thinking skills. As she matures and as she has more money to invest, making sound investments will require that she put her choices to more rigorous testing. We discuss these tests in the next chapter so that your child will learn to choose stocks wisely from here on through adulthood. For now it's enough that she wants to invest and knows what she wants. It's important to reward her "take-charge" mind-set with action. When she is ready to put her money on the line, it is time to help her get launched, to set up an account, so she can take that first solo ride.

## How Should Your Child Buy Stock?

Your child cannot literally buy stock, of course. You must buy it for her until she turns eighteen, as we explained in chapter 1. You set up what is called a custodial account; it will be her account, with stocks traded in her name, but only you can actually trade. You write the checks to cover whatever transactions you and your child decide on.

You don't have to buy stock in her name, mind you. Some parents are happy to honor their child's buy decisions but are not comfortable with the idea of creating a portfolio whose assets will revert to the child at the age of eighteen or twenty-one. We have a broker friend who feels we are running a terrible risk, giving our girls control of thousands of dollars they'll be able to access when they are just getting their wings.

By now you know that we believe in the opposite: Teaching a child to invest teaches her responsibility. She learns to save her money, to delay gratification rather than spend it on what her heart desires. She learns to be very, very careful when it comes to placing her money in the market; she learns how to optimize its earning potential by avoiding commissions and staying on top of the market. Through investing she learns just how valuable money can become if it is put to work, as opposed to being spent on shoes or clothes or CDs. In short, your kids may be like Danielle. Not a day goes by that she doesn't mention how much she enjoys having her money working hard for her while she's busy at school.

By putting our girls in charge of their portfolios from the get-go, we've given them plenty of opportunity to be impulse buyers or day traders. But guess what? They haven't! If anything, they're more conservative and protective of their assets because it's their money and they've spent years nurturing it, protecting it, and growing it.

"I do not worry about Shannon spending her college money when it's handed over to her," says Pat, "because she's earned every penny of it through her hard work and diligent efforts to understand stocks and manage her own portfolio. I've routinely told her it's *her* money for *her* college education and that whatever money she makes is going to determine the kind of college she can go to. The fact that she can control her own destiny has been a strong incentive for her to learn all she can about investing so that she can fulfill her dream—which is to go to college and then teach children around the world about stocks before she pursues her career in architecture."

By giving your child an education in long-term investing, you provide her with a long-term outlook on everything: her money, her career goals, her dreams, her destiny.

Whether it's an account in your name or your child's name (with you as custodian), where should you set it up? With a full-service broker? A discount broker? An online broker? Or no broker at all? There are so many different ways to buy stock nowadays—directly from the company, through organizations like NAIC, or through a broker—that it's hard knowing where and how to get your child an account.

There is no one right way to buy stock. Some methods require a lot of money upfront; others are expensive in the short run but cheaper in the long run; and still others require very little money but cost more of your time. The method you choose basically depends on three factors:

1. how much money your child has to invest
2. how much time you feel you (and she) can spend getting her transaction done
3. how much human help she may need or benefit from

You will find that the method that is perfect for getting one particular transaction done is not so perfect for the next. It therefore makes sense to familiarize yourself and your child with all the different methods available and to learn the pros and cons of each so that you can choose the one that optimizes your resources. We discuss them all and give you some real-life scenarios drawn from our girls' investment history as well as the club's.

## COMPARISON OF DIFFERENT STOCK PURCHASE METHODS

| Features | Full-Service Broker | Discount Broker | Online Broker | National Association of Investors Corporation (NAIC) | Direct Purchase Programs |
|---|---|---|---|---|---|
| Purchase stocks for minors (in custodial form) | * | | | | * |
| Establish account in short time frame | * | * | * | | |
| Buy and sell stocks quickly | * | * | * | | |
| Invest small amounts for low or no commission | | | | * | * |
| Identify exact purchase or sale price for stock | * | * | * | | |
| Detailed transaction information | * | * | * | | |
| Establish monthly payment schedule for stock purchases | | | | * | * |
| Advice and research information about companies readily available | * | | | * | |
| Does not require access to and basic knowledge of computer technology | * | * | | * | * |

## NAIC's Low-Cost Investment Plan

The challenge is to find a stock-purchasing method that won't require much in the way of fees, commissions, or minimums. You want every bit of your child's hard-earned money to go toward the purchase of shares. Since the commissions that brokers charge can easily consume her capital, one of the best ways to maximize her share purchase power is to go through the National Association of Investors Corporation (NAIC).

One of NAIC's programs was discussed in chapter 2. As we noted, many adults don't know where to get started, which is why we outlined the NAIC stock service program for that very first gift stock purchase. For the reasons we explained—wide stock selection, low fee structure, and single-share purchasing ability—we think you can't go wrong by having your child buy her stocks through NAIC's stock service. It is our top choice for getting kids started the cheapest, easiest, and fastest way.

You should also know about NAIC's other program, the low-cost investment plan. The low-cost program is very low cost, but there are fewer stocks to choose from. The stock service program is slightly more expensive but offers a wider variety of companies, possibly more that your child will enjoy owning. The great advantage of the low-cost investment plan is that investors with very little money can buy into some of the best companies, including such giants as AT&T, Intel, Kellogg, Texaco, Wells Fargo, and Wendy's. (For a complete listing of all 150 companies, check out the NAIC website www.better-investing.org. Participating companies do change, and the listing does grow.) Not only can your child buy a single share in these companies, but she can also participate in their dividend reinvestment programs, which are normally open only to investors who have met a minimum purchase requirement, anywhere from $250 to $1,000 or the equivalent in shares. Companies that offer DRIPs don't pay out dividends as cash; instead, the dividends are reinvested, converted into additional shares so that investment in the company automatically grows over time, whether or not additional contributions are made.

First, you have to become a member of NAIC. (For an application, call the organization headquarters toll-free at 887-275-6242.) Individual membership costs $39 a year. You join NAIC and then use your membership for your child's purchases, with you named as custodian. Benefits include the monthly magazine *Better Investing,* which has educational articles you and your child can enjoy and understand.

Once you're a member, buying a share is easy. Your child can probably fill out the half-page low-cost enrollment form. She needs to write in the name of the company in which she wants to invest and fill in the price of one share (rounded to the nearest dollar), as quoted in the daily newspaper (she can practice her stock-reading skills). She pays for the share plus $10, which NAIC requests to ensure that investors receive at least one share of stock even if the price rises significantly before the share is purchased. A onetime setup charge of $7 per company is also added to the initial purchase price.

Have your child enter your membership information (which you received upon joining NAIC). All that's left is to specify how the stock should be registered. Because minors are not allowed to purchase stock except in a custodial arrangement with an adult (see our discussion of UTMA and UGMA in chapter 2), the stock registration should read: [*your name*], Custodian for [*your child's name*], Uniform [Transfer or Gift, *depending on your state*] to Minors Act, [your state]. NAIC sends a letter of confirmation once it has received your payment, along with information about the dividend reinvestment program for the company whose stock you purchased, plus an application form. That's because, after making the purchase for you, NAIC contacts the corporation's dividend reinvestment agent on your behalf and establishes an account for you with this agent. All future payments can be sent directly to the DRIP agent; if you have any questions about your account, you contact that agent rather than NAIC. For example, if you purchase shares of Lucent Technologies through the NAIC low-cost plan, then all future payments or communications are directed to the Bank of New York, which acts as the agent for Lucent Technologies.

The beauty of getting into a DRIP is that your child can continue to invest small sums regularly at a very modest charge. (Think of these contributions as little drips accumulating into a big pool.) The DRIP agent determines when you can make these purchases—anywhere from every month to every forty-five days or every quarter; the prevailing market price determines what is paid per share. Your child can also elect to contribute to her DRIP automatically by filling out forms that enable the agent to deduct an amount she specifies from her checking or savings account every purchasing period—an arrangement she can cancel at any time. This is a great way for kids to accumulate a sizable number of shares in a major company. She can deposit her allowance into an account that the DRIP accesses for regular contributions. If your child doesn't want to purchase any additional shares, that's fine, too. The DRIP agent will keep her account open for the quarterly reinvestment of company dividends.

## Other Direct-Purchase Programs

*Direct purchase* describes any stock purchase program that allows you to purchase stock directly from the company. (The NAIC low-cost investment program is essentially a direct-purchase program. Even though you go through NAIC, the account you have is with the company in which you've invested.) Companies that offer direct-purchase programs sell you shares you request and buy them back when you want to cash out, all without a middleman or broker. You communicate with the company directly, too. Once you've purchased stock, you are allowed to enroll in their DRIP and buy additional shares, even fractions of shares. (Fannie Mae, for example, will let you invest as little as $10 at a time.) More than five hundred companies offer such programs; your child may well have chosen a stock she can purchase for herself directly from the company. (To find out, have her log on to the Internet and

---

### Dividend Reinvestment Versus Optional Cash Payment

**Dividend reinvestment programs** are offered by many major corporations, and they are an easy way to buy fractional shares of a stock instead of receiving the dividend payment directly in the form of a check. These are sometimes called DRP or DRIPs. Examples of companies that offer dividend reinvestment programs are Disney, General Electric, and McDonald's.

**Optional cash payments** are the extra cash payments you can make once you are a member of a company's dividend reinvestment program. Optional cash payments are used to buy additional shares of stock. They may be regular payments or irregular payments. One way to make optional cash payments on a regular basis is to sign up for the company's automatic withdrawal program; this way, a fixed amount, say $100, is automatically withdrawn from your checking account on the same day, every month. It is easy and requires no further involvement until you are ready to cancel the plan.

---

check out www.natcorp.com/directlist.html or www.dripinvestor.com/clearinghouse/home.htm for a comprehensive list of all corporations offering direct-purchase stock programs.)

We think direct purchase is the way to go—no commissions, low fees, and an automatic accumulation of shares in a solid company. But be forewarned: Some of these programs are simply not affordable to entry-level investors. Mattel requires $500 up front and $100 for each additional purchase. More accessible programs are those that ask for a $250 minimum outlay. Sony Corp. is one such company, as are several utility companies. McDonald's revised its program to become friendlier to kids and new young investors; with at least one share registered in a custodial name, they can open an account with a $100 initial investment and $50 for each additional purchase. Investors who authorize automatic monthly investments of $50 or more can also open a McDonald's account.

## Going Through a Broker

When Charles Dow first invented the DJIA to track stock performance, all investors purchased stock the same way: through a
broker, someone who could execute buy and sell orders with the
traders working on the floor of the stock exchange. This middleman also offered his clients financial advice and stock recommendations, and his commission usually reflected the extent of his
services.

Today, investors don't have to trade through a traditional broker and a brokerage house, but many choose to do so because they
like the full-service benefit of financial advice and stock tips. Full-
service brokers contact their clients regularly to offer their recommendations, which some people find very helpful. While the
client does not pay for this service directly, the full-service broker
charges a higher commission on each trade to recoup the cost of
his time spent on research and talking to you. This is the equivalent of an overhead charge, and for this reason dealing with a full-
service broker is the most expensive way to buy or sell stocks.

Yet establishing an account with a full-service broker offers
your child the distinct advantage of having a live human being to
talk to directly, someone to form a lasting relationship with. A
broker can provide detailed information about the companies
your child is monitoring or thinking about buying. The fact that
you can take your child to a real place to meet a real person who
will both discuss her trade and execute it before her very eyes may
make the high commission worth it—particularly if your child has
a fairly large sum of money to invest. Look at the broker's commission as an educational expense.

Don't let your child forget, however, that this person who is
being so helpful is essentially a salesperson who makes money off
her clients. Don't be surprised if the broker tries to schedule a
personal interview with *you* to give a sales pitch about the firm, its
services, and the different products that are available, such as mutual funds or retirement accounts. Just be wary of one who seems

more interested in your resources than your child—unless that is what you want from him.

A broker you like and your child likes, someone who is supportive of your effort to help your child become market savvy and who take good care of you and your portfolios, can make investing a joyful, profitable experience. But you may have to trade with a few frogs before you find your prince. There is no foolproof way to hook up with the right person. You can go with the most prominent houses—two big players are Merrill Lynch and Morgan Stanley Dean Witter. You can look in the phone book under Stock and Bond Brokers. You can ask a friend for a referral.

A word of caution: Although it's rare, occasionally a broker will try to intimidate you. After all, it seems as if a broker has access to mysterious, powerful information that could make you richer or poorer. But no one who uses his alleged power to scare you into giving up your independent judgment is serving your needs well. Remember that he is there to serve you and your child, and if your needs aren't being met or you feel the slightest bit uncomfortable, move on!

## Discount Brokers

In general, the major difference between a full-service and a discount broker is that the discount broker doesn't offer you financial information, doesn't make stock recommendations, and doesn't call you up when opportunities to invest suddenly open. You're on your own as far as figuring out what to buy and when. He will, however, execute your buy and sell transactions at a lower price than you would normally pay a full-service broker. He will also provide information about a particular company if asked—meaning that this is someone your child can talk to if she has done her homework. The discount broker can do her trade without strong-arming her into buying decisions that he profits from at her expense.

Stockbrokerage is such a dynamic field that there are nearly al-

## Special Stock-Ordering Instructions

**Market order** is the term used to describe a stock purchase or order that will be filled at the current market price.

Example: If I want to purchase McDonald's today and know the price has been fluctuating between 43 and 44, and I want that price range, then I will submit a market order and buy McDonald's at whatever price it is going for, which may be over or under the current range. McDonald's is a good stock, and I am going to hold it for a long time, so one point either way will not make a big difference. This is one of the best ways to buy stock with your children because you can let them help you place the order with the broker, and you can usually confirm that the stock has been purchased before ending the phone call. This is instantly gratifying for a child and helps him build even more enthusiasm for the process.

**Limit order** is the term used to describe a stock purchase or order that has a limit on the price.

Example: If I want to purchase McDonald's at 43, not a fraction higher, then I put in a limit order. Unless the stock trades at my specific price, I won't buy the stock. If I don't have enough money to buy shares at the current higher price but still want the stock, a limit order is a way of making sure that I don't spend more money than I have available for my stock purchase. The only risk is that the stock price may increase, and I will never get to buy the stock if my limit order is too far out of the stock's current trading range. I might put in a limit order to buy McDonald's at 42 when the stock is trading in the 43 to 45 range, but I would never put in an order to buy McDonald's at 15 when it is trading in that range. Instead, I would buy fewer shares with my funds. Again, keep in mind that children are sometimes more content to have the instant gratification associated with completing a stock purchase than waiting to save a few dollars. So if you decided to place a limit order, make it a fun experience for your child

ways changes under way. We have recently noticed, for example, that some discount brokers are responding to online trading competition by offering more financial advice. This is good for customers because it brings you more service, but you still pay only a discounted commission rate.

by making a game out of it. Talk about the thrill of getting the stock at a "sale" price instead of the retail price.

**Day order** is the term used to describe a stock purchase or order that may be filled only if the other terms and conditions are met on that day.

Example: If I want to purchase McDonald's at 43 and know that the price has been fluctuating between 43 and 44, then I will submit a day order and buy McDonald's today *if and only if* the price hits 43 today. The order is canceled at the end of the day if the price never hits 43. I cannot buy it tomorrow for 43 unless I place a separate order tomorrow. This is a good way to buy stock if you think the price is going to dip a little and you have limited cash to spend on the purchase, but you may lose the opportunity to buy the stock if the price suddenly increases while you are trying to save a point or two. Sometimes it just isn't worth the potential lost opportunity, especially since kids lose patience waiting to purchase "their stock."

**Good-until-canceled order** is the term used to describe a stock purchase or order that has a limit on the price and will be good until it is either filled or canceled.

Example: If I want to purchase McDonald's at 43, nothing higher, and I'm willing to wait a few days, weeks, or even longer, then I put in a good-until-canceled order. Unless the shares of McDonald's start to trade at my specific price, I won't buy the stock. This is a good strategy if I don't have enough money to buy shares at the current higher price but still want the stock and am not in a hurry to own it. This strategy can be very time-consuming, and sometimes people forget about the order, especially if it takes a long time to execute. Children may lose patience waiting, so parents may have to make an extra effort to keep the child involved in the transaction by talking about the stock order every day and checking the newspaper together regularly while waiting for the trade to be executed.

The tremendous advantage of a discount broker is that your child can still interact with a person interested in helping her—only with much less sales pressure and much more affordable commissions. Pat switched to Quick & Reilly, a prominent discount brokerage, after she bought stock that a full-service bro-

ker advised her to buy and watched its value dip significantly.
When Shannon wanted to place an order for the first stock she
had chosen on her own, Pat naturally took her over to the nearest
Quick & Reilly office (where she had established an account for
Shannon earlier).

Shannon had never been to the office, and this trip made her
first brokerage-based stock purchase not only an educational experience but an unforgettable one. She had $3,000—a partial
withdrawal from her account in the Stock MarKids—to invest in
America Online, a company she had tracked long enough to feel
confident in it. A broker named Ingrid invited Pat and Shannon to
watch as she entered the transaction into her computer. But at
that moment, the computers went down. While waiting for them
to come up, Shannon watched the television monitor over her
desk—and saw that the price of AOL was going up. And she was
helpless to buy!

"This is a girl who wasn't about to miss out buying stock at a
lower price due to some computer problems," her mother explains. Sensing Shannon's anxiety, Ingrid telephoned the order to
the Quick & Reilly trader on the floor of the New York Stock Exchange, and the deal was done. Pat took pictures of Shannon for
posterity; Shannon took away a valuable lesson in trading. Trying
to time the market, she says, was too anxiety-producing. It's better to leave that to the brokers!

## How to Set Up a Brokerage Account

Whether you set up an account for your child at a full-service or a
discount broker, the process is the same. First, the broker will explain what he needs in the way of fees or minimum deposits to
open the account. Usually you complete an application form that
furnishes an overview of your financial capabilities. You'll be given
a choice of account types. Be sure to open the account in custodial
form.

Once an account is established, your child can specify the price

# JOHN FRANCES "JACK" WELCH, JR.

## Chairman of the Board and Chief Executive Officer, General Electric

**COMPANY:** General Electric is made up of twelve businesses that manufacture products from lightbulbs and locomotives to industrial diamonds and includes the NBC television network. The company's current market value is $280 billion, and in 1999, for the second year in a row, GE was voted "America's Most Admired Company."

**EMPLOYEES:** 293,000

**BIRTH DATE AND LOCATION:** 1935, Peabody, Massachusetts

**EDUCATION:** B.S. in chemical engineering from the University of Massachusetts in 1957; M.S. and Ph.D. from the University of Illinois in 1958 and 1960, respectively.

**HOME:** Fairfield, Connecticut

**TIDBIT:** Nicknamed "Neutron Jack," this son of a train conductor and former high school altar boy has had a half-dozen books published about his distinctive leadership style and how he turned GE around. His number one corporate rule: Face reality as it is, not as it was or as you wish it to be.

**FIRST JOB:** Junior engineer at General Electric

**QUOTE:** "The biggest accomplishment I've had is finding great people. An army of them. They are better than most CEOs. They are big hitters, and they seem to thrive here."

she is willing to pay for a share of a certain stock, meaning the deal won't go through until the broker can get her price. That is called an open limited buy order. Or she can execute a trade at the current price: *at market.* The broker can then close the deal almost instantaneously—before you end the phone call or leave the office. We encourage you to involve your child in this decision because it's a great exercise in teaching the time value of money and the importance of delayed gratification. If your child has monitored her stock long enough to get a sense of its price range, then encourage her to hold out for a price she feels represents good value.

For instance, when Lynn placed an order with Charles Schwab to buy Microsoft for Danielle, she didn't buy "at market," which was $141.50 a share, even though she really wanted the stock. Instead, she placed an open limited buy order for seven shares at $131 per share. A month later she got Danielle her Microsoft—at $131 per share. Not even a month after that, Microsoft announced a two-for-one split, giving Danielle twice as many shares. Those 14 shares appreciated 134 percent in the next six months, and then there was another stock split. "It just shows how, if you're willing to wait, you can pay a bargain price and get anything but a discount return," says Lynn.

Once your trade goes through, you have three days to get your money into your broker's hands (or, in the case of a sale, three days to deliver the stock certificate to the broker's office). As the custodian for the account, you, the parent, are responsible for writing the check to cover the price of the stock your child purchases and getting the funds to the broker in time. For this reason, many people prefer to leave money in a money market account that the broker can access. (Likewise, to facilitate a sale, many shareholders also leave their stock securities in their broker's hands—or, as they say in the trade, "in the street name," meaning in the name of the Wall Street broker.) Ask your broker if there are any other payment options, such as wiring funds from your bank account (usually at a cost) or setting up a bank account from which he can electronically transfer funds to make the trade. Or you can write a check and mail it the day you request a trade; typically, your broker will get the payment by the time the transaction clears.

## Online Trading

As exotic and high-tech as online trading may seem, it is really just another form of discount brokering. The whole idea behind a discount brokerage is that you get deals done for cut-rate commissions because you're asking for no-frills service. Online trading simply takes that concept to a higher level by providing even deeper commission cuts and the ability to execute a trade without ever interacting with another human being.

Online trading requires access to a computer and a fairly good comfort level with the Internet—two qualifications most children today meet easily. Kids like the idea of being online, so hooking them up to online trading sites may fuel their interest in investing in general. But don't be fooled by the apparent sophistication of the Internet into thinking you're going to have better returns on your investments. Online trading, whether with E*trade or some other online broker, requires the same amount of effort by you and your child in choosing a stock, monitoring the stock, and then making the "buy" decision. Online trading is a tool, not a substitute, for stock monitoring and learning about the market.

If you and your child feel more comfortable with a modem than a telephone, then by all means go online to set up an account. The downside is that cut-rate commissions don't guarantee cut-rate setup costs. Even though their commissions on trades can be as low as $5, online brokers can require $1,000 to set up a custodial trading account.

To open an online account, check out these sites:

DLJdirect: www.dljdirect.com
Web Street Securities: www.webstreet.com
Suretrade: www.suretrade.com

Ameritrade: www.ameritrade.com
E*trade: www.etrade.com
Datek: www.datek.com

## Which Method for Which Purchase?

Ideally, you'll expose your child to all the methods we've outlined above because only by using them will she really know how to choose the one that's best for the purchase she has in mind. First-hand experience will acquaint her with the pros and cons of each in a way that our discussion cannot.

When it came time for the Stock MarKids to put their dues into the market and buy stock for the club, we had them use a different method for each of their purchases. They bought McDonald's through that company's direct investment program, called McDirect. They bought EMC through a discount broker. They bought Johnson & Johnson through a dividend reinvestment program offered by a subscription service called the MoneyPaper. And they bought Intel through NAIC's low-cost investment program.

Their purchase choice depended on how much money they had to spend, how quickly they wanted their transaction completed, and how much broker involvement was necessary. For example, the only way they could buy EMC was through a broker; it wasn't available any other way at that time. They decided on a discount broker, and since they were buying fifty shares, they didn't bother trying to shave down the commission by going through the NAIC stock service. We cared more about trying different purchase methods than saving on commissions. It took the club months to save up $1,000 for the shares (EMC was trading at 19 to 20 at the time) plus another $50 for the broker. When the club decided to buy Johnson & Johnson and General Electric, the kids elected to reduce the number of shares they bought rather than spend months building up the club treasury again. They had so little money to spend that the only method open to them was to buy one share of each through dividend reinvestment programs.

**How We Bought the Stocks in Danielle's Portfolio**

**American Century Giftrust:** direct purchase (fractional shares through DRIP)
**EMC:** discount broker (Charles Schwab; established a DRIP account)
**General Electric:** stock transfer (fractional shares through DRIP)
**The Limited:** subscription service (MoneyPaper; fractional shares through DRIP)
**Mattel:** subscription service (MoneyPaper; fractional shares through DRIP)
**McDonald's:** NAIC low-cost program (Note: This option is no longer available.)
**Microsoft:** discount broker (Charles Schwab; established a DRIP account)
**Netegrity:** NAIC stock service (fractional shares through DRIP)
**Stein Roe Young Investor Fund:** direct purchase (fractional shares through DRIP)
**Yahoo:** discount broker (Charles Schwab; established a DRIP account)

We weigh the same factors of money, time, and ease of transaction every time we execute a trade for ourselves or our girls. We look at how much money we have, how willing we are to pay commissions, how quickly we want the deal done, and how easily we can get it done for the money. For example, when Shannon wanted to buy AOL, she had almost $3,000 to invest. How did she want to make her stock purchase? She and Pat decided against a full-service broker because she did not have an established account, and Pat didn't see the point of paying a high commission for a trade Shannon had already researched thoroughly herself. Trading online was something Shannon felt comfortable doing, having played the Yahoo stock-trading game, but her mom nixed that option, feeling that it was important for Shannon's education to remain concrete and live. Buying through NAIC's low-cost investment program was not an option because AOL wasn't among the 150 participating companies. Neither did AOL offer any direct-purchase or dividend reinvestment programs at the time; even if it had, Shannon would have passed on it because getting into a DRIP takes time, and she wanted to buy immediately.

In the end, Shannon went with the discount broker, making her purchase in person, as recounted earlier in this chapter. She already had an account with Quick & Reilly, which facilitated things. But the main reason for choosing this option was that Shannon could go into the office, speak with the broker, watch as the transaction was completed, and walk away with not only a new stock but a lifelong memory of the actual process. She also did well in terms of saving on the commission: $49 for $2,827.13 worth of AOL.

If Shannon had had less money to invest, the hands-down winner would have been NAIC's stock service. Pat was already a member of NAIC, after all, and with $1,000 or less, Shannon could have saved herself the $49 in commission. It would have taken more time for the transaction to be completed, however, and Pat felt that Shannon had waited long enough, researching the stock and making sure AOL was "the one." Besides, the broker's commission worked out to be only 1.73 percent of the stock's purchase price.

Some parents may not mind paying a full-service brokerage firm to manage their child's transactions. They feel the ease of use and extra service, especially at this early stage in their child's investment education, is worth the cost. We won't argue. If you are like Pat and hate to pay fees and commissions, you'll put in the extra time and work required to participate in such programs as General Electric's or NAIC. Pat has done it many times and doesn't even see it as work anymore. When she wanted to buy one share of Intel for her husband's newborn granddaughter, Pat chose to go through NAIC's low-cost investment plan, not her bro-

## How We Bought the Stocks in Shannon's Portfolio

**America Online:** discount broker (Quick & Reilly)

**Coca-Cola:** subscription service (Money Paper; fractional shares through the DRIP)

**Disney** (first share): full-service broker (Charles Schwab)

**Disney** (after first share): optional cash payments (automatic monthly withdrawals of $100 for shares purchased directly from Disney plus fractional shares through the DRIP)

**EMC:** discount broker (Quick & Reilly)

**General Electric:** subscription service (MoneyPaper fractional shares through the DRIP)

**Intel:** NAIC low-cost program (fractional shares through the DRIP)

**Lucent** (first share): NAIC low-cost program

**Lucent** (after first share): optional cash payments (automatic monthly withdrawals of $100 for shares purchased directly from Lucent plus fractional shares through the DRIP)

**McDonald's** (first share): NAIC low-cost program (option no longer available because McDonald's is no longer a participant in the program)

**McDonald's** (after first share): optional cash payments (initially, infrequent optional cash payments; later, automatic monthly withdrawals of $100 for shares purchased directly from McDonald's plus fractional shares through the DRIP)

ker at Quick & Reilly, because his commission would have been too high for one share. She knew she could fill out the NAIC paperwork in about five minutes and walk it to the mailbox in another five. True, the transaction would take an additional two months to clear, but as a gift for a child who was only four months old, Pat reasoned, it made no sense to shell out extra money for a quicker transaction.

There is no right or wrong way to buy stock, just as there is no appropriate amount of money to spend on investments. It is all a matter of family attitude and personal resources. The amount of time you spend, the number of shares you buy, the amount of money your child invests, and the method by which you invest for her are entirely up to you and your child.

There is, however, a right and wrong way to build a portfolio. Now that your child has the foundation—how to identify a winning stock, how to monitor it, and how to buy it—it is time to help her with the construction. It is not the number of bricks that make a sound building, it's how they fit together. In the next chapter we'll show you how to teach your child to become a master builder.

## TIME TO BUY QUIZ

## Circle one:

*1. The different ways to buy stocks are:*

(a)   through a discount broker

(b)   by establishing an account with a full-service broker

(c)   directly with some publicly traded companies

(d)   with one of the NAIC stock investment programs

(e)   all of the above

*2. You may invest small amounts of money on a regular basis for a low fee with:*

(a)   direct-purchase programs

(b)   a full-service broker

(c)   a discount broker

(d)   an online broker

*3. When you invest in the stock market, it is possible to:*

(a)   invest in companies whose products you recognize

(b)   buy stocks without paying a lot for commissions

(c)   start investing with a small amount of money

(d)   buy stocks even if you are under the age of majority

(e)   all of the above

*4. When you purchase shares in a company, you are:*

(a)   an investor, a shareholder, and a part owner of the company

(b)   stuck with the stock no matter what happens

(c)   unable to buy shares in a competitor's company

5. When you buy stocks, you need to consider:

    (a)  how much money you have to invest

    (b)  whether or not you want help in selecting stocks

    (c)  how much money you want to spend for fees or commissions

    (d)  all of the above

## True or false:

6. Stocks may be purchased at the checkout counter of your local grocery store.

          ____T   ____F

7. You need to have lots of money before you start buying stocks.

          ____T   ____F

8. The term "DRIP" stands for Dividend Reinvestment Plan.

          ____T   ____F

9. Once you start investing, you can never use your money again.

          ____T   ____F

10. Stocks may be registered in a minor's name using a special form of registration.

          ____T   ____F

## Answer key:

| | |
|---|---|
| 10. T | 5. d |
| 9. F | 4. a |
| 8. T | 3. e |
| 7. F | 2. a |
| 6. F | 1. e |

## COMPUTE THE COST OF PURCHASING MCDONALD'S

1. Compute the cost of 100 shares of McDonald's stock at a value of 42⅛

   Answer: $_____

2. Compute the cost of 100 shares of McDonald's stock at a value of 46½

   Answer: $_____

3. The difference between the two prices:

   Answer: $_____

4. Which is the better price for buying McDonald's stock?

   Circle the answer: 42⅛ or 46½

5. Which is the better price for selling McDonald's stock?

   Circle the answer: 42⅛ or 46½

Show all work here:

## Answer key:

1.    Step 1: Convert ⅛ to a decimal (1 ÷ 8 = 0.125)
      Step 2: Add 42 (42 + 0.125 = 42.125)
      Step 3: Multiply by 100 (42.125 × 100 = 4,212.5)
      Step 4: Convert to dollars (4,212.5 × $1.00 = $4,212.50)

2.    Step 1: Convert ½ to a decimal (1 ÷ 2 = 0.5)
      Step 2: Add 46 (46 + 0.5 = 46.5)
      Step 3: Multiply by 100 (46.5 × 100 = 4,650)
      Step 4: Convert to dollars (4,650 × $1.00 = $4,650)

3.    Step 1: Determine which price is higher ($4,650.00 is greater
              than $4,212.50)
      Step 2: Subtract the lower from the higher price
              ($4,650.00 − $4,212.50 = $437.50)

4.    Step 1: Equate a price with the stock price of 42⅛ (42⅛ = $4,212.50)
      Step 2: Equate a price with the stock price of 46½ (46½ = $4,650.00)
      Step 3: Compare the two prices and determine which is lower
              ($4,212.50 or $4,650.00)
      Step 4: The lower price is $4,212.50 and therefore 42⅛ is a
              better "value"

5.    Steps 1–3 are the same as above
      Step 4: The higher price is $4,650.00 and therefore 46½ yields more
              profit from a sale


Always remember: Buy *low* and sell *high*.

# 6

## How to Build a Portfolio and Profit by It

As our children developed more and more market savvy, we realized we needed to teach them how to assess not just the individual merits of a stock, but how it contributed to the value of their portfolio as a whole. Buying a stock because the company offered a product or service the girls liked or enjoyed was no longer a sufficient criterion. We wanted them to ask questions about their stock choice. Was it at the top of its industry? Would it diversify their holdings enough to reduce their risk of losing money in a down market? Would it grow at a reasonable rate for years to come? Could it carry some of their other stocks through rough times?

We also wanted them to start checking their existing stocks regularly to be sure they still "fit" in the portfolio, which is an individual's entire set of investments. We wanted them to start asking questions like "Are these holdings of mine going up in value?" and "What are each company's prospects for growth?" In other words, we wanted them to acquire a portfolio manager's perspective. A diversified portfolio can avoid a situation where one industry or one stock can pull down the entire portfolio.

We developed a stock-picking strategy—a list of six traits that every chosen stock of theirs should have. While the concepts are those of the most sophisticated investors, we made our checklist of traits simple enough that our girls could grasp them quickly, remember them easily, and apply them consistently. Your child can, too. Choosing sound stocks is nowhere near as complicated as it might sound. We came up with the ADDING acronym to remember these traits. Good portfolio-building companies:

✓ **A**re high-ranking in their industry
✓ **D**iversify your existing holdings
✓ **D**eliver a reasonable rate of return
✓ **I**ncrease in earning power or show potential for growth
✓ **N**eutralize risk
✓ **G**row the value of the portfolio overall and long term

Using this ADDING strategy, the girls have learned a lot, have had fun, *and* have made money. Now we'll show you how to use ADDING with your own children.

## What Are Your Goals?

Your primary objective is to teach your child how to build a portfolio. He should have fun while he's learning the finer points of trading. Your object is not to discover the next Amazon.com or turn your kid into a high-tech day trader. The portfolio you're helping him build doesn't rely on flashy newcomers and doesn't require timing the market. You want to acquire stocks together that offer a comfortable balance between reward and risk, and you will buy them with an eye to holding them for the next ten, twenty, thirty, or even forty years.

## "A" Is for Companies That Are High-Ranking in Their Industry

A successful investment starts by choosing a successful company. That should be rather obvious, but how can you determine if a company is successful?

One of the best ways is to compare it to its competition—to the companies in its industry that are trying to provide the same or similar goods or services. Many financial publications and online services do this comparison for you: They rank companies within each industry. Sometimes they assign an actual number. Each rating service uses its own proprietary formula to evaluate and generate a composite rating for each stock, using factors such as historical earnings per share, projected earnings growth, broker recommendations, and price-earnings ratio.

Often, however, industry rankings are given according to which quartile (or twenty-five out of one hundred) a company falls in. A company in the top quartile is one that performs among the top 25 percent of all the companies in that industry. A company in the bottom quartile is one that is worse than 75 percent of the industry—not much of a performer! Usually, a company worth looking at for your child's portfolio will fall within the top two quartiles—somewhere in the upper half of the industry. Companies that rank within the top 25 percent are even better bets.

Of all the places to find industry rankings, we like the Internet best because the information is *free*. There are other sources as well: *Fortune* magazine, for instance, publishes an issue annually that ranks all the major companies, including all the Dow stocks. You can find this at www.fortune.com. *ValueLine* is another printed source for industry rankings, and you can find it at any library. It's also free, but using it is more time-consuming because most libraries don't allow you to borrow it. You have to stay at the library to do the research. Wherever you go for your rankings, be aware that they will vary from source to source because each source uses different rating methods and criteria to determine its list.

To try Yahoo for your research, as we do, just log on to your computer and follow these simple instructions:

Step 1. Go to the Yahoo website at http://quote.yahoo.com.

Step 2. Enter the symbol for your stock in the box labeled "Get Quotes." Let's say, for example, you're looking up Intel. Enter the

> **Successful companies rank high within their respective industries:**
>
> Top 10%—Best
> Top 25%—Better
> Top 50%—Good
> Top 75%—Questionable
> Bottom 25%—Not a good place to be

symbol for Intel, which is INTC. (Note: If you do not know the symbol, use the "Symbol Lookup" feature.)

Step 3. Click on the "Research" feature (under the column title "Other Info").

Step 4. Scroll down to the area labeled "Earnings Estimates & Recommendations."

This is the information that was available for Intel in October 1999:

Industry: ELEC COMP-SEMIC
Ranked 38 of 81
Earnings Date (Approx.): 12-Oct-99

Step 5. Compute the percentage ranking.

Intel is number 38 out of the 81 companies in the semiconductor electronics industry. Divide 38 by 81, and you have its percentile ranking: 46.91.

Step 6. Analyze the data. Does this company rank high within its respective industry? The numbers indicate that Intel is in the top half of its industry, which is an okay place to be. Ideally, we would prefer to purchase stocks that rank higher than this because the closer a company gets to the top of its industry, the more revenue it generates. The more revenue it generates, the more people want to own it. The more people want to buy it, the higher its stock price will climb. The market is like an auction: Buyers bid up the price of a share when they're competing against each other to get hold of a stock.

While industry ranking is important, it's too early in ADDING to decide to buy. Intel has passed its first test, giving your child a green light to proceed to the next.

## "D" Is for Companies That Diversify the Portfolio

*Diversify* is a word that investors of all kinds and ages love to mention, but what does it really mean?

In 1994, concerned that Shannon's portfolio was too concentrated in the fast-food industry, Pat made her choose between selling McDonald's and selling Wendy's—two of the three stocks that Shannon owned (Disney was the third). Shannon didn't want to choose. She loved Wendy's fries and Frostees (she thought they were the best in the industry), and she loved McDonald's burgers and Happy Meals (also the best in the industry). She felt she was already diversified across product lines; she didn't see why she had to be diversified across industries. Pat went ahead and sold her shares of Wendy's. Shannon was so upset, she never let her mother hear the end of it.

Lynn faced a similar situation. Danielle's portfolio was too top-heavy with McDonald's stock. Danielle did not want to sell any of her McDonald's stock, which she'd been attached to since the age of three. Lynn compromised by selling half and using the proceeds to purchase shares of EMC, a high-tech stock that Stock MarKids had tracked and purchased with great success. Initially, Danielle was so upset that she refused to accept the new shares and tried to give the shares to Lynn.

Pat feels she made a mistake in strong-arming Shannon into selling Wendy's. "I violated my own principle, which was that Shannon should remain actively involved and empowered in her own decision making at this stage," she says. "Her happiness

## Four Diversification Strategies

✓ **Different Industries**
Example: Consider Disney and Campbell's Soup

✓ **Different Market Capitalizations**
Example: Consider Microsoft and Netegrity

✓ **Different Types**
Example: Consider GE (diversified/blue-chip stock) and Cisco (technology/growth stock)

✓ **Different Countries**
Example: Consider McDonald's and Intel

was more important than the little money we made selling her stock."

Lynn, on the other hand, feels that sometimes the adult has to intervene on behalf of the portfolio, especially when there are financial outcomes that the child may not understand. She points out that after she sold half of McDonald's, the company had a stock split that restored Danielle's total shares to 110.108, which was 2.45 shares more than she had before the split, thanks to the additional dividend reinvestment. "Danielle loves her McDonald's stock and will not allow me to sell any more of it," says Lynn. "Since her portfolio is now diversified, I don't feel the need to sell any more."

When it is time to diversify your child's existing portfolio, you might meet resistance. If you decide to go ahead against your child's wishes, the only advice we can give you is to explain your decisions, compromise where possible, and then wait because eventually the child will understand. (Danielle did, as soon as she saw how much money EMC was making for her!)

It is easier when your child selects *new* stocks, as opposed to selling existing shares. Be sure to stress the importance of settling on one that diversifies her current holdings. Explain that diversifying a portfolio is like making sure you eat a variety of foods. Just as it is important to eat fruits, vegetables, grains, and some sort of protein every day, it is essential to the health of a portfolio to buy a variety of stocks—ideally, from different industries. And just as your child knows to eat different-size portions for balanced nutrition—a lot of vegetables, a little meat, and a tiny bit of dessert—so you can explain that it's important to buy companies in different sizes: big, medium, and small. Finally, in the same way you want your child's tastes to broaden and include foreign cuisine—Chinese stir-fries, Mexican burritos, Japanese sushi—you want to encourage him to buy companies that are active in global markets. The wider variety of stocks your child chooses, the healthier and more balanced he and his portfolio will be!

Or try the eggs-in-a-basket metaphor: If all your eggs are in one basket and it accidentally falls to the ground, then you break all your eggs. Likewise, it's smart to hold your stock "eggs" in different industry baskets so that even if an entire industry drops, you won't break all your eggs.

While there are probably endless ways to achieve diversity in a portfolio, we found that the following four work best:

1. *Don't pick too many stocks from the same industry.*
   Ideally, the companies in your child's portfolio should provide very different products and services. A stock in the pharmaceutical industry along with one in the oil and gas industry, another one in the financial industry, and possibly another one in the computer technology field makes for a lot of diversity, certainly according to the adult interpretation of that word. If your child insists on diversifying along product lines, don't despair. Shannon has started buying a mix of high-tech stocks this way: Intel for chip manufacturing,

## Diversification with Stocks from Different Industries

Diversification with stocks from different industries means looking for companies with different products or services.

Example: A diversified portfolio may include McDonald's from the fast-food industry, Microsoft from the high-tech area, and General Electric, a diversified conglomerate.

There is little diversification in a portfolio composed of McDonald's, Wendy's, Coca-Cola, and Pepsi because two of the companies are in the fast-food business and two are in the beverage industry; therefore, all four companies are subject to the changing whims of consumer tastes.

The following are some different types of industries:

Aerospace
Financial
Transportation
Technology
Pharmaceuticals
Utilities

EMC for data storage, and Lucent for networking. It might turn out to be a pretty good strategy!

2. *Mix together market capitalizations: small cap, mid cap, and large cap.*

Market capitalization is a mathematical calculation used to determine the size of a company. When you multiply the number of shares outstanding by the price of the stock, the resulting number is the value or market capitalization of the company. A large company or one that has a high value is called a *large cap,* and a smaller company or one with a low value is called a *small cap* company. As you might expect, those companies in between are mid cap. Microsoft and GE are good examples of large cap companies, and almost everyone has heard of one or both of them. Sedona Corporation, a company that specializes in imaging systems and software, is a small cap firm—so small that you may never have heard of it.

Since any change in the price of the stock can affect the company's value or capitalization, some financial advisors believe that small cap stocks are the ones with the most potential for stock appreciation. There have also been times—the late '90s, for example—when investors holding small cap stocks lost out on major growth opportunities in the rest of the market; for this reason, counsel your child to buy companies in an array of sizes. One source for information about market caps is the Yahoo website mentioned earlier: http://quote.yahoo.com.

3. *Balance favorite stocks in known industries with some from other segments of the market you're not as inclined to buy.*
Since the stocks your child tends to research and buy will reflect his interests, hobbies, and personal preferences, his portfolio may get thematically heavy. Danielle and Shannon are always ready to buy Internet stocks, for instance, because this is their world, where they function comfortably every day with their friends. On the other hand, we are a lot more leery of this new segment, not having grown up with it as they have; our portfolio holdings tend to be more blue chip and technology heavy because that is what we feel we know well.

We should take tips from each other. Should the Internet boom suddenly lose favor, Danielle and Shannon might wish they had some of our blue-chip steady performers, while right now we could probably use a little Yahoo in our holdings to take advantage of the tidal wave.

It pays to diversify. If your child is heavy in the high-tech stocks, help him see how important it is to come by a blue chip or two, and vice versa: Too many McDonald's and Wendy's is a signal to diversify into, say, Intel and Lucent.

4. *Choose companies that are active overseas.*
   We like to expose our children to companies with overseas business because it makes them more globally aware and allows us to talk to them about issues that go beyond our own local communities. Buying stock in companies that do business in markets outside the United States also makes good investment sense: If there is a downturn in the U.S. economy, then holding shares in companies doing business elsewhere in the world—Europe, Asia, or Latin America—is a way of minimizing its impact on a portfolio.

We do not recommend foreign companies per se. We prefer to get foreign exposure by investing in U.S. companies that invest in foreign countries. Companies such as GE, Microsoft, McDonald's, Intel, Netegrity, Wal-Mart, General Motors, and AT&T are American companies, but they invest and sell their products worldwide. Many companies are still penetrating into foreign territories and derive much of their revenues from operating there. For example McDonald's is still opening new stores in Latin America, Europe, and other areas. Microsoft's products are sold worldwide.

The easiest way to find out if a company has a global presence is to check out its annual report. You can request one over the phone by calling investor relations, or you can get the information by logging on to the company's web page. Newspaper or magazine articles can also give you this information, but you'll have to wade through a lot of copy to find what you're looking for.

## Events That May Increase the Price of a Stock

### Internal Events

✓ Increases in earnings and sales resulting from good products and a good marketing strategy

✓ A favorable court ruling or new patents (especially for drug companies)

✓ Release of new products (such as Microsoft's newest version of Windows or a new "miracle" drug by a pharmaceutical company)

✓ Stock buybacks by the company (indicating the management has confidence in the company)

✓ Winning new contracts, especially for large amounts of money or over an extended period of time (such as Dell's contract to supply PCs to a large government agency)

✓ Buyout by another company (such as when Trusted Information Systems shares moved from approximately $13 a share to $19 a share after the company announced it had agreed to a buyout by Network Associates)

✓ New managers, especially at the top levels

### External Events

✓ Political stability

✓ Economic stability with low interest rates and low inflation

✓ Recognition for superior products by an awards body

✓ Positive comments in a financial magazine or on a financial talk show

✓ Upgrades in ratings by analysts

## "D" Is for Companies That Deliver a Reasonable Rate of Return

The story made headlines everywhere: RETIRED CLERK GIVES $22M TO YESHIVA. It was about one of the most amazing investors of our time: Anne Scheiber, a woman who turned her $5,000 portfolio into a $22 million portfolio in fifty years. When she died in 1995 at the age of 101, she willed her estate to Yeshiva University to help young girls realize their full potential.

Once the word got out about Scherber's endowment, everyone wanted to know her portfolio-building strategy. She invested in companies she admired, favoring firms with growing earnings—a strategy that should be familiar to you and your child by now. But here is what's unusual: According to *Money* magazine, she posted an annual return of 22.1 percent, earning her a place "among the investing giants of our time. Her performance tops Vanguard's John Neff (13.9%) and investment legend Benjamin Graham (17.4%), and falls just shy of superstars Warren Buffett (22.7%) and Fidelity's Peter Lynch (29.2%)."

We all wish we could be as savvy as Anne Scheiber. More reasonable rates of return—in the vicinity of 12 to 14 percent per year—are what your child should aim for. In fact, a return of 14.8 percent is pretty darn great. His money will double in just five years. If your child earns just 10 percent, in five years he'll have $1.61 for every dollar he originally invested. Not bad!

Understand that this does *not* mean every stock in his portfolio has to achieve a 10, 12, or 14 percent return per year. The rate of return for each individual stock will vary. Some will balloon in returns; others will deliver a small but steady return; still others may lie stagnant for a while and then suddenly get active. That's to be expected. Their average by year's end should amount to at least a 10 percent increased growth. This is what we call a reasonable return, one that will allow your child to feel good about his stock choices and his buying decisions. If he feels he has to aim for bigger returns, the pressure on him might take all the fun out of

## Different Types of Stocks

Stocks can be roughly categorized as belonging to one of the following groups:

**GROWTH STOCKS:** Should deliver consistent revenue and earnings performance. They may be accompanied by more volatilility and more risk (examples: Microsoft, EMC, Qualcomm, Netegrity, Cisco).

**BLUE-CHIP GROWTH STOCKS:** Established companies with long records of earnings and dividends (examples: General Electric, American Express, Wal-Mart, Intel, Citigroup).

**INCOME STOCKS:** Have a record of paying higher-than-average dividends and are especially good for those who seek safe investment holdings (examples: Washington Gas, Southern Company, Occidental Petroleum).

**CYCLICAL STOCKS:** Those whose earnings are closely linked to the general level of business activity. They tend to go up when the economy is booming and down when the economy is backsliding (examples: Caterpillar, General Motors, The Gap).

Please note; These stocks are not intended to be investment recommendations or advice, merely examples. Each stock may have a different amount of risk. The reader should conduct his or her own test using the ADDING strategy before purchasing.

---

investing his own money—and at this stage in his education, that would be a shame.

Besides, as we've said, a stock's annual return is but one measure of its worthiness. If your child chooses a "winning" stock that has what seems like a low rate of return, do not automatically dismiss this stock as unsuitable for your child's portfolio. Instead, go to the next test in our strategy.

## "I" Is for Companies That Increase in Earning Power

Everyone wants to buy shares in companies that are growing because the bigger a company gets, the more revenue it takes in and
the more valuable the company's stock becomes. Bigger earnings
translate into bigger returns.

Your child might have a good intuitive sense of which companies are "high growth." If he's going to be a truly savvy investor, he
needs to examine more than his own instincts. He needs to look at
a stock's share price trends and its earnings growth potential.
Looking at a company's shareholder returns for the past year can
help your child determine, to a degree, what to expect in the way
of returns down the road. Looking at a company's earnings—past,
present, and future, based on projections—can help your child figure out just how fast and how big the company is growing or expects to grow.

Help your child understand these concepts by having him
look at share price trends the way baseball team managers look
at batting averages. Price trends are a lot like batting averages: They can't predict the future, but they can give you some
idea of what to expect. We use the Yahoo finance website at
http://quote.yahoo.com to look at charts that show the price
movements for a stock we currently own or are considering owning. The chart feature allows us to view charts for the past year,
two years, five years, and maximum. We look at the maximum
data chart because it shows stock price trends for the company for
the longest period of time, although we usually make estimates
from data in the one-year chart.

For example, McDonald's stock price increased from approximately 32 on October 1, 1998, to approximately 42 on October 1,
1999, the day we did this particular calculation. This means that
over the latest one-year period McDonald's stock price increased
10 points, or 31 percent (which is the amount of the stock price increase divided by the price at the start of the period, or 10 divided
by 32).

If your child is more comfortable looking up stock information in a newspaper, just have him find the stock's fifty-two-week low. Use that as his starting point and use the stock's most recent ending price to determine how much the stock has increased in share price. For example, the fifty-two-week low for McDonald's is 31, and the closing price on October 12, 1999, is 42$^{15}/_{16}$, which we'll round to 43. The resulting calculation shows an increase of 12 points, or 39 percent.

While the numbers will vary depending on the beginning and ending days you choose, the data show the same thing: McDonald's was a home run hitter last year for its shareholders. That's no guarantee the company will generate equally stunning returns in the years to come, but it indicates some solid talent to bank on. Plus, anybody who sees this 39 percent statistic is going to want to acquire McDonald's stock. As in baseball, when everybody is trying to acquire a hot player, his price goes up. In this way, a big upward move in share price affects a company's ability to grow because the more money it's worth, the more money it can invest in itself, developing new products or expanding its distribution to generate even greater earnings.

But there is another, more direct way for your child to determine if a company is likely to grow. Once again, have your child go to the Yahoo website, enter the symbol for his stock in the box labeled "Get Quotes," and click on the "Research" feature (under the column title "Other Info"). Then have him scroll down to the area labeled "Earnings Growth."

This is the earnings growth information that was available for McDonald's on September 23, 1999:

| | Last 5 Years* (%) | This Year (Dec 99) (%) | Next Year (Dec 00) (%) | Next 5 Years* (%) |
|---|---|---|---|---|
| McDonald's Corporation | 11.0 | 11.6 | 12.5 | 12.2 |
| Retail Restaurants | 11.9 | 16.3 | 21.2 | 19.8 |
| S&P 500 | 10.3 | 10.2 | 10.3 | 6.7 |

* These numbers represent the average growth per year over a five-year period.

Compute the difference between Next 5 Years and Last 5 Years: 12.2 − 11.0 = 1.2. Notice that this number is positive, which means the company is projecting more growth for the next five years than the last five years. Have your child ask himself: *Does this seem like a reasonable projection? What might happen in the next five years that is different from the last five years? What is going to make more people eat at McDonald's?* See if your child can provide some insight; maybe he knows something that you don't know about the menu or his friends' eating habits. He might have some insights worth submitting to McDonald's executives or board members!

One night while Pat and Shannon were discussing her staying after school with her flag squad before the Friday evening football game, Shannon abruptly announced that Domino's Pizza, which the flag squad ordered every Friday, was going to go out of business. Why? asked Pat. Shannon explained that Domino's had been running a promotion every Monday following a Redskins game, promising to deduct $1 for every touchdown the Redskins scored. Since the Redskins had scored a record seven touchdowns the previous Monday, Domino's pizzas were selling for 99 cents apiece, which cost the company $400,000 in revenues in one day. (This was information that Shannon had gotten off the Internet.) "Based on this loss," Shannon explained, "and my prediction that the Redskins will continue to have a good football season, I bet that Domino's Pizza will go out of business."

Her assessment got her mom and stepdad thinking. Pretty soon the whole family was trying to figure out how many touchdowns Domino's management was gambling on, how much profit they needed to make on each pizza, and other aspects of Domino's business model. "This is our idea of fun," explains Pat. "And I have to say, Shannon's critical thinking skills are much sharper as a result of these discussions." (So sharp, in fact, that two weeks later *The Washington Post* ran an article about the Domino's Pizza offer that addressed some of the very issues Shannon had pointed out to her family!)

Earnings growth drives
the stock price:

5–10 percent = low growth *(cold)*
11–15 percent = moderate growth *(lukewarm)*
16–20 percent = close to high growth *(getting hot)*
21 percent or more = high growth *(hot)*

As for McDonald's future, we didn't have to guess: Looking at the figures posted on the Yahoo site, we could see that exceptional growth isn't in the cards. McDonald's has lagged behind the industry for the past five years. For next year and the next five years, McDonald's still doesn't expect to do as well as the industry. It expects to perform better next year than it has this year, which is reassuring; at least it is going in a positive direction.

But a company's future growth projections are not as reliable as past performance figures. They are just a "best guess" based on the information available at the present time, and they are subject to change as circumstances change. A better gauge of growth potential might be to compare your child's company to the S&P 500, which many believe is the most representative index of the overall market. Since McDonald's growth rate was 11.0 percent over the past five years, it beat the S&P 500 growth rate of 10.3 percent by .07 percent over the past five years. This is a good sign. Whenever you beat or exceed the S&P, you can assume you are doing well. In other words, a company's growth in earnings, like its rate of return, is *relative*. McDonald's growth relative to the S&P was high even though what we consider a high-growth stock shows a 20 percent gain in earnings per year.

In the end, your child should realize that a company projecting a 20 percent growth spurt in earnings is a much better bet than

one projecting 5 percent. But don't be worried if your child gravi-
tates to companies whose growth rates, like McDonald's, aren't all
that dazzling. As long as a company's growth is going in a positive
direction, it is capable of increasing in earning power.

## "N" Is for Companies That Neutralize Risk

Every time your child buys a stock, there is a chance he might lose
money. For certain stocks the risk is rather great, but for others,
it can be small. Risk is something an investor learns to live with,
although the amount of risk an investor can tolerate varies from
one person to the next. If you are not comfortable losing money
at all, you are what the industry calls "risk averse." Your child, on
the other hand, may feel more inclined to take chances—because
he's less experienced in terms of living through the consequences.
Your job as parent is to help him acquire experience without
paying too great a price. So just as you would insist he wear a
helmet when he rides his bike, you should insist that he avoid
high-risk stocks when he invests. Your job is to protect him from
getting hurt, whether it's his head or his portfolio that's in
danger.

Our feeling is that there are so many terrific stocks out there to
invest in, it does not make sense to choose one that might lose you
money. Stock prices can plummet for reasons beyond anyone's
control. No matter how much money you have and no matter what
your child says he can tolerate personally in terms of risk, there is
no reason to choose a high-risk stock.

Risks to businesses are constant. What changes is your comfort
level. Has a medium-risk stock become a high-risk one? As new information becomes available, it is important to reassess the risk
levels of the stocks your child owns or is contemplating owning.
Keep talking about the company and changes that might impact
its business environment.

What makes a particular stock risky? Again, there is no absolute measure. What some of us might consider high risk, others

## Events that May Decrease the Price of a Stock

### Internal Events

✓ Earnings decline warning (a company-issued public announcement that it is not going to meet the earnings amounts it had previously forecast)

✓ Loss of customers (Fads change, and when teen consumers no longer wanted the fashion styles at Merry-Go-Round, the company went from being the darling of the fashion industry to bankcruptcy.)

✓ Loss of contracts, especially one for a large amount of money or over an extended period of time (example: EMC lost a major contract with Hewlett-Packard)

✓ Poor marketing and inventory buildup

✓ Loss of patents (which expire after a number of years)

✓ Events that cause profits to decline, such as increases in expenses, labor strikes, or excess inventory that cannot be sold

✓ Mergers or acquisitions (the acquiring company's stock frequently goes down while the acquired company's stock goes up)

✓ Product recall

### External Events

✓ Lawsuits

✓ Increased interest rates

✓ Negative comments by senior administration officials such as the Federal Open Market Committee or the chairman of the Federal Reserve (currently Alan Greenspan)

✓ Negative press, such as the company being accused of using child labor

✓ Negatively impacting economic data about inflation, employment, or the consumer price index

✓ Downgrades in ratings by analysts

might label medium risk. Likewise, what we would term low risk might be considered medium risk by someone more conservative than us. However, it is generally agreed that risk levels rise in the following four situations:

1. *A company goes public*

   Immediately following its introduction to the public through an "initial public offering," or IPO, a new stock is more volatile than at almost any other time in its life cycle. This is because no one knows much about the company yet. There is no track record to analyze and no performance numbers to crunch. As investors respond to the company's news, good and bad, the stock changes hands frequently. That makes the price fluctuate, sometimes wildly for months, until the public feels it knows enough about the company to stop buying and selling it reactively.

   As one of the first investors to buy shares in Microsoft, Lynn knows firsthand how risky it can be to "get in on the ground floor." When Microsoft first went public, the stock price rose. However, when the price started to nose-dive, Lynn, being too risk averse, sold immediately. Later—with the luxury of hindsight—she would say that selling Microsoft was the biggest mistake she ever made, a mistake that took her months to recover from. What hurts is realizing that if she had waited only a year or so, allowing the company to get better established and allowing herself more time to learn about its product and growth potential, she might have held the stock. If she had, she would be managing a portfolio worth millions of dollars today.

   This is why we tell our girls that if it is a truly good stock today, it will also be a truly good stock a year from now. Don't get caught up in the frenzy. Wait a while to see if a product fizzles and dies before jumping on the bandwagon and spending ridiculous amounts of money (the Furby phenomenon comes immediately to mind). Let a stock prove itself or allow a company's new product enough time to show up on the company's bottom line before you buy into it.

In our estimation, brand-new companies or products are always high-risk stocks to own. We suggest you avoid them until they're no longer brand new.

2. *Lawsuits raise eyebrows and lower returns*
Whenever a company gets involved with litigation or federal regulators, it raises its level of risk. We would automatically rate any company involved in litigation as a medium-risk or high-risk stock depending on the type and extent of the litigation.

The risk of owning stock in a company at the losing end of a lawsuit is especially high. Consider what happened to Apple when it sued Microsoft in the late 1980s. Apple alleged that Microsoft's Windows infringed on Apple's copyrighted operating system. The two companies had previously reached a settlement over the original version of Windows, but this time they went all the way to trial—and the courts sided with Microsoft. It took nearly a decade for Apple stock to recover from losing this lawsuit, while Microsoft just moved onward and upward.

Scrutiny by federal regulators is not something to ignore, either. Although Microsoft survived the Apple lawsuit, it didn't fare so well in its antitrust suit with the U.S. government. The Justice Department ruled that Microsoft was indeed a monopoly, although it has not been decided whether Microsoft will be broken up. Currently the case is in the hands of a mediator. A lawsuit of this magnitude hanging over a company no doubt scared off some Microsoft investors, although most were probably safe in assuming that a company as large as Microsoft will never go out of business. (Some investors are even betting they'll make out better

# WILLIAM H. "BILL" GATES

### Chairman and Chief Executive Officer, Microsoft

**COMPANY:** Microsoft develops, produces, licenses, and supports software products such as operating systems, business and consumer applications, and Internet software. The company's current market capitalization is $470.8 billion as of (September 8, 1999).

**EMPLOYEES:** 31,396

**$$$:** $85 billion (as of October 1999), the richest man in the United States in 1999, according to *Forbes* magazine

**BIRTH DATE AND LOCATION:** 1955, Seattle, Washington

**EDUCATION:** Gates attended public elementary school and the private Lakeside School. In 1973, Gates entered Harvard University as a freshman. He dropped out during his junior year to work with friend Paul Allen on their new company, Microsoft.

**HOME:** Seattle, Washington

**TIDBIT:** Gates enjoys reading and puzzles, and also plays golf and bridge. He lives in a 40,000-square-foot house containing all the latest technical wizardry. Gates is interested in biotechnology; he sits on the board of the Icos Corporation and is a shareholder in Darwin Molecular. Recently, Gates has received a lot of attention for the large public donations of his Gates Foundation, which his father oversees for him.

**FIRST JOB:** In 1975, Bill Gates and Paul Allen created BASIC, the first language written for personal computers, and licensed it to their first customer, MITS of Albuquerque, New Mexico.

**QUOTE:** "The Bill of Rights is the foundation on which our nation is built. The Internet is an enormously valuable place in which those rights must continue to thrive. Both the Bill of Rights and the Internet are potentially fragile. Mess with either of them too much, and we might ruin them. We can't let this happen."

based on the fact that AT&T's breakup actually benefited shareholders!)

If nothing else, look at litigation as a terrific opportunity to expose your child to the legal system. Even if you don't understand all the charges and countercharges yourself, it is still a lot of fun to gather news accounts and try to untangle the story—kind of like a puzzle but one with real people and companies and important issues being decided. Whenever we see a newspaper or magazine headline featuring a company we own stock in, we bring it to the dinner table for discussion. It has gotten to be sort of a family contest to see who can bring the most thought-provoking news item. Everybody gets in on the analysis and debate. Dinners are more interesting and fun this way, and our girls are learning how to gauge risk for themselves.

3. *Challenges from competitors are always worrisome*

Whenever a company develops a great product, you can expect that its competitors will rush to copy it to seize back market share. Intense competition will test just how "winning" a stock you chose. Can it survive threats from the rest of the industry?

The best defense is to know ahead of time how well your company can handle external threats. Look at its management, its product, its competition, and its history of fending off competitive threats in the past. EMC is a good example. We were attracted to it early in its history, when it overtook IBM as the leading provider of mass storage solutions for high-end computers—no small feat. We were concerned about its ability to fend off Dell, but that threat faded when Dell shifted its marketing focus to storage solutions for mid-sized machines. We were concerned again when Hewlett-Packard canceled a long-standing alliance with EMC in favor of another storage solutions provider, but EMC's managers, in anticipation of this decision, had hired more salespersons to counter the threat—a strategy that proved effective. What turned a potentially high-risk situation into a medium- to low-risk one was (a) an impressive track record of over-throwing such huge competitors as IBM, (b) management that continually prepared for a counterattack, and (c) a superior product.

If your research leads you to believe that your company is poised to answer a competitor's threat, then it is a low-risk stock—or possibly a medium-risk stock for a small period of time. If a company has a good product but no defensive strat-egy, we'd term it high risk.

4. *Expect the unexpected*
Even when your child screens for all these risks, it's impor-tant to discuss with him the very real fact that some risks cannot be anticipated because they cannot be imagined. Say your child owned McNeil Laboratories, the maker of Tylenol, back before everything was sold in tamper-proof packaging. Remember when some sociopath put cyanide into Tylenol? It was a disaster for the shareholders of McNeil, one that no one checking out the stock could have anticipated.

Companies do business in a world full of these unexpected risks. Your child should bear in mind that no matter how carefully he has assessed a company's risks, unexpected events can alter his assessment. If you look hard enough or long enough, you're bound to find something that can cause you anxiety about a company you're invested in or are plan-ning to invest in. Shannon found out that Johnson & Johnson was implicated in the death of a woman who died while hav-ing a J&J medical device implanted under the supervision of a J&J representative in the operating room. Shannon used this piece of information to try to persuade the Stock MarKids Investment Club not to invest in it. Pat supported

Shannon in her position even though it was contrary to her own estimation of J&J. She wanted to encourage Shannon to develop her research and analytical skills and form independent opinions even when they were minority ones. But she also used the opportunity to explain to Shannon and the Stock MarKids that any company, especially if it's a leader in the industry, can suffer setbacks that impact its stock adversely. What is important, Pat emphasized, is to expect the unexpected and use it to continually reassess a company's risk status.

## "G" Is for Companies That Grow the Value of the Portfolio

The final step of our ADDING strategy is to synthesize all the traits we've discussed so far. At this point your child should be able to add up all he has learned from subjecting his stock to the different queries and to determine whether it is a winning stock—meaning that it is going to enhance the overall value of his portfolio.

We suggest you make up a checklist and hand your child either colored markers to indicate green, yellow, or red lights, or have him write, next to each statement, GO, PROCEED WITH CAUTION, or STOP. Here's one we made for our girls:

1. ___ This stock ranks high in its industry—at least in the top 50 percent but ideally in the top 25 or even 10 percent.
2. ___ This stock diversifies my holdings because
    (a) it is in a different industry
    (b) it is in the same industry but features a different product
    (c) it is a different size from my other companies
    (d) its market segment is different from what I usually invest in
    (e) it is not limited to the U.S. market

3. ___ This stock delivers a reasonable rate of return—anywhere from 10 to 15 percent per year.

4. ___ This stock is increasing in earning power or shows potential for growth.

5. ___ This stock has very few inherent risk factors, meaning it
      (a) isn't brand new to the market
      (b) isn't involved in litigation or regulatory issues
      (c) has shown it can fend off competitive challenges

How much of a green light does your child get now? A number of yellows or even a few reds tell you that he should look at another stock and subject it to these same criteria. After all, there are more than nine thousand stocks for him to choose from!

If the signal is to buy, congratulations! He'll really enjoy owning it because, having applied the ADDING strategy, he knows so much more about it than he did at first. He isn't likely to panic if the stock or the market takes a sudden downturn. He knows enough about the company, its product, its management, and its share price history to feel confident the stock is worth hanging on to. This will help him weather the inevitable ups and downs of the stock market.

That's how Shannon weathered mad cow disease as a McDonald's shareholder. "My stock went down a lot," she observed. "But the news stopped affecting me when I went to McDonald's and saw people eating. The mad cow thing was just a phase. I knew I was invested in a company that was going to fill a need for a long time to come."

## What Long-Term Investing Looks Like

The ADDING strategy works only if your child is planning to be in the market for the long haul. This means planning to buy and hold stocks, not sell them at the first dip in share price or downturn of the market. The only time your child should sell a stock is when he is so heavily invested in it that it is affecting the overall balance or diversity of the portfolio or something happens to change the company's underlying structure or its prospects for the future.

Holding a stock for the long term is the key to financial success, and we want you and your children to experience the pleasure of being successful investors. *Long haul equals big haul.*

There are other rewards to adopting a buy-and-hold strategy. When we review the history of a stock we've come to own, it triggers memories of what we were doing or living through at the time. For example, whenever we check our McDonald's stock, we're reminded of what led to its acquisition: the outbreak of mad cow disease and the inception of our investment club. Those two events were linked in history; we can't think of one without being reminded of the other. That one investment conjures up a whole page of snapshots in our minds—our first meeting at the McDonald's restaurant with the other kids and parents; us sitting around the table at Martin Luther King, Jr. Library discussing what impact mad cow disease might have on the fast-food industry.

Looking at our girls' portfolios, we see more than just numbers. Every investment they've made has a story behind it, a story of both a growing company and a maturing investor. The portfolios are like family albums because so much of their growth reflects the development of our kids into young women and sophisticated investors.

## PORTFOLIO QUIZ

## Circle one:

*1. How would you rate the diversification of Lynn's portfolio with the following stocks: Merck, Microsoft, American Express, McDonald's, and General Electric?*

- (a) well diversified
- (b) not diversified
- (c) needs to add more stocks
- (d) needs more blue-chip stocks

*2. How would you rate Danielle's portfolio, consisting of Microsoft, General Electric, AT&T, and Intel, as to mix of stocks and different market capitalizations?*

- (a) good mix of stocks with different market caps
- (b) too many stocks with low market caps
- (c) too many high-tech stocks
- (d) too many stocks with high market caps

*3. How would you rate Shannon's portfolio as to mix of industries if it contains Intel, Sun Microsystems, Cisco, McDonald's, and Network Associates?*

- (a) portfolio needs more high-tech stocks
- (b) good diversification
- (c) too many high-tech stocks
- (d) needs to add more stocks

*4. Pat's portfolio has General Electric, Netegrity, Amazon, and Yahoo. Do you think these companies have a proven track record?*

- (a) All these companies have been around a long time.
- (b) Only General Electric has been around a really long time.
- (c) All these companies have been around a long time except Amazon.

**5. Would you suggest that Danielle buy shares in Yahoo to add to her portfolio, which currently contains McDonald's, EMC, Intel, Cisco, and Mattel?**

    (a) No. Danielle already has too many high-tech stocks.

    (b) Yes. Yahoo is a very good stock.

    (c) Not sure. Need to learn more about Yahoo.

Review the following chart and then answer the questions that follow.

### EARNINGS GROWTH CHART

| | Last 5 Years (%) | This Year (%) | Next Year (%) | Next 5 Years (%) |
|---|---|---|---|---|
| XYZ Corporation | 9.9 | 14.0 | 21.5 | 19.9 |
| Retail Restaurants | 12.5 | 17.5 | 15.0 | 12.5 |
| S&P 500 | 10.3 | 10.2 | 10.3 | 6.7 |

Cold = 5–10%        Getting hot = 16–20%
Lukewarm = 11–15%    Hot = More than 20%

**6. Identify the years when XYZ Corporation was cold (low growth):**

**7. When was the S&P lukewarm (moderate growth)?**

**8. When is the XYZ Corporation expecting to be hot (high growth)?**

**9. Does the XYZ Corporation expect to perform better than the S&P in the next five years? Circle one:**
                    YES    NO

**10. When does the XYZ Corporation's earnings growth exceed the rest of the industry's growth rate?**

## Answer key:

5. a    10. Next year and the next 5 years
4. b    9. Yes
3. c    8. Next year
2. d    7. Never
1. a    6. Last 5 years

## WINNING QUIZ

**Circle one:**

*1. Some of the different principles for managing children's portfolios are:*

    (a)  avoid high-risk stocks

    (b)  build a diversified portfolio

    (c)  choose "winning" stocks

    (d)  select companies with potential for high earnings growth

    (e)  all of the above

*2. You should select "winning" stocks based on:*

    (a)  whatever your uncle tells you

    (b)  something you read in a chat room on the Internet

    (c)  your own experience and observations

    (d)  the advice of a friend

*3. Some of the characteristics of "winning" stocks are:*

    (a)  no other company makes products as good as this company

    (b)  the company provides goods or services that will always be needed

    (c)  the company makes products that you or your family members like and enjoy using

    (d)  there is a trend for people to use the company's products more

    (e)  all of the above

*4. When you look for companies with the potential for high earnings growth, you are:*

    (a)  hoping to find a stock that will grow 6 inches a year

    (b)  trying to find a stock that is *hot,* so it will appreciate over time

    (c)  looking for a stock with the potential for 2–5 percent growth over the next year

5. When you think about risk, you need to consider:

   (a)  how long you plan to hold the stock

   (b)  whether or not the company is involved in any lawsuits

   (c)  the stock's historical rate of return

   (d)  none of the above

   (e)  all of the above

## True or false:

6. Stocks that have high risks are good to own.

                 \_\_\_\_T  \_\_\_\_F

If false, why?


7. You should invest only in companies that are the same size.

                 \_\_\_\_T  \_\_\_\_F

If false, why?


8. The term "market cap" stands for market capitalization, which is the size of the company.

                 \_\_\_\_T  \_\_\_\_F

If false, why?


9. When you buy stocks, you should expect at least 75 percent price appreciation per year.

                 \_\_\_\_T  \_\_\_\_F

If false, why?


10. A long-term investor sells his stocks after a long time and only if something changes.

                 \_\_\_\_T  \_\_\_\_F

If false, why?

## Answer key:

| | |
|---|---|
| 1. e | 6. F |
| 2. c | 7. F |
| 3. e | 8. T |
| 4. b | 9. F |
| 5. b | 10. T |

Explanation for question 6: The opposite: Stocks that have *low* risks are good to own.

Explanation for question 7: When you diversify, you invest in companies that are different sizes.

Explanation for question 9: It would be highly unusual for a stock to appreciate this much. A much more reasonable goal is to expect 15 percent or less appreciation per year.

## PRACTICE CHOOSING "WINNING" STOCKS

Read each paragraph about a particular stock and choose all the reasons it is a "winning" stock.

1. Danielle attends a private school where all the kids wear uniforms. One day she came home and told Lynn that she wanted to go shopping for a new pair of shoes. Since they had just bought school shoes only one month before, at the beginning of the school year, Lynn was surprised by the request and was reluctant to spend money for a new pair of shoes when the old ones were perfectly fine. Talking to Danielle, she learned that many of the girls were wearing a new kind of shoe called Doc Johnson's, and she wanted them because she wanted to fit in with the crowd. Identify one or more of the reasons that Danielle might consider the Doc Johnson Company a "winning" stock:

   (a) __ Doc Johnson makes products that Danielle or her family members like and enjoy using
   (b) __ Doc Johnson makes products that Danielle's friends like and use
   (c) __ Danielle noticed that many of her friends like Doc Johnson products
   (d) __ No other company makes products as good as Doc Johnson shoes
   (e) __ There is a trend for people to use Doc Johnson products more
   (f) __ Doc Johnson products will always be needed

2. When the weather turned cold, Shannon started to wear long-sleeved cotton shirts to keep warm. After about a week of the cold weather, she told her mother that she needed more shirts. She said these shirts kept her warmer than any others, and she really liked the feel of cotton against her skin in cold weather. Shannon reminded her mother that the shirts she was wearing were from last year and that she really hadn't bought any new shirts for cold weather. Shannon also said the kind of shirts she liked were available at only one store: Pacific Moonwear. What makes Pacific Moonwear a "winning" stock to Shannon?

(a) __ Pacific Moonwear makes products that Shannon or her
family members like and enjoy using

(b) __ Pacific Moonwear makes products that Shannon's friends
like and use

(c) __ Shannon noticed a lot more of her friends like Pacific
Moonwear products

(d) __ No other company makes products as good as Pacific
Moonwear shirts

(e) __ There is a trend for people to use Pacific Moonwear
products more

(f) __ Pacific Moonwear products will always be needed

3. Last spring at one of Shannon's softball games Pat got into a conversation with some of the other parents about the high school policy ban-
ning cellular phones at school. One mother told a story about her
daughter receiving a two-day suspension for using her phone in the
school parking lot. Several parents talked about what their children did
to avoid being caught on school premises with their phones. Pat was
surprised to learn how many high school girls actually had their own
cell phones. Why would Pat consider investing in Apple Electric, a local
company that makes cell phone products?

(a) __ Apple Electric makes products that Pat or her family
members like and enjoy using

(b) __ Apple Electric makes products that Pat's friends like and use

(c) __ Pat noticed a lot more of her friends like Apple Electric
products

(d) __ No other company makes products as good as Apple
Electric cell phones

(e) __ There is a trend for people to use Apple Electric products
more

(f) __ Apple Electric products will always be needed

## Answer key:

3. b, c, e
2. a, d, f
1. a, b, c, e, f

## LEARN TO ASSESS RISK LEVELS

Read the facts about each company and decide if the company should have a high-, medium-, or low-risk rating and why.

1. California Candy Company makes many popular cookies and candies for distribution to stores throughout California. The company recently decided to begin selling its products to specialty stores throughout the United States. The company believes it can increase production from eight hours to sixteen hours a day to meet the increased production requirements. This means training some new employees, but that should be easy. The equipment is a little old, but the company has a very good engineer who says he can be reached at home through his pager if there are any problems. There are some concerns about the candies because they stay fresh for only about one week, and that is why the company never expanded beyond California. However, managers believe that if they add a preservative, the candies will stay fresh for two or three weeks. How would you assess the risk level for this company?

   (a) __ Low risk. The managers really know what they are doing.
   (b) __ Medium risk. Adding a second shift is a little bit of a concern, and so is product freshness.
   (c) __ High risk. Many "new" variables make this company's "new" plans shaky.

2. Macrohard Software Company makes systems that help stockbrokers keep track of stock orders and sales. Macrohard has been in business for over ten years, and the company has been developing a loyal following among the discount brokerage firms. A new firm, Brokers Friend Company, has just introduced a competing software system and has started offering it to all the brokers for a free ninety-day trial period. Salespersons for Macrohard say that full-service brokers really like the Brokers Friend system and plan to use it after the trial period ends. Macrohard managers are not too worried because most of their

customers are the discount brokerage firms, and none of the brokers at the discount brokerage firms likes the new system. How would you assess the risk level for the Macrohard Software Company?

    (a) __ Low risk. Macrohard has absolutely nothing to fear from its competitors.

    (b) __ Medium risk. Macrohard should wait and see what happens in ninety days.

    (c) __ High risk. Macrohard's software may be replaced by the Brokers Friend product.

3. Orion Company, a large firm that makes many household products such as lightbulbs and toilet paper, has been on the New York Stock Exchange for over fifty years. The company has experienced a steady increase in earnings over the past ten years, and this year is no exception. Everything the company does is successful, mainly because the president and chief executive officer, John Warren, insists on careful planning and rigorous attention to detail by all the executives who work for him. As a result, employees like to work for this company, and investors like to invest in it.

    (a) __ Low risk. Orion Company sounds like a great company.

    (b) __ Medium risk. There must be something wrong here.

    (c) __ High risk. No company is this perfect!

## Answer key:

1. High risk. The company is embarking on a new venture that has several areas of concern, such as hiring and training new employees, equipment wearing out, unavailability of the engineer to fix problems, and product freshness. This is *not* a good time to invest in the California Candy Company.

2. Medium risk. Macrohard is facing some very stiff competition from the Brokers Friend Company, and this is always cause for concern. However, since most of the Macrohard customers are discount brokers who like its system, Macrohard is likely to be only mildly affected by the competition. It would be wise, though, to avoid investing in Macrohard at this time and wait to see what happens in the future with its competitor, Brokers Friend.

3. Low risk. That's right. This is a *great* company, one that every investor would love to own. Try to find stocks like this in your search for "winning" stocks.

# 7

## Many Happy Returns

**C**an you tell how well your child is doing? Is she profiting from the experience? Can you point to some positive returns?

There are many ways to gauge profit, and not all of them are financial measurements. Whatever the current dollar value of our girls' portfolios, we need only look, listen, or watch them to know they are profiting from their investing. When her neighbor, a NASA scientist, invites Danielle over to meet and mingle with his college graduate intern because she's every bit as poised and mature, Lynn sees just how much her granddaughter has profited from putting her money in the market. Pat sees similar high returns for Shannon. It is Shannon who is consulted for her opinion on Yahoo stock when Pat's friend calls for investment advice. And Shannon is an entire grade level ahead in math ever since her stock market savvy got her selected for a program for high-achieving girls in the fourth grade.

We know without ever crunching the numbers or tabulating current market value for their portfolios that the girls have profited immeasurably from their investments. We can also tell how well they're doing in very quantitative ways. We have an array of tools for the task, much as a contractor has a measuring tape, a

T square, and a plumb line to give him an idea of how his project is coming along. While the project we'll be assessing in this chapter is not a building, it still is something that has been built: a portfolio. The tools we discuss are those your child can use, just as our girls are using them now to measure their own returns.

## Tabulating Returns

Whenever your child makes a profit on her investments, the amount she makes is termed her *return*. To borrow a description from the IRS, investment returns are unearned income, or money earned without having to go to work. Even children can appreciate the beauty of that! Their money will grow without their lifting a finger, and they won't have to pay taxes on it as long as it is invested.

To know whether your child is indeed profiting from her portfolio, you must compute something called the gain or loss on investment. It is a simple calculation, one your child can learn. It is best done on a regular basis—every week, every month, or even every quarter—because over time, the gains or losses tell a story worth listening to. A stock that goes up and down may still earn a gain over time; that's a stock worth holding on to long term. But a stock that loses ground rather steadily over a year's time is possibly one asking to be sold. Either way, the gain-or-loss calculation is invaluable for telling your child when or if she needs to rethink her investment decisions.

While the following computations may look a little scary, we promise they're only fifth-grade math. Take them one step at a time. Remember, you're in no rush!

## How to Calculate Gain or Loss

*STEP 1.* Compute the current market value.
No. of shares owned × Current share price = Current market value

# JOHN T. CHAMBERS
President and Chief Executive Officer, Cisco Systems Inc.

**COMPANY:**  Cisco Systems Inc. is a $14 billion company and a worldwide leader in networking hardware and software for the Internet. It has the third largest market capitalization behind Intel and Microsoft on NASDAQ as of 1999.

**EMPLOYEES:**  21,000

**$$$:**  His Cisco stake is worth nearly $400 million

**BIRTH DATE AND LOCATION:**  August 23, 1949, West Virginia

**EDUCATION:**  Bachelor's degree from West Virginia University and MBA in finance from Indiana University

**RESIDES:**  Los Altos, California

**TIDBIT:**  John Chambers has been called the best boss in the country. Having a self-described sweet tooth himself, he regularly roams the halls of Cisco giving out candy and ice cream, and says modestly that as the CEO he has to do something. He is also known for generous stock option plans for employees. He overcame dyslexia to graduate near the top of his high school class and his best friend is his dad.

**FIRST JOB:**  Started with IBM

**QUOTE:**  "I think nice people can win. I don't think you have to be mean to be a good leader."

Current market value (or CMV) tells you how much the shares you own are worth today based on the closing price for the stock listed in today's newspaper.

*STEP 2.* Compute the total cost paid

No. of shares owned × Average cost per share + Fees and commissions = Total cost paid

**Total cost paid** (or TCP) is the amount you paid for all the shares of this stock that you have purchased. Over time you may have bought shares at different prices; you look at your statements to tally up the purchases and compute the average price. If you've purchased shares through a dividend reinvestment program, then the total costs are usually listed on the statements, and you can just use that figure.

*STEP 3.* Compute the net gain or loss.

CMV − TCP = Net gain or loss

**Net gain or loss** (or NET) tells you whether you have made money or lost money on the stock you purchased. If your NET is a positive number, then congratulations! You have made a profit on your investment. If NET is a negative number, then your investment is worth less today than what you originally paid for it. This may be just a temporary situation and no cause for concern, especially if you bought the stock very recently.

*STEP 4.* Compute the percent of gain or loss

$$\frac{\text{NET}}{\text{TCP}} \times 100 = \text{Percent of gain or loss}$$

**Percent** tells you how much you are making or losing as a percentage of the amount that you invested. If you have a 3 percent gain on your investments, then it means that for every $100 you invested, you have earned $3 without lifting a finger!

How much has Danielle gained or
lost on her McDonald's stock?

We need to look at the data first. The total cost includes fees paid, which totaled only $16.25.

| No. of Shares Owned | Total Cost | Current Share Price |
|---|---|---|
| 110.324 | $971.24 | $41.69 |

The total cost represents the sum of what Lynn and Danielle spent for Danielle's 110.324 shares. This was easy to figure out because Lynn saved all of Danielle's statements. The current share price is what a share was selling for at the close of the market on November 1, 1999.

Now that we have the raw data, we can do the calculations:

STEP 1. Compute the current market value.
No. of Shares Owned × Current Share Price = Current Market Value
110.324      ×      $41.69      =      $4,599.41

STEP 2. Compute the total cost.
No. of Shares Owned × Average Cost Per Share +
Fees and Commissions = Total Cost

This exercise should be done for each stock. It will give your child excellent practice in these basic math skills. After she has calculated her gain or loss on each stock, have her compute the gain or loss for her entire portfolio. If she performs these calculations at the end of the month (or the end of the week if she is really ambitious), she will notice a pattern emerging—one she can graph, just as she took the stock prices and plotted them on a graph to see whether they were headed up or down. Pictures of performance tell a stock's story better than words.

## Relative Strength Is a Strong Indicator

Yet another way to measure success is the Relative Strength Indicator. It's a tool that helps an investor compare the performance

We already know the total that Lynn and Danielle paid for all their McDonald's shares: $971.24. The dividend reinvestment forms actually showed a figure twice that—$1,942.48—but since Danielle sold half of her shares, she divided this figure in half to come up with what she spent on what she still holds.

STEP 3. Compute the net gain or loss.
CMV − TCP = Net Gain or Loss
$4,599.41 − $971.24 = $3,628.17

STEP 4. Compute the percent of gain or loss.
$$\frac{NET}{TCP} \times 100 = \text{Percent of Gain or Loss}$$

$$\frac{\$3,628.17}{\$971.24} \times 100 = 373.56$$

Danielle has gained $3,628.17, 373 percent, on her McDonald's investment. Wow!

of an individual stock to the performance of the market as a whole. When the market goes up and down, up and down—what is called "volatility"—it is sometimes hard to know how a particular stock is doing. You compare its volatility to the market's by comparing the percentage of change in the stock's value in relation to the change in the overall market.

Relative strength is a good way to get perspective on your stocks versus the universe of stocks out there. Are you beating the market, lagging behind, or keeping up with it? Shannon and Danielle compute relative strength as often as they compute gain or loss: every month (unless they're feeling particularly motivated, and then it's every week). See the activity on page 198 for how you and your child can calculate relative strength.

What you want to see is a stock that generally outperforms the overall market because it generates the greatest returns from its steady and constant stock price increases. A stock that consistently underperforms, according to the relative strength indicator, is one that is likely to generate a loss down the road. Remember, however, that this is a tool whose results are best interpreted over time—a few quarters at least—before leaping to any conclusions about buying more shares or selling those you have.

## Trend Analysis the Easy Way

Trend analysis sounds like some complicated data processing best left to Wall Street geeks. In fact, it used to be a tedious exercise. You had to gather data on stock prices that spanned months and years of time, and then manually plot the prices on charts. But now, thanks to the Internet and sites like Yahoo Finance, all it takes is glancing at a colorful chart with a bold line plotted on it to figure out where a particular stock is headed.

As helpful as it is to have a stock's price plotted and graphed in a line, it's even more telling to compare one line to another. A great way to illustrate the differences is to compare a stock you're interested in to a benchmark you've held for a long time and know very well. Without this basis for comparison, you'd have no idea whether the trend line you were looking at was good, bad, or mediocre. Trend analysis helps investors understand if positive returns are good or positively outstanding—or, conversely, if a loss is bearable or frightening.

Trend analysis is not just a tool to measure the performance of stock already owned but an excellent way to examine potential investments as well. Yahoo's trend charts are a great place to check out a stock your kids are thinking about buying, to flesh out the picture you get from applying our ADDING strategy to that stock.

Trend analysis needn't be limited to what you see on your computer screen, either. Without doing any math, without comparing any returns or charts showing gain or loss, your child probably has a good sense of a favorite company's past growth and future prospects if she thinks about people's buying habits. Will people be as interested in her company's product five years from now? Ten? Twenty? Are the last five years an indication of how the company's growth will continue? Shannon decided to commit her first real investment earnings (from the club) to AOL despite her mother's misgivings. As a loyal user, Shannon felt that AOL had features that would continue to ensure its dominance in the industry and that the Internet would only get bigger, with even more first-time users subscribing to AOL. She identified a trend based on looking around at what people needed and would need down the road. (Apparently her trend analysis is solid, if the recent announcement of the AOL–Time Warner merger is any indication!)

Trend analysis can be as straightforward as identifying what people need now and will continue to need in the future. People will always eat food. People will always get sick and need health care and pharmaceuticals. As the Internet carries more and more information that is vital to our lives—including, literally, patients' vital signs and other data that doctors rely on—people will need the Internet, along with all the providers that use it or make it possible, including the vast network of telecommunications we're still assembling.

The bottom line: Take a peek into the future based on what you see today. Look beyond increased sales and earnings, price trends, and management's expectations.

Getting your children invested and learning how to invest is a lot like planting a tree. The sapling you start out with is so small, you just can't imagine how it can turn out to be much of anything. We know because we've planted them. Lynn planted a tiny pine tree that Danielle won at a science fair one year; at the time it seemed hardly worth planting. Nonetheless, she watered it regularly, mulched it occasionally, and sometimes gave it a dose of fertilizer. And you know what? Today that pine tree is taller than Danielle. It has grown nearly to maturity, as she has. For that

### Trend Analysis Examples

Shannon often uses EMC as her baseline for comparison because it's a stock she knows and it has performed consistently well. Plus, EMC is a useful benchmark for technology stocks. When it came to checking her Intel stock to see how strong a performer she owned, EMC was a natural choice for comparative purposes.

First, she figured out EMC's return. On November 15, 1994, the price of a share was $5.75, after adjustments for subsequent stock splits. The price on November 15, 1999, was $80.25—an increase of $74.50 over five years. She did the math—74.5 divided by 5.75 times 100—and got a return of 1295 percent. Pretty spectacular! Next, she looked at the trend line for EMC over the same period. EMC had been on a steady course, with the price increasing most noticeably over the last three and a half years. EMC's trend line is the type we really like because we like to see a pattern of steady increases over a period of time.

Finally, Shannon can compare Intel to EMC. Intel's price increased $66.38 over the same period of time (from $7.68 to $74.06), and its trend chart showed a steady pattern of growth over the entire five years. Intel generated a return of 864 percent over five years, she learned—not as much as EMC but still a fabulous rate of return. Shannon's trend analysis of Intel persuaded her that it is a keeper, one that can generate many happy returns.

small but constant investment, the pine has tripled in size and value—just as Danielle's portfolio has.

With time and regular nurturing and persistent investing discipline, you and your child will also experience the joy of many happy returns.

## GAIN OR LOSS?

This activity involves many facets of math, including multiplying, adding, decimals, and percentages. An example is given to show how to calculate the gain or loss. It is simple, easy, and fun—particularly when there is a gain.

Determine the net gain or loss for each stock transaction. Calculate the broker's fee (3 percent or .03) for each purchase and the sale. Do you have a gain or loss? If the number is positive, it is a gain. If number is negative, it is a loss.

Example: 100 shares of Expedia brought at $14 and sold at $45

(Number of Shares × Price of Stock) + Broker Commission = Total Cost of Purchase
      (100 × 14)             + (100 × $14 × .03)
       $1,400             + ($1,400 × .03)
       $1,400             + $42           = $1,442
(Number of Shares × Price of Stock) − Broker Commission = Total Received from Sale
      (100 × $45)       − (100 × $45 × .03)
      $4,500            − ($4,500 × .03)
      $4,500            − $135         = $4,365

**250 shares of EMC bought at $32 and sold at $55**

Purchase _____

Sale _____

Gain or loss _____

**50 shares of Mattel bought at $25 and sold at $12⅝**

Purchase _____

Sale _____

Gain or loss _____

**300 shares of Netegrity bought at $13⅜ and sold at $44**

Purchase _____

Sale _____

Gain or loss _____

150 shares of AOL bought at $93 and sold at $147

Purchase  _____

Sale  _____

Gain or loss  _____

500 shares of Sedona bought at $5 and sold at $2$^{15}/_{16}$

Purchase  _____

Sale  _____

Gain or loss  _____

325 shares of Nike bought at $38⅜ and sold at $25½

Purchase  _____

Sale  _____

Gain or loss  _____

100 shares of Motorola bought at $69 and sold at $55

Purchase  _____

Sale  _____

Gain or loss  _____

400 shares of Qualcomm bought at $168 and sold at $264

Purchase  _____

Sale  _____

Gain or loss  _____

25 shares of Johnson & Johnson bought at $71¼ and sold at $59¾

Purchase  _____

Sale  _____

Gain or loss  _____

150 shares of PEPCO bought at $25½ and sold at $23

Purchase  _____

Sale  _____

Gain or loss  _____

## COMPUTE PERCENTAGE OF CHANGE IN STOCK PRICE

This activity can be used after you have advanced your skills and are comfortable calculating the gain or loss.

$$\text{Percentage of Change} = \frac{\text{Amount of Change from the Original Purchase Price}}{\text{Purchase Price}} \times 100$$

Determine the amount of change in dollars, the percentage of change in price, and the gain or loss. Place + (plus) or − (minus) in the Change in Dollars column and the Change in Price column to indicate an increase or decrease.

| Stock Name | Purchase Price | Selling Price | Change in Dollars | Change in Price (%) | Gain or Loss |
|------------|---------------|--------------|-------------------|---------------------|--------------|
| Johnson & Johnson | 69⅝ | 65½ | | | |
| AOL | 95 | 144¼ | | | |
| Cisco | 71⅞ | 99⅛ | | | |
| Wal-Mart | 17⅛ | 13 | | | |
| MCI WorldCom | 33½ | 86 | | | |
| Sedona | 5 | 2¹⁵⁄₃₂ | | | |

## COMPUTE THE RELATIVE STRENGTH

This way of gauging a stock's performance is a shortcut method of checking the percentage of change in a stock in relation to the change in the market. Check the relative strength every week or every month, for example, every Wednesday or every Saturday, using Friday's closing price.

Relative strength must be computed on the same day every week for the entire month.

Divide the stock price by the DJIA for the day and move the decimal place three spaces to the right.

An example is provided by Danielle for CMGI, a stock she is researching.

---

### NAME OF STOCK: CMGI
### MONTH: OCTOBER 1999

---

| | Date | Stock Price ($) | DJIA | Stock Price ÷ DJIA | Results |
|---|---|---|---|---|---|
| Week 1 | 10/1 | 99.1875 | 10,273 | 99.1875 ÷ 10,273 | 9.7 |
| Week 2 | 10/8 | 112.50 | 10,649.76 | 112.50 ÷ 10,649.76 | 10.6* |
| Week 3 | 10/15 | 97.8125 | 10,019.71 | 97.8125 ÷ 10,019.71 | 9.8* |
| Week 4 | 10/22 | 103.125 | 10,470.25 | 103.125 ÷ 10,470.25 | 9.8* |

* Outperforming.

Explanation: Any result above 9.7 (the starting point in this example), means the stock is "outperforming" the overall market; while any result below 9.7 would have meant the stock was "underperforming" the market. Therefore, after just three weeks of following the stock, Danielle concluded that CMGI was outperforming the overall market, as measured by the DJIA.

Try computing the relative strength of your favorite stock.

---

**NAME OF STOCK:** _____

**MONTH:** _____

---

| | Date | Stock Price ($) | DJIA | Stock Price ÷ DJIA | Results |
|---|---|---|---|---|---|
| Week 1 | | | | | |
| Week 2 | | | | | |
| Week 3 | | | | | |
| Week 4 | | | | | |

Is the company outperforming the market (yes or no)?
Is the company underperforming the market (yes or no)?

# 8

## Beyond the Basics

To celebrate three years of successful investing through the Stock MarKids, our girls cashed out the majority of their stake in the club to invest in stocks of their own choosing for their own portfolios. By this time they were quite savvy about the market, so we decided to have them visit a broker's office and place the buy orders themselves. That is, we did not pick up the phone. We had the girls make their purchases in person.

Pat took Shannon to the nearest office of Quick & Reilly, where she had already established an account for her; likewise, Lynn took Danielle to Charles Schwab, where Danielle actually picked up the broker's phone and placed her order (although Lynn had to confirm it "officially"). Shannon and Danielle came away with a sense of empowerment. As Danielle said, "It really makes you feel as if you're moving up in life, placing an order with a broker!"

Keeping your kids interested in investing is simple if you keep them *active*. Money management can be so abstract in our technological age. You can transfer funds, pay checks, buy into mutual funds, open and trade a brokerage account, and create and manage an entire portfolio all by looking at a computer screen and moving a mouse. That's great for busy adults, but for kids just learning about money and the infinite ways in which to put it to work, this kind of virtual management is too remote, too conceptual. Kids learn best when they are physically engaged in a process that involves other people. They need to interface with people and establish relationships with individuals. They need to go places and see how things work firsthand. Learning investing is like learning any other topic: Time at your desk is important, but field trips can make the whole subject come alive. Here are various extracurricular ideas for getting the most out of the very vivid stock market world.

## Visit a Stock Exchange

In chapter 4 we talked about some of the biggest and oldest stock exchanges in the country. Of course, your child can visit them online (see the list of exchanges and their websites), but, again, there's just no substitute for going in person. The sheer physical energy, noise, and commotion of the actual trading floor really impress most kids we know. The floor provides them with a visual image of the concept of buying and selling stock and provides an opportunity for them to ask plenty of questions, such as: What are those weird letter combinations? What do all those numbers stand for? Who are those guys in the jackets, and what are they yelling about?

Depending on the exchange, you may have a human tour guide, audiophones, or other automated system. Lynn recalls taking Danielle on her first trip to the New York Stock Exchange: "On a rainy, dreary spring morning, we left Washington, D.C., early and arrived in Manhattan around lunchtime. There in the financial district, only a few blocks from the exchange, we had lunch in one of the most elegant McDonald's that Danielle or I had ever visited. We were greeted by a doorman, a hostess seated us, and we enjoyed live music from a grand piano. We ate our meal on marble tables, each with its own vase of fresh flowers. Our food was served on real plates, with ice cream for dessert and real espresso or cap-

## Marketplaces to Visit in the United States

New York Stock Exchange (NYSE)
20 Broad Street
New York, NY 10005
(212) 656-4298
**Website:** www.nyse.com
*Admission tickets are free. The admission counter is located outside 20 Broad Street. Open Monday through Friday from 8:45 A.M. to 4:30 P.M. (Trading ceases at 4:00 P.M.)*

Chicago Mercantile Exchange
30 South Wacker Drive
Chicago, IL 60606
Telephone: (312) 930-8249
**Website:** www.cme.com
*The Chicago Merchantile Exchange is happy to host any visit. All presenta-tions can be scheduled from 9:00 A.M. until 12:00 noon, Monday through Fri-day, for groups of 10 to 50 people.*
    *Smaller groups and individuals are welcome to join a scheduled group. Call in advance for presentation times.*

Minneapolis Grain Exchange
130 Grain Exchange Building
400 S. 4th Street
Minneapolis, MN 55415
(612) 321-7101
**Website:** www.mgex.com
*Tours are offered Tuesdays, Wednesdays, and Thursdays at 8:45 A.M. and 10:30 A.M. by appointment only. Call for more information or to schedule an appointment.*

The National Association of Securities Dealers, Inc. (NASD)
The NASDAQ Stock Market
1735 K Street, N.W.
Washington, DC 20006
(202) 496-2500

The NASDAQ Stock Market
33 Whitehall Street
New York, NY 10004
(212) 858-4000
**Website:** www.nasdaq-amex.com

American Stock Exchange (AMEX)
86 Trinity Place
New York, NY 10006
(212) 306-1000
**Website:** www.amex.com

Arizona Stock Exchange
2800 N. Central Avenue
Suite 1575
Phoenix, AZ 85004
**Website:** www.azx.com

If you are in New York City, don't limit your tour to the NYSE. Check out the Museum of American Financial History, founded in 1988 to chronicle the role of finance and the capital markets in American history. The museum's permanent collections include priceless antique stocks, bonds, and currency, historic documents and photographs, and equipment once used on Wall Street. It is located in the Standard Oil Building at 28 Broadway and is open to the public Tuesday through Saturday, 10:00 A.M. to 4:00 P.M. Every Friday at 10 A.M. the museum sponsors a two-hour walking tour of New York's financial district that includes a visit to the NYSE. Call (212) 908-4110 to make reservations or check out the museum online at www.mafh.org.

puccino—definitely not your ordinary McDonald's. We were so proud to be shareholders in such a company!

"After lunch we joined a guided tour of the NYSE that allowed us to use the data terminals to get stock quotes. We also used the interactive displays, watched a video that explained the hows and whys of the exchange's market system, and viewed the trading floor from a balcony because only traders are permitted on the floor. It was very exciting to see all the activity beneath us. There seemed to be hundreds of traders, each in a color-coded trading jacket and running around and shouting. It is a busy, busy situation, especially when the Dow is going up or down fast. The traders were taking buy orders and sell orders and throwing their paper notes on the floor. That's what left such an impression on me: There was so much paper on the floor, and hardly any in the trash cans!

"Danielle was so impressed by this visit that she convinced her eighth-grade class to tour the NYSE as part of their graduating class trip to New York. But unlike Danielle, her class had very little understanding of what was going on around them. The whole group kept turning to her with questions. Danielle was happy to explain everything to her classmates. (She's also the only teenager we know with a poster of the New York Stock Exchange on her bedroom wall!)"

## Participate in a Shareholders' Meeting

The annual shareholders' meeting is open to every shareholder of the company, no matter how young. A shareholders' meeting allows the board of the company to receive input from its investors on various issues affecting the financial health of the firm. Every shareholder gets to participate by voting—one vote for every share held. While it is possible to have this say by proxy—by filling out a form with your votes and mailing it in—it is worth attending at least once or twice with your child to experience this meeting live.

As a parent, you might consider buying a share in a local publicly traded company just so your child can experience a share-holders' meeting. Even one share will entitle your child to cast his vote in the proceedings of the company, and there's nothing like exercising his right at the actual meeting. To arrange for your child to attend, call the company's investor relations department. Any shareholder is welcome, but it's a good idea to arrange for your child's participation in advance. As we discovered, some companies go to quite a bit of effort to welcome their youngest shareholders.

Soon after the club purchased Trusted Information Systems (TISX), we contacted its investor relations department and arranged for the club to attend. Our young shareholders got more of an eye-opening experience than we bargained for. On April 28, 1998, at the corporate office in Glenwood, Maryland, Trusted Information Systems turned the company over to its new buyer, Network Associates (NETA). The buyout was something the kids knew about in advance; in fact, they had voted in favor of the acquisition by NETA because they felt it would impact favorably on the company's stock value. But at the shareholders' meeting the kids could see that their decision had more than just financial implications.

Shannon arrived early enough to chat with Mr. Steve Walker, president of the company. She presented him with the club proxy—the Stock MarKids' vote to okay the merger. The actual shareholders' meeting lasted no more than ten or fifteen minutes. First, Walker announced it would be too hard for him to run the meeting. His attorney then conducted the business. At the end of the meeting almost everyone who had worked for the company was crying. Many people had lost their jobs in the takeover. Others were upset because they were losing their friends and because the company would never be the same family-run sort of operation.

"It was a once-in-a-lifetime experience," recalls Shannon. "I learned a lot. I learned that just because shareholders are happy

---

### Educational Websites

You and your child can find out all sorts of general finance and investing information on these sites.

Museum of American Financial History:  www.mafh.org
U.S. Treasury Department:  www.treas.gov
                                          www.treas.gov/educational.html
                                          www.treas.gov/currency
Looking for a Parent Company:  http://dir.yahoo.com/
                                          Business_and_Economy/Companies

---

with a buyout, it doesn't mean the employees will be happy at all. Even though it's not necessary for every shareholder to vote, the votes are tallied at the meeting, and decisions are made based on those tallies. I like feeling that I had a say in those decisions!"

## Financial Seminars

As more and more Americans enter the stock market (and about half the populace has already), companies are becoming aware that kids, not just adults, are ready and eager to become investors. It has always been in a company's best interests to educate the next generation of shareholders, but now as never before certain companies are taking the lead in that education and sponsoring financial seminars specifically for the under-eighteen crowd.

Salomon Smith Barney, for example, sponsored a pilot Boston Financial Camp for Girls, consisting of a series of intensive two-day seminars. Julian Krinsky Enrichment Camp in Pennsylvania teaches entrepreneurship. If you look around at the financial websites on the Internet—pick any major mutual fund or brokerage house—you will no doubt find one in your area. Better yet, look at the financial magazines geared to children such as *Young Money Matters* and *Young Entrepreneur.* NAIC's adult publication, *Better In-*

*vesting,* includes a list of workshops and seminars organized regionally. And don't overlook the literature you get from your own stock holdings and mutual funds. Just because a lecture series or workshop isn't directed at your child doesn't mean it's over his head. Stay tuned to what your local community college or continuing education programs are offering, and you might find something both you and your child can profit from by attending.

## Attend an Investor Fair

For the last two years Lynn has taken Danielle to the NAIC Regional Investor Fair held at the University of Maryland. These fairs give investors of all ages an opportunity to learn more about publicly traded companies. Their representatives give presentations and hand out quite a bit of material. NAIC sponsors these events all around the country; once you become a member, you'll hear about the next one that will be in your area. For more information on how to attend or host a fair, contact the NAIC toll-free at (877) 275-6242.

Fairs are quite interactive. It's hard to imagine how a child wouldn't be interested. In her first year Danielle went from booth to booth picking up whatever the company was giving away—everything from Fannie Mae mugs and annual reports to company refrigerator magnets and other gadgets. She didn't hesitate to talk with the different representatives even though she was only eleven years old. One of them asked her if she owned any stocks; when she answered yes, he asked her which ones. "Which ones do you want to know about—my club's portfolio or my personal portfolio?" she replied, to the man's astonishment.

## Other Ways to Be an Active Shareholder (or Practice Being One)

Field trips are fun. We've found them to be highly educational as far as investing is concerned. But if you can't get to a stock exchange or can't make a shareholder's meeting, don't despair:

There are lots of hands-on ways to keep your kid engaged as an investor without ever leaving home. With the advent of the Internet, we've found that the tools available to us to teach investing get more varied and more incredible every day. And even the more traditional tools such as reading annual reports and writing letters to investor relations have a place in your child's education. Acquaint your child with all of them. You might be surprised at what catches and keeps his interest.

## Our Favorite Investing Websites

Many companies, such as GE, include a website address for downloading annual reports and provide a direct link for shareholder feedback. The CNBC website, which is owned by General Electric, runs an ongoing stock tournament; it also lists national NAIC conventions plus links to stock-investing information sites. There are all kinds of information here that may lead your child to even more interesting activities and websites.

**INVESTING FOR KIDS:** http://library.thinkquest.org/3096/index. htm
This extensive site was designed by three high schoolers for entry in the ThinkQuest competition for Internet education. Catering to kids, it helps beginner investors learn the basics of stocks and investing, such as the reasons for investing in the first place, how to buy stocks, and where to find financial information. The online stock game feature enables kids to pick and track an imaginary portfolio, gaining a feel for the stock market and its fluctuations. As visitors learn more, they can move up to the intermediate level, which offers a host of investing strategies and resources.

**THE YOUNG INVESTOR:** www.younginvestor.com
Although younginvestor.com is a commercial site sponsored by Liberty Financial Group and Stein Rowe that aims to get kids to invest in the Stein Rowe Young Investor Fund, there are some as-

pects of this site that are educational and fun for kids. The Young Investor Fund claims to educate investors about personal finance while providing a solid, long-term growth vehicle.

**BETTER INVESTING YOUTH:** www.better-investing.org/youth/youth.html

The youth section of the National Association of Investors Corporation, a nonprofit organization committed to investment education, is aimed at adults wishing to teach their children about investing. It includes several excerpts from NAIC publications, most reporting on youth investment clubs around the country. The site does not provide many resources or actual information, offering only the sale of educational software.

**YOUNGBIZ:** www.youngbiz.com

Youngbiz is an enthusiastic website aimed at all young people interested in money, business, and investing. It provides basic financial information for people in their teens on such topics as investing and savings, the Dow, and credit cards, in a fun, easy-to-read format. The site lists resources that aspiring entrepreneurs can use, such as several entrepreneurship camps and internship information. A particularly interesting feature is its section profiling successful entrepreneurs who started out at a young age, many of them in their teens.

**YOUNG FOOL AT THE MOTLEY FOOL:** www.fool.com/Family Fool/1998/FamilyCollection980325.htm

You've probably heard of the Motley Fool, the investing site started by two brothers who recommend that in today's world, with tools such as the Internet providing vast amounts of information, individuals should take personal control of their finances. The Young Fool is the Motley Fool's section devoted to young people, and it teaches basic aspects about money and the financial world. In a manner most teens will relate to, the site explains

what stocks and mutual funds are and how young people can
begin investing for themselves.

## The Stock Challenge Games

Most kids seem to think that anything on the Internet is automatically more cool, more fun, and more educational than what can
be found in other sources. We agree in at least one regard: The Internet wins hands down as far as making investing fun and educational with fantasy stock investment games.

A typical game starts registrants with $100,000 in "play" money
and gives them a month to make it grow. Players can buy and sell
as often as they want, but they are "charged" a commission, usually around $10 a trade. So they are penalized for too much trad-
ing, just as you would be in real life.

Games are very similar to the real market in that the stocks go
up and down in sync with the Dow, and the hours you can trade are
from the opening of the NYSE to its close at 4 P.M. EST. But games
can offer a feature that the real market does not: Your child can
see where he stands each day as compared to all the other investors playing (4,451 out of 75,651, for example). These games
give kids—and grown-ups—an opportunity to trade online without putting their personal money on the line.

In school systems around the country there's an investor training tool called The Stock Market Game, an electronic simulation
of Wall Street trading that more than 6 million students have
played since its inception in 1977. Sponsored nationally and on the
state level by a consortium of securities industry firms, founda-
tions, corporations, and Securities Industry Association Districts,
SMG targets kids in grades four through twelve. But anyone can
register as a team for a modest fee. (We paid $25; it varies from
state to state. To check out SMG, go to www.smgww.org.) As a
team, kids compete with other kids nationwide to assemble the
winning portfolio by investing $100,000 in fantasy money over a
ten-week period (there are two annual sessions, one in the fall, one

## Beyond the Basics

Here is a summary of extracurricular ideas for having fun with your child while continuing to learn about investing:

✓  Visit a stock exchange (either in person or through interactive website).

✓  Visit a local broker's office.

✓  Invite a guest broker to speak (to a group or in your home).

✓  Attend a local annual meeting (you don't have to be a shareholder to attend).

✓  Visit an investor fair.

✓  Invest in and play the stock challenge games.

✓  Have kids compile a company profile that includes the firm's name; address; phone, fax, and e-mail numbers; industry in which it competes; contact person's name and title; description of company products or services; recent news; name of owner; whether company is publicly traded; how stock is doing; and a copy of the annual report.

✓  Have kids obtain hands-on experience about the company. If the company makes candy bars, eat a few. Read its magazines, visit its store, talk to its employees, and so on.

✓  Talk to your school principal to see if the school wants to host an investor fair. Local publicly traded companies could be invited to participate.

in the spring). They play on the Internet, but the game can be played on paper for those who aren't online or who don't have access to a computer. Teams then have to mail their transactions to the state administrator. Some states award prizes to winning teams, such as an all-expenses-paid trip to the NYSE. In most state there are regional and state-level awards, and recognition is given to individuals and teams for their research or game strategies.

This particular stock challenge promotes in-depth study and understanding of the securities industry. It also reinforces economic concepts that encompass math, social studies, business, economics, language arts, and even computer proficiency skills. But it is by no means the only game in town. Stock investment challenge games are popping up all over the Internet, and your child may find one we don't even know about.

While we believe that real investing with real money ultimately imparts the greatest lessons, there is one lesson the stock challenge games teach very well: not to become a day trader. Maybe more adults should play these games before getting online to trade with the real thing! Pat likes to tell the story of how she experimented with short-term trading, buying Cisco at 53.88 in the morning and selling it that evening for 55.25. At the time, Pat was thrilled to be making that much money in such a short time. But Shannon, who had learned quite a bit about Internet stocks and short-term trading by playing the Yahoo stock challenge game, saw better than her mother that it wasn't a winning strategy. "Mommy, you're crazy!" she told Pat. "Buy and hold!"

And Shannon was right. Had Pat bought and held Cisco, she would have doubled her money because it went up to 68 in less than a year after splitting two for one. "I learned a lot about myself during that period," says Pat. "Maybe because she has played the stock game, Shannon doesn't seem to be drawn to that kind of trading."

## Annual Reports

We know what you're thinking: *What kid could make sense of these financial summaries?* Maybe your child!

While it's true they're not written with a young audience in mind, you owe it to yourself and your child to flip through them when they come in each year (or scroll through them; many can be viewed at the company's website and downloaded or printed). Annual reports are an insight into the future of the company and the

> ### Investment Game Websites
>
> These are some of the best virtual stock investment games. Try them all to decide which one is your favorite.
>
> Yahoo Investment Challenge: www.yahoo.com
> Stock Market Game 2000: www.smgww.org
> CNBC Student Stock Tournament: http://sst.cnbc.com
> The Street.com Investment Challenge: www.thestreet.com

industry it operates in. They tell you how much and how fast the company has grown, how much market share the company has gained, and how many new companies it has added to its portfolio. They also tell you what the company anticipates in the way of growth or income in the future, and what its challenges may be in its particular industry.

Some bright, colorful annual reports are expressly intended to appeal to a younger audience. Shannon loves to look at Coca-Cola's annual report because its clever graphics impress her. One year the bar graphs were stacks of Coke bottles; another year the symbols were bottle caps in pie graphs as well as bar graphs. She likes the catchy inspirational messages throughout the report— "Only 99 million to go" and such. Shannon owns only one share of Coca-Cola, but you wouldn't know that to watch her pore over its report.

Other annual reports may include a coupon for investors to give a product a try. In addition to a coupon for a packet of fries or other food item, McDonald's has a kit designed especially for kids as a result of the many requests from students who want to know more about the company. The kit includes interesting McFacts, some of them downright inspiring: Senior Chairman Fred Turner started his career with McDonald's by working in a restaurant.

## What to Look For in an Annual Report

**FINANCIAL HIGHLIGHTS:** Generally found in the front of the report as a spreadsheet or on the first page.

**LETTER TO SHAREHOLDERS:** The CEO's assessment of the past year.

**FINANCIAL REVIEW AND NARRATIVE INFORMATION:** Where management discusses the company's performance in good and bad times, its upcoming research and previous developments, competition, and other information including the investor relations contact person. Look for:

✓   Selected financial data

✓   Management's discussions and analysis

✓   Statements of operations (Net Sales and Net Income)

✓   Accountants' report

✓   Stock market information

✓   Directors and officers

Chairman and CEO Mike Quinlan began in the mail room. And President and CEO of McDonald's USA Ed Rensi worked on the grill in his first McDonald's job.

Annual reports generally include four sections: financial highlights, review of operations, financial summary, and narrative information. Financial highlights are a spreadsheet or similar snapshot of the recent performance of the company. They are often accompanied by a letter to the shareholders in which the CEO gives his overview and analysis of the year's performance and a perspective on the company's future. We tend to zero in on this letter because it sums up the year's performance in a way everyone can understand—in plain English, that is.

The second section, the review of operations, gives summaries of the products or services that the company provides. You get a sense of its various holdings without even having to read the discussion of its operations.

The financial summary gives the really key data in a narrative format: an interpretation of sales, revenues, costs, taxes, profits, and shareholders' equity. It is followed by the section least likely to interest your child but the most highly useful in terms of understanding the company's performance in good and bad times, its research and development, its competitors in the industry, and where the industry is going based on management's analysis. In this section you will find the income statement, balance sheet, and statements of changes in financial positions and shareholders' equity in actual graphs. Usually the report ends with an investor contact's name, phone number, and e-mail address in case you want to call and ask questions or comment as a shareholder about the company.

## The Proxy

As we've discussed, all shareholders in a company receive, in addition to an annual report, a proxy form (the report and proxy are often mailed together) by which they may vote on key issues affecting the company without having to show up at the annual shareholders' meeting. Proxy votes are important to management. Sometimes shareholders decide on an issue strongly enough to sway management's own inclinations.

Proxies, as we've noted, allow you to vote as many shares as you own. You will have more voting power if you own 10,000 shares than someone who owns 1,000 shares, 500 shares, or 100 shares. But even one share carries a vote, and that's a privilege and a responsibility your child should exercise. Shannon recently learned just how much her vote mattered after she took her proxy to the AOL shareholders' meeting in Virginia. During the meeting she checked her votes as each issue was discussed. Later that evening, after the proxies had been collected and tallied, the board of directors announced a two-for-one stock split—a decision made possible because earlier in the day the shareholders had approved an increase in the number of outstanding shares.

Have your child fill out the proxy himself, whether or not he attends the shareholders' meeting. The more active he is as a shareholder, the more closely he will follow his investments.

## The Investor Relations Office

If there is an issue your child doesn't fully understand, she can contact investor relations. The investor relations office is a place you can call, e-mail, write, or even visit in order to ask questions about the company, share views or opinions, or set up meetings with management (such as attending the shareholders' annual meeting). Whether you own one share or a thousand, the people in this office are usually happy to express your views to management, answer your questions, or possibly even set up a meeting with a senior official if possible. You might also meet some of the managers after an annual meeting, as Shannon did at the AOL meeting when she shook hands with General Colin Powell (Ret.), who sits on the board of directors. Shannon also offered CEO Steve Case a hot stock tip (she urged him to buy eBay). Acquaint your child with his contact at the investor relations office early on in his ownership of company stock. It's a wonderful resource, and it will personalize his relationship with a company that otherwise can seem too huge and faceless to feel a part of.

Whether your child approves or disapproves of the way his company does business, have him contact investor relations by phone, letter, or e-mail. Many companies have an e-mail section at their website for this very purpose. Danielle was very upset when Mattel's stock price fell 30 percent in one day and her stock value fell more than 50 percent, so she wrote a letter to the CEO asking very detailed questions about the company progress.

The experience of writing the letter was so satisfying to Danielle that a day after sending her letter to Jill Barad she de-

Danielle M. Flythe
Washington, DC 20024

October 11, 1999

Ms. Jill E. Barad, Chairwoman/CEO
Mattel, Inc.
333 Continental Blvd.
El Segundo, CA 90245

Dear Ms. Barad:

I am writing to you to let you know that I am very unhappy with the company. I have followed the progress of the company closely. I am a 14-year-old investor and cannot understand what is happening to my company. Would you please respond to me and answer the following questions:

✓   Why has the value of my stock holdings dropped more than 50% in this past year?

✓   As CEO why is it that you do not know what happened with the acquisition of The Learning Company and how it dragged the company's earnings down?

As CEO you are supposed to know everything that is going on in the company. It is unacceptable for you to tell us shareholders that you do not know what is going on. I am a young investor, and even though my custodian has advised me to sell the stock, I am willing to keep it because I like Mattel and the products it produces. I hope I will not be too disappointed by holding on to my Mattel stock.

Sincerely,


Danielle M. Flythe
Mattel Shareholder

## Sample Letter to Investor Relations Office

(date)

Dear Sir or Madam:

I am interested in your company as a potential investor. Could you please send me the (company's name) annual report and any other information that would be helpful to me? I am _____ years old and would like to receive any special material your company provides for young investors.

Thank you for your help.


Sincerely,
(Your name)

cided to write to Bill Gates. She wanted to tell him that she
started out with seven shares of Microsoft and those seven had
now grown to twenty-eight in two years as a result of stock splits.
She was very pleased! Danielle wrote to Gates, telling him to keep
up the good work and to ignore those people who accused him of
being the bully of the software industry because they were simply
jealous. That letter made her feel just as empowered. And as a
shareholder, she *is*.

## Maintaining Your Child's Interest

In this chapter we've reviewed a number of ways you can expand
your child's knowledge and interest in stocks and the stock market. Whether it's a trip to a brokerage, exchange, or shareholders'
meeting, a trip to a store or restaurant he holds stock in, a day at
an investor's fair, a letter-writing campaign to investor relations,
or a stock challenge game, the key is active engagement.

If your response is "I don't have that much time in my day now.
I can't possibly find time to add one more activity," then you're
missing an important point. We don't schedule our kids' exposure
to the markets every day. Aside from the field trips we mentioned,
we often don't schedule their investment education at all. The
topic comes up either because of something we read, some place
we go, some food we eat, some service we use, some piece of mail
we get. For the most part we're just seizing the opportunities that
present themselves—and you can, too.

One thing we did notice from the beginning: No matter what
activity we used as a teaching tool, it was always much different—
often better—when other kids were involved. Ultimately, that fact
is what prompted us to form the Stock MarKids.

You don't have to form an investor club to keep your child investing. There are other ways to make his education more social.
But if you should decide that's the way to go, read on. We show you
just how easy, fun, and rewarding the club experience can be.

# SUMNER M. REDSTONE

Chief Executive Officer and Chairman, Viacom

**COMPANY:** Viacom is one of the world's largest media companies. Its holdings include MTV, Nickelodeon, Paramount, VH1, Showtime Networks, and Blockbuster Video.

**EMPLOYEES:** 111,730

**$$$:** $9.4 billion net worth (as of October 1999)

**BIRTH DATE AND LOCATION:** 1923, Boston, Massachusetts

**EDUCATION:** B.A., Harvard, 1944, and L.L.B., Harvard, 1947

**HOME:** Newton, Massachusetts

**TIDBIT:** Redstone is a visiting professor at both Harvard Law School and Brandeis University. He enjoys playing tennis and spends time working with organizations such as the Dana-Farber Cancer Institute, the American Cancer Society, and the Will Rogers Memorial Fund.

**FIRST JOB:** Legal secretary with the U.S. Court of Appeals

**QUOTE:** "Viacom is me. I'm Viacom. That marriage is eternal, forever."

220            Wow the Dow!

## BEYOND THE BASICS QUIZ

1. Annual reports are issued three times a year. ____T ____F
2. The NYSE is located in Jersey City, New Jersey. ____T ____F
3. A subsidiary is owned by the parent company. ____T ____F
4. More young people are investing today. ____T ____F
5. A parent company can own only one company. ____T ____F
6. Stocks are the only type of investment. ____T ____F
7. The letters on the ticker are called symbols. ____T ____F
8. Shareholders' meetings generally are held once a year.
   ____T ____F
9. Annual reports give a peek into the company's future.
   ____T ____F
10. Annual reports sometimes can be found online. ____T ____F
11. Company representatives visit investor fairs. ____T ____F
12. Stock-investing games can be used as an educational tool.
    ____T ____F
13. The NYSE is an exciting place to visit. ____T ____F
14. A company's annual meeting is another learning experience.
    ____T ____F
15. There is a museum dedicated to American financial history.
    ____T ____F
16. Shareholders receive a proxy statement each month.
    ____T ____F

## Answer key:

| | |
|---|---|
| 8. T | 16. F |
| 7. T | 15. T |
| 6. F | 14. T |
| 5. F | 13. T |
| 4. T | 12. T |
| 3. T | 11. T |
| 2. F | 10. T |
| 1. F | 9. T |

## 9

## All About Investment Clubs

Investment clubs are really very simple: A handful of like-minded people meet every month or so to share market strategies, company research, stock tips, or other investment knowledge they've picked up. Each member of the club also contributes dues, which are then invested to create a club portfolio. Everybody contributes both their research and their money so that everyone benefits, both financially and educationally.

While neither of us had ever belonged to an adult investment club, the idea of forming one with our girls seemed like a natural. We knew they'd have fun if their friends were involved, and if they had fun, we reasoned, they'd stay interested and keep learning. And so, at the end of 1995, we started calling parents (our friends plus parents of the girls' friends) who we thought might also want to educate their kids about the stock market. We told them we wanted to form a club of young investors (ages nine through eleven) whose parents would act as investing partners. We told them we needed their ongoing participation, not any special investing experience or knowledge, and that we were looking for a long-term commitment.

The response was overwhelming. Everyone we called wanted to

be a part of this new venture. About a month later, on February 5, 1996, six children accompanied by four adults joined us in one of the meeting rooms at the Martin Luther King Library in Washington, D.C. The Stock MarKids Investment Club was born. It would take another meeting for us to come up with that name and add a few more members, and it would be another two years before we got it officially trademarked. But we had begun an educational journey that would teach them not just investing skills but teamwork, leadership, and conflict resolution.

Forming an investment club is not hard. We did it, and you can, too, whatever your own level of investing expertise. As Pat says, "I'd never have the time or energy to invest in a club of adults, but this way I can educate my daughter while I indulge my own interests!" Forming a club of children and their parents is by far the most "hands-on" of all the activities we've discussed so far. It can also impart the most valuable lessons of all.

## How to Find Kid-Friendly Investment Clubs

Of course, you don't necessarily have to start your own club. You may be able to join an existing club. They come in all shapes and sizes, although to date there isn't a central clearinghouse for clubs that include minors. Even the National Association of Investors Corporation does not keep a breakdown of the types of memberships in a club, that is, whether there are kids in a club. Your best bet is NAIC's *Better Investing* magazine. It has a Regional Notices section in every issue that lists 110 regional chapters located in or near most major cities across the country, along with regional chapter contacts. (If you do not receive the magazine, you can go online to NAIC's website at www.better-investing.org.)

For example, say you are looking for a club in Oklahoma. The Greater Tulsa chapter entry includes the contact person's name, telephone number, and e-mail address. To find a club with young investors you would first contact this person, and if he cannot help you, he probably can direct you to someone who can.

## A Sampling of Family Investment Clubs

**The Family Investors Investment Club,** Fall River, Massachusetts
Contact: Gabe Patricio
npatricio@msn.com
family_investors@hotmail.com

The young investors in this club hold what we call "junior" accounts. They have slightly different rules for minimum upfront investment and monthly contributions, but otherwise they function like other accounts. Of fourteen accounts, five are for children or are managed for children by parents.

Although the club is a partnership in Massachusetts, where most of its members reside, it has members in New Jersey, California, Virginia, and Japan (two members are in the military, but all are family or friends).

**Mutual Investment Club of Montgomery,** Montgomery, Alabama
Contact: Dave Anderson
dave.anderson@prodigy.net

Although this club has just one young member, Dave Anderson has embarked on a program of planting young student investment clubs in the Montgomery area. The Evangel Family Christian Academy Student Investment Club, for example, is made up of seventeen home-schooled students and has been through a year of instruction from Dave. They are currently preparing to select their first stock.

Mr. Anderson says, "I became active in planting student clubs as a result of attending several functions related to the NAIC investment clubs and noting that nearly everyone who attended was forty years of age or older. Although it is wonderful to have these folks involved (I am fifty-four myself), it was apparent to me that the people who could gain the most from fundamental, conservative investing (as presented through the NAIC principles and practices) were not there. So I decided to do something to fix that."

**Share Family Investments,** Tucson, Arizona
Contact: Brian Reilly
reilly@specent.com

Currently has three young members, ages seven, fourteen, and sixteen.

## Pros and Cons of Parent-Child Investment Clubs

Here are the advantages of joining or starting an investment club with your child:

✓ It allows quality socializing and develops teamwork.

✓ There is a lower risk as a group because all investment decisions are discussed and analyzed by the members.

✓ The costs of investing are less.

✓ You can enjoy more diversification than is possible in an individual portfolio.

✓ When actively participating in all aspects of the club, especially as officers, kids learn leadership skills.

✓ Kids learn oral presentation skills when they provide regular reports as stock monitors.

✓ Parents can work with other parents to actively guide their kids toward becoming financially responsible and prepared for the "real world."

✓ Kids can talk to their peers about delayed gratification and making decisions about large purchases with their money: Will a CD player outweigh the gains of investing?

✓ Kids learn how to do financial research and increase their critical thinking skills in a nonschool setting. They see how others do it and share the results of their own research.

✓ It leads to kids wanting to invest on their own.

Although a club worked beautifully for us, we feel it's only fair to present a few warnings regarding the challenges a club might involve and reasons that a club might not work for some families.

✓ Some people may think it's merely a get-rich-quick scheme and do not understand that investing is a long-term commitment that requires discipline. There may be disappointment when a stock does not perform as expected.

✓ Investment clubs require time. Many parents and children have many extracurricular activities. It is sometimes difficult to find the time to prepare for and attend club meetings.

✓     Learning about investments requires a commitment from the parents, and when parents want their kids to learn but are not willing to learn along with them, then neither will learn much.

✓     Much of the educational value of a club is lost if members do not commit to starting their own personal investing program, which enhances the total learning process.

✓     Children learn at different rates, so it is challenging for the parents to try to keep all the children learning at the same rate.

✓     Group dynamics are sometimes stressful, especially for children, when members are trying to resolve issues as a group. It's hard enough to get two people to think alike, let alone ten or more. Reaching agreement within the club takes some effort.

✓     Club administration can be boring to children. It can be a challenge to keep the children interested in such matters as taxes and partnership agreements.

✓     Some people find they just are not interested in being in a stock club. Not everyone who starts out with a club stays with it. Be prepared for dropouts.

## How to Begin if You Want to Start Your Own Club

We can't emphasize enough how important it is to choose your potential members very carefully. A club, like a portfolio, works best when it has a big-picture perspective. It needs parents who are committed not only to getting their child financially savvy but to walking hand in hand with him through the maze of stock and financial markets. The parents you contact should have the same philosophy as you do: that teaching kids how to invest is best done as partners, over the long term, and with an emphasis on fun and firsthand experience rather than making money. You may want to limit your list to parents of children who fit within a certain age range—for us it was parents of children between the ages of nine and eleven.

All parents should understand what will be required of them and be willing to fulfill their obligations month in and month out.

That means they will strive not to miss a monthly meeting; they'll make sure the homework their child is assigned is completed; they'll pay dues regularly; and they'll put the club's agenda and interests ahead of their own.

Above all, you can't have parents dropping off their child at the meeting and then running out to do errands. For one thing, a child cannot invest without his parent on hand to sign contracts, open a broker's account, or approve anything legally binding. For another, even teenagers can be surprisingly short on information and know-how when it comes to investing their hard-earned money. One teen investor we know who started his own Teen Investment Club lamented to Lynn in an e-mail that while it was easy to get forty or even fifty teens to join his club and talk investing with him, very few had any experience. "I can't say that I have learned much from my peers. One of my friends inherited some money and now has it invested in mutual funds. If I'm not mistaken, though, her mother invested the money for her. She likes to think of herself as an investor, but she really has no idea what she is doing."

Look for parents whom you know to be fairly "hands-on," already committed to helping their children grow and learn, both in school and out, in sports and other extracurricular activities.

You might also consider as prime candidates parents who don't know all that much about investing themselves but are eager to learn. Investment knowledge, we found, was not as important as an interest in acquiring it. Parents who are learning a step or two before their children sometimes make the best teachers because their experience as students themselves is so fresh. Parents eager to learn tend to inspire their children to learn alongside them. It helps if they also share your basic buy-and-hold investment strategy. You'll spare yourself some heated disagreements later on if you can agree the club should avoid, say, day trading on margin.

## Before the First Meeting

Once you have a response from your potential members, it's time to prepare for your first meeting. You'll need to set a date and time and arrange for a meeting place, of course. But your first meeting will be far more productive and exciting if you take care of some paperwork beforehand.

Prior to your initial meeting, contact the National Association of Investors Corporation (NAIC), which, after all, exists in order to facilitate the formation of investment clubs. NAIC will send its *Investor's Manual* and other brochures to give you pointers on how to go about setting up your club. You can also request its green sheets, which are financial reports on more than one hundred companies provided free to members. It's a good idea, too, to request an SS-4 form from the Internal Revenue Service. This is an application for a tax identification number, something a club needs before it can start investing. The NAIC materials also help formulate the agenda for your very first meeting. This is what we discussed at our first club meeting:

✓ our organizational structure

✓ our club mission

✓ where we would meet and how often

✓ the role of club officers

✓ the way in which the club would operate

## Getting Launched

The children came to that first organization meeting full of energy and excitement. We came armed with the NAIC *Investor's Manual,* the green sheets, and materials on how to start an investment club, in anticipation of people's questions. The green sheets provided us with a great activity to plunge into right away: The kids picked through them and easily identified companies they wanted to check out for investment potential: Babysitters Club

(Scholastic), Marvel Comics, Nike, Adidas, Disney, Nickelodeon, Sega, Wendy's, Boeing, Limited, Dial, General Electric, and Eastman Kodak. Every child and adult chose one or two green sheets for further study at home. We also showed everyone how to determine the value of a share of stock using the business section of the newspaper. Everyone had an opportunity to randomly select a stock from the New York Stock Exchange, NASDAQ, or American Stock Exchange, and as a group we practiced how to zero in on the price of a share.

Here's the agenda we used for our first meeting that you might follow:

✓ Have people introduce themselves, telling their age and what experience they've had, if any, investing in the stock market.

✓ Explain the need for operating procedures—the ground rules by which the club will select and purchase stocks, handle individual withdrawals, add new members, and disperse funds when a member leaves the club. The NAIC material can be very helpful with suggestions on how the club might operate.

✓ Discuss the structure of a partnership—the structure most clubs adopt to do business. A partnership is set up in the name of the club, which is then assigned a tax identification number. This is why it is important to name your club immediately and fill out the SS-4 form from the IRS for your tax identification number. A partnership is not taxed but acts as a conduit to pass on any club income to the individual partners. (That means members are taxed differently on the same proceeds based on each member's individual tax bracket.) While club members may not become legally recognized partners until they reach the age of majority (eighteen or twenty-one in most states), parents may register their child with their city and state in the partnership agreement in custodial form.

✓ Discuss joining NAIC. While it is not necessary, club membership provides considerable benefits: access to the stock plans, subscription to *Better Investing* magazine, free green sheets, free investor reports, and an ongoing roster of special events, investor fairs, and tournaments—at a reduced rate. Additionally, kids and their parents who belong to NAIC can start their own individual portfolios with very little money, in addition to building up the club portfolio. Membership is $40 for the club and $14 annually for each member. (It takes only one member per family to qualify for NAIC benefits.)

✓ Establish dues to cover the cost of buying stock. In a club for kids, dues should be at a level everyone can pay out of his or her allowance. We asked our group what they could afford to pay and settled on $10 per month per member. This figure eventually doubled to $20 as the kids discovered they needed more money to buy the stocks they selected.

✓ Determine your club mission. It's helpful to have it in writing to ensure that everybody understands the order of priorities and their own obligations. Our group arrived at the following wording:

> This is a stock investment club for kids and their parents. Members will attend meetings at least once a month, where each junior member performs his/her elected-officer functions under the tutelage of his/her parent. While the primary emphasis of the club is education, members are actively involved in conducting stock transactions that will increase the value of the club portfolio over time, and old and new stocks are studied regularly so that each member, regardless of age, can be knowledgeable about stock trends, industry events, and other related issues.

The kids also decided to impose a time frame on membership: No one would be allowed to withdraw funds from the club's portfolio before three years were up. This allowed enough time to build a profitable portfolio and hindered members from taking their money out of the club and still remaining members. If a child wants to drop out of the club before the three years are up, then he is paid out in full, either with cash on hand or by selling a stock, whichever is feasible at the time.

✓ Discuss the need for club officers. Again, NAIC offers some excellent guidelines on officers and their roles. Explain these roles:

PRESIDING PARTNER (PRESIDENT): Calls each meeting to order; requests that minutes be read and approved; leads discussion on each item on the agenda; conducts votes; helps determine the agenda for the next meeting.

ASSISTANT PRESIDING PARTNER (VICE PRESIDENT): Stands in for the president in his/her absence; may also oversee educational activities.

FINANCIAL PARTNER (TREASURER): The keeper of the money. He/she collects and logs dues; tracks the portfolio and keeps a record of how much each individual is entitled to of the total income; purchases stocks; makes monthly valuation reports; and prepares the club's accounts for verification and tax reporting.

RECORDING PARTNER (SECRETARY): Writes down what happens at each meeting and submits minutes for approval at the next meeting. Also makes sure everyone is given notice of the next meeting's time, place, and agenda. May also be the club's contact person.

SERGEANT AT ARMS: Ensures that the meeting runs smoothly and that members abide by club rules and remain orderly even if debate heats up. Ask the kids if they want to hold these positions themselves or have their parents fulfill them. We agreed in our club to appoint only kids as officers, in keeping with our philosophy of learning by doing. It was a role reversal that appealed to everybody!

Alert those who want to run for office to prepare a speech for the next meeting, during which elections will be held. Each candidate will be expected to present to the group why he/she should be elected for the position.

✓ Decide who will be the contact person for the group—the person to whom all club correspondence is sent. This person is called the club agent.

✓ Decide on where you will continue to meet as a club. We didn't always meet at the same place, but we did consciously decide to meet in a businesslike setting. Meeting at one another's homes was out. Can you imagine having the kids steal away from the meeting to go play Sega in the host child's bedroom?

Try your local library or university. Often there are rooms available for meetings on a regular, cost-free basis. At our Martin Luther King Library we filled out a simple form that allowed us to meet there regularly, free of charge. We also held meetings at Southeastern University and later, thanks to Pat's business contacts, at the office of J. G. Van Dyke & Associates (which later became our corporate sponsor).

✓ Close the meeting by reminding everybody of what next month's agenda will be:

## The Campaign Trail

**In the second year of Stock Markids, Danielle ran for president and came up with this speech:**

Good afternoon. My name is Danielle, and I would like to be your president. I think I would make a good president because I am hard-working and willing to do the job. To me being president doesn't just mean being the head of everything and not producing, but making sure all the work that needs to be completed gets done, showing leadership, and helping the club run smoothly. For example, yesterday I went to the NAIC investor fair and discussed our club with Kenneth Janke, the president of NAIC, and other participants. Many people were so impressed that they kept verifying that parents and children were involved, which showed leadership on my part. I will try my very best to make sure the kids run the club instead of the parents, and also try to make it fun so that each and every one of you will actually be excited to come to meetings. I don't want people coming to meetings and possibly falling asleep or not paying attention. So I hope you make the right choice and vote for me.

**Danielle was voted president, and, of course, Lynn acted as assistant to the president. Danielle's duties were to schedule meetings and develop the agenda, call the meetings to order, report on any new developments with the club, and perform other leadership roles. Danielle continues to hold the presidency position.**

1. Naming the club (everyone should come prepared with a list of possibilities)
2. Electing club officers (candidates should prepare their speeches)
3. Solidifying your partnership agreement

## Choosing a Name, Electing Officers, and Other Essential First Steps

The six kids and four parents who attended our first official club meeting came prepared. They had generated quite a list of names for the club, such as MoneyMakers, Metropolitan Millionaires,

Future Millionaires Club, Long-Term MoneyMakers, and Kids Investment Club. We held a vote, and Stock MarKids won out. (We later contacted NAIC and had them run our name through their computers to see if anyone else had the same name. When told we had the name exclusively, we registered with NAIC as an investment club.)

Elections were a lot of fun. The kids had prepared speeches and presented them with all the formality of adults. It was excellent practice in public speaking. We gave the treasurer a receipt book and log for tracking dues, and gave Shannon, who was elected recording partner, a notebook for taking notes during the meeting. Shannon had the opportunity to use the notebook during our first meeting, and the treasurer got to use his new receipt book as he collected dues for the first time.

It's important for club officers to fully and routinely perform their duties because there is much to be learned by "being in charge." For example, Danielle, in her role as assistant to the presiding partner, developed the agenda for the meetings and introduced new educational concepts relative to the stock market (with Lynn's help). In the absence of the presiding partner, she called meetings to order. She also undertook the responsibility of maintaining a running glossary of new words the kids learned. (Our glossary on page 253 grew out of it!) The officers' roles are not set in stone, however. While it was Shannon's job, for example, to read the minutes of the previous meeting, we agreed that as a club it would be better if each child was assigned a portion of the minutes to read aloud to the group. Oral reading and presentation are worthwhile experiences for kids. Club meetings can be an excellent tool for reinforcing these valuable skills.

Once your club has elected officers, it's time to formalize yourselves with several authorities. First, as we mentioned, you need to submit that SS-4 tax identification number (TIN) request to the IRS. You need to register with your city as a partnership in order to be recognized by the IRS as such; contact your city's department of finance and revenue to learn what is required of your club in the way of paperwork. If you've joined NAIC, it's important to register with the organization as soon as you've determined that no other club has claimed your name.

Your club must also choose a bank and/or brokerage account in order to purchase stocks. We assigned our treasurer (and his mom) the task of researching banking options for the club at this first official club meeting, with a report due back to us at the next meeting. Among the options we considered was opening a money market account at a discount broker (such as Schwab or Quick & Reilly). We wanted someone to transact our trades, not give us advice or charge us hefty commissions.

The club should decide on certain operating procedures and keep refining the details of the partnership agreement at each meeting. We agreed, for instance, that we would use the cash method for accounting and the calendar year as the accounting period. We also established the thirtieth of each month as our valuation date, the date the club's assets would be calculated.

NAIC recommends that clubs establish a verification committee and file a verification report to its members at the end of the year. A verification report basically assures all members that our records are in order, all funds have been spent in accordance with their wishes, and all expenses have been accounted for and verified. It is like an annual audit. We established a verification committee of three people; each year different children volunteer to serve on this committee. Because this function is extremely important and fairly time-consuming, it made sense to rotate the duties so that no parent felt unduly burdened in this role.

## Learning by Doing

It is a good idea early on to get everyone on the same page of the hymnal—the hymnal being NAIC's *Investor's Manual*. These are NAIC's Proven Principles:

✓   Invest regularly.
✓   Reinvest all earnings.

✓   Invest in growth companies.
✓   Diversify to reduce risk.

As novices we started with these Proven Principles and urged all members to study them. In addition, four of the kids prepared a presentation, one on each principle. At the following meeting Danielle explained how, by investing regularly, she had built up shares in McDonald's; another child explained how, by reinvesting dividends, shares build up "automatically"; a ten-year-old member noted that by investing in growth companies the club's portfolio would grow, too; and Shannon recounted how owning Wendy's and McDonald's wasn't a great idea because both companies were in the same industry, and if fast food took a dive, then her whole portfolio would, too.

In short, by having the kids learn and present these concepts to the group, they used examples and explanations even our youngest members could grasp—in addition to cementing their own knowledge. After this discussion the kids were so eager to get investing that they agreed unanimously to ask each member for a $100 entrance fee to put toward the purchase of the club's first stock.

The kids' enthusiasm and interest spilled over to the adults. Even adults who weren't members liked what we were doing and made valuable contributions. Lynn's husband, Wallace, donated calculators to each member. Pat's husband, Russ, helped create the professional spreadsheets that Shannon and Pat brought to the monthly meetings. Gary Van Dyke, a friend of Pat's, allowed us to hold meetings in his offices in Bethesda, Maryland. Some Sundays when we met at Van Dyke & Associates, he'd stick his head in our conference room, and what he saw and heard so impressed him that he became our corporate sponsor. This meant we could use his facilities and resources, including the computers for online stock research and a photocopier so that everyone would have his own copy of important materials. Van Dyke also spon-

> ### Order in the Club!
>
> Pat loves antiques. One day while antique shopping, she purchased a gavel that had belonged to former Speaker of the House Sam Rayburn. She donated the gavel to the club, and we were able to tell the kids a little bit about history. From this time forward the gavel was a cherished club artifact. The club's sergeant at arms loved it, used it when needed, and staged a formal "passing of the gavel" ceremony for his successor.

sored our trip to the New York Stock Exchange by donating $1,000. We suggest that you ask the parents in your club to consider whether any of their business contacts might be interested and supportive enough of your venture to offer meeting rooms—or more!

Take every opportunity to have your club members learn by doing. Many of the activities we've included in this book were developed to keep club members interested, engaged, and critically involved: Use them. Seize what "live" opportunities present themselves. Since we held meetings in the library, for instance, we took advantage of our surroundings to introduce the kids to the different financial tools housed there—research tools such as Value Line, Standard & Poor's, and other reference books.

Resist the temptation to act as lecturer. If you need to convey a difficult concept (such as P/E ratios) or a dry piece of business (taxes), ask for kid volunteers to pull together a presentation, or form a committee of kids to study it and present it.

This isn't to say you can't invite outside speakers to make presentations. At the end of our first year we got the former president of the Maryland NAIC Council, Salvador Waller, to speak to us about investing. He was so impressed with the kids that he volunteered to teach us the methodology behind the NAIC Stock Selection Guide (SSG) over a three-class training session, free of charge. The kids actually met three times over a Christmas holiday break at a conference table with Waller to learn every step of the SSG, including how to prepare one. We enjoyed a potluck dinner with him and his wife after the last session, and the kids presented him with a thank-you gift. Instead of being force-fed information by us, the kids wound up acquiring solid skills, a lasting memory, and a new friend.

## Curriculum Basics

Have club members chart and track every stock they intend to purchase as well as every stock they have purchased. Each member should understand the company and industry under consideration. For each company in the club portfolio, have a member (or his parent) monitor that stock for the group. Monitoring a stock means tracking the stock's price movements over the month, computing the gain or loss for that stock since the date of purchase, and compiling recent news about the company or industry. Adult members as well as kids can be assigned their own company to monitor; this means each household will be keeping a close eye on at least two companies.

Stock monitoring helped the kids become versed in research techniques. They vied with one another to see who could produce the most complete and interesting picture of their particular company. At one meeting, after a young member had completed his report on Johnson & Johnson, Shannon said, "Is that all you have to say? Because in the news this week I found that Johnson & Johnson allowed a sales representative to be in the operating room to monitor the new equipment, and the patient died." (Shannon was not too keen on the company; her hostility toward J&J motivated her to do some particularly thorough research.)

It's a good idea to change the assignments on a regular basis so that each member gets a new company to monitor and learn about. At the end of our first year, during our celebration at a local eatery, we decided that we would change everybody's monitoring assignment annually. We did this by way of a grab bag.

Once our kids had a clear understanding of at least one company, we started assigning readings from Peter Lynch's *Learn to Earn: A Beginner's Guide to the Basics of Investing and Business*. Again, it was the kids who made a presentation on what they had learned about alternative investment instruments.

Whether or not you use Lynch's books as a springboard, your members should become familiar—through presentation to the group—with the following financial instruments:

Savings accounts
Money market funds
Treasury bills
Certificates of deposit
REITs and other real estate investments
Bonds, from municipal to government to zero-coupon
Stocks
Mutual funds
Load and no-load designations (front- and back-end loads, for
     instance)
Collectibles and other nonsecurities

## Investing as a Club

To get the biggest educational bang for each buck, try to vary how the club buys stock. For instance, our club bought McDonald's directly from the company through its McDirect program; Johnson & Johnson and General Electric through the MoneyPaper subscription service; EMC through our broker, which turned out to be the discount broker Quick & Reilly; and Intel through the NAIC low-cost program. As a lesson in risk management we decided to purchase Trusted Information Systems and Sedona as our risk stocks. (We did not want to avoid risk altogether, but we did keep our investment in these two stocks to a minimum.) As a lesson in shareholding we bought Trusted Information Systems because it

was local and we could attend its annual shareholders' meeting.
(That acquisition turned out to be a lesson in mergers and acquisitions when Network Associates bought out Trusted Information Systems.)

On a regular basis, make sure everyone in the club understands exactly where she stands in terms of individual assets in the club. It's all right to see how well you're doing as a group, but kids want to know how much money *they're* making. Most clubs keep track of individual standings by assigning a sum of money as an investment unit. In our club every $10 invested equals one unit. A member with thirty units has contributed $300. The unit reflects what each member contributes but not what each member is worth because the actual value of the unit changes as the portfolio goes up or down in value. To compute the valuation of a member's account, you create a ratio: Total club units are to individual club units as total portfolio valuation is to individual valuation.

If your club is successful with its investing and the portfolio exceeds $5,000, you may want to consider insuring those assets (up to $25,000) with the NAIC Fidelity Bond Coverage. The cost is minimal: $30 per year for the first $25,000. As with any insurance, the club is protected from losses due to theft or other irregularities in fund management by the treasurer. And as with any insurance, you probably won't need it, but if you do, it will be invaluable. Our own portfolio was growing so fast during this bull market that we had to raise our bond coverage to $50,000. The fee was a little more, $98 annually, which provides coverage for a portfolio ranging from $1,000 to $50,000.

## Getting a Trademark

Once your club is well established, it may make sense to trademark yourselves. A trademark basically locks in your club name. No one else can use it without consulting you first and possibly paying you for the privilege. The only downside is that you must make sure everyone uses your trademark correctly every time it appears in print and that businesses you deal with use it correctly.

We felt that getting a trademark on Stock MarKids was yet another way to underscore our legitimacy. Running an investment club is a lot like running a business, and to that end we had the kids conduct themselves in a professional manner and take their responsibilities seriously. They were rewarded for this: Business cards were ordered for the officers as a perk for holding office, for instance. Everybody was given a weekly budget-planning sheet and a spending diary for their personal use as well. They responded so well to these measures that, as club founders, we felt they deserved their own trademark.

The process is time-consuming but not difficult. There are libraries throughout the country that are designated as Patent and Trademark Depository Libraries; they receive patent and trademark information in various formats from the U.S. Patent and Trademark Office. All information is available for use by the public free of charge. To find the library nearest you or for answers to other questions, contact the Trademark Assistance Center at (703) 308-9000, Monday through Friday, 8:30 A.M. to 5:00 P.M. EST, except holidays. The Trademark Assistance Center provides general information about the trademark registration process and responds to inquiries pertaining to the status of specific trademark applications and registrations. There is also a new online database that allows users to do research via computer. Further information is available at the website: www.uspto.gov.

The application fee is $245 and is nonrefundable, so it's critical that you conduct a thorough search on your club name before submitting an application. You don't want to be turned down because someone else has already claimed your name. After you've applied, there's a period during which the public may object to your trademark, which is published by the U.S. Patent and Trademark Office in its *Official Gazette*. Pat and Shannon worked on this project, and on January 6, 1998, we received a certificate of registration for Stock MarKids.

*Doug Carter is seventeen now and lives in California. His father came up with a creative way to get him and his siblings involved in the stock market.*

**How did you start investing?**

One summer, I must have been thirteen, we had a contest in my family. My brother was twelve, and my sister was sixteen. My dad gave each of us an imaginary $1,000, and we had to invest it. We got to choose our own stocks, and the winner would get a real $1,000. My dad sat down with us and taught us how to read the stock quotes in the paper and stuff.

**How did you choose your investments?**

I can't remember which ones they were exactly, but they were high-risk, short-term investments—smaller companies that were most likely going to be absorbed by larger companies. My sister stuck with Nordstrom and a sporting company like Adidas and, I think, Snapple—things people would know about. She chose things that sounded cool, not necessarily the wisest investments.

**Where did you get your information on your choices?**

From my dad, some on the web, and I just took the time to think about it. I researched them a little bit more, and that's why I won.

**How often did you check your stock quotes?**

I would check about three times a week in the NASDAQ. I charted the changes.

## A Parent's Mission

Learning about the financial markets is a continuing education. The business world is ever changing; the markets are ever volatile. To keep your child learning you must keep her engaged, and while the club adds a social, even competitive element to her education, you must always present something new. Those young brains are constantly processing data, sometimes faster than the adults'.

### Did you make or lose money?

I ended up making between $400 and $500. It was an introduction, really. You're not going to make that much in eight weeks. The point was to learn about stocks and see them in the newspaper and find out what it means. Over such a short time it's really insignificant. You're not going to gain or lose that much unless something dramatic happens in the market. But over a longer period it would have a greater effect.

### So you won the contest. Do you feel that you learned something?

Definitely—the process of how you invest, how you choose your stocks and research them, and how to check profits and know when to pull out. It's not really the numbers or how much the company is earning, it's how people perceive how the company is doing. That's what drives the price up or down.

### Has there been anything particularly hard about investing?

Choosing the stocks was the biggest challenge.

### Was the game a good idea?

Yes. You have nothing to lose. It's a figurative $1,000, so you can only gain something. During the summer it's a really good thing to do, to keep kids' brains working and keep kids thinking, and they can learn an important economics lesson.

Don't make the mistake of presuming your kids are not "taking it all in" or will tune out if they're presented with things they don't immediately grasp. We were astounded at how our kids joined in discussion every chance they could in order to make a point. They weren't bored even though we had to discuss some tedious things like tax numbers, establishing a bank account for the club, and other administrative matters. Sometimes it wasn't the topic they objected to but the fact that we insisted on presenting it. They would say, "You adults are doing all the talking!" This happened primarily when meaningful decisions had to be made relative to taxes and related club business. The kids really wanted to run the show.

But your role as parent remains pivotal. The club and your participation in it qualify as an essential course in the University of Life. Sometimes we forget, as our children become teenagers and act so adult, how much they continue to need us. We're reminded of the letter that our young friend Nick e-mailed us about his teen investment club. We had written to him thinking he might have some tips or activities that his teen members had found particularly helpful, but he wrote to say he had none. "One of the definite cons of having a teen start an investment club," he explained, "is that the founder and all the members wander around aimlessly like lost puppies." He added, "I am very pleased to hear that you are writing a book about teen investing. It always works out better when someone more experienced tries to teach us how to invest."

# Putting the Tools to Work

**H**ow does a portfolio grow? We're going to show you, using both Shannon's and Danielle's. The numbers chart two growth stories, actually. One is measured in dollars, the other in maturity, judgment, and wisdom.

Shannon's portfolio began with one share of Disney as a Christmas present in 1993. But it was after Pat met Lynn that her education—and her investments—headed skyward. Here were Shannon's holdings as of May 27, 1994:

| Stock Name | No. of Shares | Total Cost ($) | Current Share Price ($) | Current Market Value ($) |
|---|---|---|---|---|
| Disney | 1.0000 | 42.25 | 44.25 | 44.25 |
| McDonald's | 3.2860 | 190.00 | 61.00 | 200.45 |
| Wendy's | 1.5909 | 28.00 | 17.50 | 27.84 |
| Total | | 260.25 | | 272.54 |

At the age of ten, Shannon chose stocks whose products she knew and liked—hence the McDonald's and Wendy's. Over the course of the next eleven months she was content to purchase additional shares of McDonald's and Wendy's through the company's dividend reinvestment programs. She used birthday money and money from her grandparents for Christmas.

Not until April 1995 did Shannon consider branching out—again, to a company whose product she knew and liked (and that NAIC offered through its low-cost program). Dial fit the bill; its liquid pump dispenser was in her bathroom. Meanwhile, Pat was helping her add to her McDonald's holdings through an automatic deduction from her bank account of $100 a month. Shannon was such a happy McDonald's shareholder that Pat cashed her out of her savings bonds to buy even more stock.

So by November 1, 1996, Shannon's holdings looked like this:

| Stock Name | No. of Shares | Total Cost ($) | Current Share Price ($) | Current Market Value ($) |
|---|---|---|---|---|
| Dial | 9.5480 | 259.00 | 14.00 | 133.67 |
| Disney | 1.0000 | 42.25 | 65.50 | 65.50 |
| McDonald's | 86.7410 | 3,511.44 | 45.375 | 3,935.87 |
| Viad | 9.5480 | Free | 15.00 | 143.22 |
| Wendy's | 21.7570 | 375.08 | 20.625 | 448.74 |
| Total | | 4,187.77 | | 4,727.00 |

When we purchased Dial, we didn't realize the company had a division devoted to food service for airlines. This division was spun off into a separate company called Viad, and suddenly we were shareholders in it. At no cost we got one share of Viad for each share of Dial that we owned.

By June 24, 1998, however, Shannon's portfolio looked very different. For one thing, she sold the Dial and Viad stocks. They hadn't done much to retain her interest as products or stocks.

| Stock Name | No. of Shares | Total Cost ($) | Current Share Price ($) | Current Market Value ($) |
|---|---|---|---|---|
| Coca-Cola | 1.0060 | 69.82 | 84.125 | 84.63 |
| Disney | 6.4173 | 636.98 | 112.688 | 723.15 |
| EMC | 80.0000 | 2,225.00 | 45.688 | 3,655.00 |
| GE | 1.0081 | 65.94 | 89.813 | 90.54 |
| McDonald's | 120.0000 | 5,088.56 | 67.500 | 8,100.00 |
| Cash | | | | 865.42 |
| Total | | 8,086.30 | | 13,518.74 |

Through the Stock MarKids' subscription to the MoneyPaper, she signed up for Coca-Cola and General Electric, two blue-chip companies offering DRIPs. Shannon loved Coke; she chose General Electric when she realized that GE made all the lightbulbs in our house.

But her big investment was in a company called EMC, which made data storage systems for large companies. Shannon knew quite a bit about EMC because we purchased shares in the stock club and she heard reports every month from the stock monitor, who actually visited the Library of Congress where EMC was installing a lot of disk storage systems. She used the cash from the remainder of her savings bonds to buy 80 shares through Quick & Reilly.

Shannon bought EMC on the condition that she wouldn't end up owning more shares of it than McDonald's, her absolute favorite stock. But on Pat's urging, Shannon agreed that it was time to start building up some of her other stocks. She terminated her participation in the McDonald's automatic withdrawal program and starting adding to Disney. (Pat helped her build Disney through a similar automatic deduction program of $100 a month but canceled it after accumulating more than 50 shares in order to move on to yet another company.) With huge reluctance, Shannon also allowed Pat to sell her stock in Wendy's—a tale of diversifying we've already told.

Proceeds (cash) from the stock sales of Dial, Viad, and Wendy's went into a money market account at Quick & Reilly so that it was readily accessible for stock transactions.

As of September 10, 1999, Shannon's portfolio looked like this:

| Stock Name | No. of Shares | Total Cost ($) | Current Share Price ($) | Current Market Value ($) |
|---|---|---|---|---|
| AOL | 18.0000 | 2,827.13 | 96.313 | 1,733.63 |
| Coca-Cola | 1.0190 | 69.82 | 55.125 | 56.17 |
| Disney | 56.0000 | 1,784.39 | 27.875 | 1,561.00 |
| EMC | 160.0000 | 2,225.00 | 68.125 | 10,900.00 |
| GE | 1.0196 | 65.94 | 119.188 | 121.52 |
| Intel | 2.0020 | 69.87 | 87.375 | 174.92 |
| Lucent | 11.8624 | 700.29 | 67.438 | 799.97 |
| McDonald's* | 240.000 | 5,088.56 | 43.375 | 10,410.00 |
| Cash | | | | 121.83 |
| Total | | 12,831.00 | | 25,879.05 |

*Stock split 2-for-1 on March 8, 1999.

You can see how Shannon's stock picks have changed, in part to reflect her interests but in much greater part to her exercise of the ADDING strategy along with trend analysis. Lucent, a communications company that has grown by leaps and bounds, was Shannon's choice from the list of companies participating in the NAIC low-cost investment program. Using the ADDING strategy she chose America Online and Intel as well. AOL's growth rate had been great: 92.5 percent for the last five years, 87.1 percent this year, and 49.9 percent anticipated over the next five years. It was also ranked in the top half of its industry. This stock was completely her choice. So was Intel, but only after Pat hammered away at her for three years! Shannon resisted because she said she didn't understand the stock; as she matured, she was more comfortable owning companies whose products she hadn't actually seen or touched.

The huge jump in the value of Shannon's portfolio came primarily from her shares of EMC. The company had a terrific spurt starting in late 1998. EMC was now closing in on McDonald's in terms of value, which made Shannon nervous. She still kept insisting that she wanted McDonald's to be her "biggest" stock in her portfolio. She was very pleased when McDonald's announced a two-for-one split that suddenly doubled her holdings to 240 shares! But then EMC announced a two-for-one split effective June 1, 1999, so Shannon suddenly had 160 shares of EMC—overtaking McDonald's in terms of value in Shannon's portfolio. Shannon's reaction? "We need to buy more McDonald's."

## Putting the Tools to Work: Danielle's Bull Run

Danielle owned her first stock when she was three years old. Understandably, for years she was content to be part owner of "her" company and no other. For her eighth birthday Lynn bought her shares in American Century Giftrust, a mutual fund–with a jokey reminder on the statement that this investment was from Nana for Danielle's future Porsche. Hence, as of December 31, 1993, Danielle was this far on her way to owning a fancy sports car:

| Stock Name | No. of Shares | Original Cost ($) | Closing Price ($) | Value ($) |
|---|---|---|---|---|
| McDonald's | 52.5090 | 1,745.90 | 57.00 | 2,993.01 |
| American Century Giftrust | 17.9430 | 280.77 | 17.53 | 314.54 |
| Total | | 2,026.67 | | 3,307.55 |

By her eleventh year, however, Danielle had gotten serious as an investor. For one thing, she was a club officer in the Stock MarKids club, and that exposure increased her confidence tenfold. She told her grandmother that she'd like to buy Mattel because, as a collector of Barbies for years, she felt she knew the company's product history enough to predict its future. She had read its annual reports, from which she had learned all about the new Barbies and toys in addition to the company's acquisition of The Learning Company, which designed educational software. With $40 she acquired one share.

Over the course of the next year, Danielle's portfolio swelled considerably. Lynn had her two shares of GE transferred to Danielle's name after Danielle served as club monitor of it for a year. Danielle purchased seven shares of Microsoft, a company she loved because she had studied Bill Gates and wanted to grow up to be a software designer. Lynn gave her shares in The Limited as a Christmas gift because Danielle shopped there and was eager to support it. Stein Roe Young Investor Fund was another Christmas gift. And together, with proceeds from selling half of her McDonald's stock, Danielle and Lynn used the club's research and bought 50 shares of EMC.

As of December 31, 1997, her portfolio looked like this:

| Stock Name | No. of Shares | Original Share Price ($) | Total Cost Paid ($) | Current Share Price ($) | Current Market Value ($) |
|---|---|---|---|---|---|
| McDonald's | 54.7390 | (Avg) | 935.81 | 47.75 | 2,613.79 |
| American Century Giftrust | 27.8910 | (Avg) | 507.54 | 23.30 | 649.86 |
| Mattel | 2.3814 | (Avg) | 140.20 | 37.25 | 88.71 |
| GE | 7.4711 | (Avg) | 210.33 | 73.38 | 548.23 |
| The Limited | 4.3550 | 20.00 | 115.52 | 25.50 | 111.05 |
| EMC** | 50.0000 | 31.87 | 1,648.75 | 27.44 | 1,372.00 |
| Microsoft** | 7.0000 | 131.00 | 962.59 | 129.25 | 904.75 |
| Stein Roe Young Investor Fund | 4.4660 | 22.39 | 100.00 | 23.29 | 104.01 |
| Total | | | 4,620.74 | | 6,392.40 |

** Purchase with gains realized from sale of McDonald's
** Total proceeds of sale           $2,426.29
** Gains realized from sale of McDonald's    $1,508.23

Danielle's most ambitious purchase to date has been Yahoo. She bought it with her earnings from the Stock MarKids. Lynn was against it, but Danielle argued convincingly that there was no other company whose product she used more often with more satisfaction (she used the website every day). It was expensive, but Danielle anticipates a stock split soon. She is certain her reasoning is sound and her stock will generate returns down the road.

Looking at her portfolio of stocks (listed in order acquired) as of November 1, 1999, it takes only a glance at the bottom line to see the results: nearly $20,000!

| Stock Name | No. of Shares | Original Share Price ($) | Total Cost Paid ($) | Current Share Price ($) | Current Market Value ($) |
|---|---|---|---|---|---|
| McDonald's* | 110.3240 | (Avg) | 971.24 | 41.69 | 4,599.41 |
| American Century Giftrust | 27.8910 | (Avg) | 507.54 | 26.92 | 750.83 |
| Mattel | 3.4677 | (Avg) | 142.37 | 13.56 | 47.02 |
| GE | 11.2137 | (Avg) | 688.88 | 129.38 | 1,450.83 |
| The Limited | 6.0860 | (Avg) | 190.29 | 39.81 | 242.28 |
| EMC** | 100.0000 | 31.87 | 1,648.75 | 74.50 | 7,450.00 |
| Microsoft** | 28.0000 | 131.00 | 962.59 | 92.38 | 2,586.64 |
| Stein Roe YIF | 34.3120 | (Avg) | 865.80 | 15.01 | 515.02 |
| Yahoo | 10.0000 | 161.62 | 1,671.25 | 180.69 | 1,806.90 |
| Total | | | 7,648.71 | | 19,448.93 |

** Purchase with gains realized from sale of McDonald's
** Total proceeds of sale                    $2,426.29
** Gains realized from sale of McDonald's    $1,508.23
*Stock split

Since the bottom line almost never tells the whole story, Lynn has another way to illustrate Danielle's Bull Run. Using the financial records she has kept over the eleven years Danielle has been an investor, Lynn has constructed a graph. On this graph, "cost" is the amount of money that Lynn and Danielle actually invested in stocks. The "value" is what the stocks were worth each year. Following the chart from left to right, one can see just how Danielle's net worth moved from $95.49 in 1988 to $19,663 at the close of the

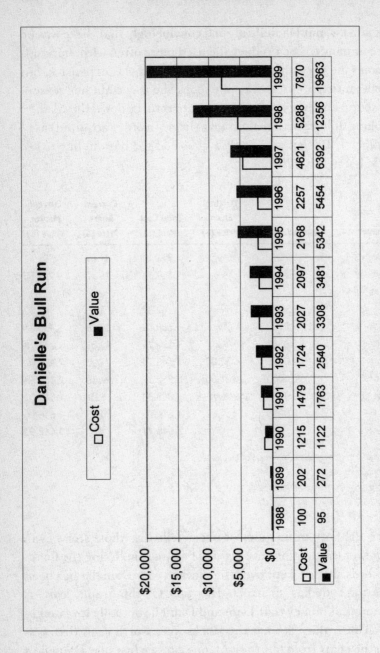

## Danielle's Bull Run

|  | 1988 | 1989 | 1990 | 1991 | 1992 | 1993 | 1994 | 1995 | 1996 | 1997 | 1998 | 1999 |
|---|---|---|---|---|---|---|---|---|---|---|---|---|
| ☐ Cost | 100 | 202 | 1215 | 1479 | 1724 | 2027 | 2097 | 2168 | 2257 | 4621 | 5288 | 7870 |
| ■ Value | 95 | 272 | 1122 | 1763 | 2540 | 3308 | 3481 | 5342 | 5454 | 6392 | 12356 | 19663 |

1997 and subsequent-year figures include purchase with gains realized from the sale of McDonald's. The total proceeds of the sale were $2,426 and the gains realized from the sale were $1,508.

century. Even though the family invested only $7,649 of its own money in the market, eleven years of small, steady contributions plus an amazing bull market have nearly tripled that investment.

Wow!

# GLOSSARY

You can use this simple glossary as yet another learning tool for you and your child. Try giving each other spot quizzes as you read through the book. Terms in italic refer to other entries in the glossary.

**American Stock Exchange (AMEX):** The second largest stock exchange in the United States after the *New York Stock Exchange (NYSE)*, listing the issues of around 800 companies. AMEX-listed stocks tend to be smaller than the companies listed on NYSE.

**analyst:** A person who works for a brokerage, insurance company, bank, mutual fund, or other investment business, who studies the market and produces reports that include buy and sell recommendations on particular stocks and industries.

**annual report:** The formal financial statements issued yearly by a public corporation. The annual report shows *assets*, liabilities, revenues, expenses, *earnings*, and *profits* during the year and other information of interest to share owners. Annual reports are available to the public on request.

**antitrust laws:** The federal laws that prevent businesses from monopolizing a market or restraining trade. Antitrust legislation opposes large trusts or combinations of business and capital and is used to promote and encourage competition and free trade.

**asset:** Something of value to an individual or company. Company assets may include factories, machinery, intellectual property such as copyrights, trademarks, patents, and accounts receivable, and all outstanding money due to the company.

**bankruptcy:** The condition in which corporations or individuals legally declare in federal court that they cannot meet their financial obligations. If you own stock in a company that goes bankrupt, then you lose all the money you paid for your shares. The Bankruptcy Reform Act includes Chapter 7, which deals with liquidation or converting assets to cash to pay debt, and Chapter 11, which deals with reorganization.

**bear market:** Describes the stock market when stock prices go down for a prolonged period of time. Opposite of *bull market*.

**bear stock:** A stock that keeps going down in price for a period of time.

**blue-chip stock:** Term used to describe the stock of a large, well-established company, named after the blue chips in a poker game, which have the highest value. AT&T, IBM, and General Electric are blue-chip stocks.

**bull market:** Describes the stock market when stock prices continue to rise for a prolonged period of time. Opposite of *bear market*.

**capital gain:** Amount an investor earns by selling a stock for more than the price paid for it.

**capitalization:** The total value of the securities issued by a corporation, calculated by multiplying the price of the stock by the number of shares outstanding. Microsoft, as of October 1999, has the highest capitalization of any stock on the *NASDAQ*.

**capital loss:** Amount an investor loses by selling a stock for less than the price paid for it.

**closing price:** The cost of a stock as listed at the end of a trading session.

**commission:** Fee paid a broker for buying or selling securities; it is usually a percentage based on the size or number of transactions.

**conglomerate:** A large company consisting of many diversified businesses under one corporate name. General Electric is a conglomerate with businesses that make lightbulbs and airplane engines.

**corporation:** A form of business that is registered with the state and considered an independent entity with legal rights and responsibilities separate from the individuals who own it.

**debt:** Something owed as money or goods; the less debt a company has, the better its stock value.

**discount broker:** An agent who charges lower fees than traditional agents for stock transactions but does not provide investment advice.

**diversification:** Investing in more than one kind of stock and more than one kind of industry to create a more stable *portfolio*.

**dividend:** A payment made to shareholders out of a company's earnings, usually quarterly. The amount is determined by the company's board of directors and may be given in cash or stock. Also known as *payout*.

**Dividend Reinvestment Program (DRIP):** A plan that allows investors to purchase more stocks regularly using the dividends received from the company.

**dollar cost averaging:** One method of computing the cost of stocks when they have been purchased at regular intervals over a period of time so that the cost per share overall is averaged.

**Dow Jones Industrial Average (DJIA):** This is an indicator that is considered to show generally the overall health of the U.S. economy by averaging the prices of thirty blue-chip stocks. Founded in 1884 by entrepreneur Charles H. Dow, whose financial newsletters evolved into *The Wall Street Journal,* the Dow 30 is made up of stocks selected by the editors of *The Wall Street Journal* and changes infrequently.

**earnings:** A corporation's revenues minus cost of sales, operating expenses, and taxes.

**earnings per share:** The profits allocated to each share outstanding; generally, as earnings per share increase, so does the stock price. To determine the earnings per share, a company divides its net income by the number of shares outstanding.

**face value:** The nominal dollar amount assigned to a *security* by the issuer. The face value is printed on the stock certificate, bond, or other financial document.

**52-week high:** The highest price of a stock during the previous twelve months.

**52-week low:** The lowest price of a stock during the previous twelve months.

**fractional share:** Less than one whole unit of stock. For example, .599 is a fractional share, or less than one whole share.

**income:** The amount earned by an individual through employment or investment, or a corporation's *earnings.*

**index:** A benchmark against which financial performance is measured, such as the *Standard and Poor's 500 Stock Index.*

**initial public offering (IPO):** The first public selling of shares in a company that previously was owned privately. Registration with the *SEC* is required by law, and it is during this process that the company's investment banker works with prospective investors to determine an appropriate selling price for the new shares. News that a company is "going public" often generates excitement among investors.

**institutional investor:** An organization with large amounts to invest, such as an investment company, insurance company, brokerage, *mutual fund,* bank, or endowment fund.

**market:** A public place where buyers and sellers make transactions; often refers to the stock market, where organized stock trades take place.

**market value:** The current resale value of a stock.

**mutual fund:** A company that invests the money of its *shareholders* in other corporations.

**National Association of Investors Corporation (NAIC):** A nonprofit umbrella organization that provides educational materials and programs to individual investors and investment clubs.

**National Association of Securities Dealers Automated Quotations (NASDAQ):** A stock exchange that trades orders through a computer network without a stock-trading floor, as on the *New York Stock Exchange.* Many high-technology companies are listed on the NASDAQ.

**net change:** The comparison of the stock closing price to the purchase price, or the comparison of portfolio value from one time period to another.

**net worth:** The *assets* minus the liabilities of an individual or a company.

**New York Stock Exchange (NYSE):** The largest stock exchange in the United States, located on Wall Street in New York City. This exchange lists the stocks of well-established companies on its trading floor.

**no-load:** With no sales charges. For example, a no-load *mutual fund* does not impose a sales charge. A no-load *stock* may be purchased via a direct-purchase program and without any additional charges or transactional fees.

**odd lot:** Stocks purchased or traded in a "lot" or amount ranging from 1 to 99 shares; it is the opposite of a *round lot.*

**optional cash payment:** A system that allows regular stock purchases through additional cash payments as opposed to dividend reinvestment alone, through which individuals can build ownership in a company over time.

**payout:** The taxable payments made to *shareholders* out of *earnings;* also called *dividend.* May also refer to the percent of a company's earnings paid as dividends.

**percent return:** The money gained on the investment or stock expressed as a percentage. It is calculated by dividing the money gained by the amount of money invested and multiplying by 100.

**portfolio:** All the securities held by an individual investor, institutional investor, or investment club; a collection of investments.

**price-earnings (P/E) ratio:** A way to compare stocks selling at various price levels. The P/E ratio is the price of a share of stock divided by earnings per share for a twelve-month period. For example, a stock selling for $50 a share with earnings of $5 a share is said to be selling at a price-earnings ratio of 10. Generally, investors think that a stock with a lower price-earnings ratio will increase more in price or value than others.

**profit:** The amount of earnings after expenses are deducted; the amount made on a transaction.

**proxy:** An absentee ballot for shareholders to vote on issues within a company.

**quarter:** A three-month period of time used to measure financial results. Companies usually announce these results four times a year.

**revenue:** Income from all sources.

**reverse stock split:** The reduction of the number of shares outstanding by increasing the dollar value of the shares. A one-for-four reverse split means the shareholder will receive one share for every four held and the value of each share is increased four times. Companies sometimes do this to make the stock more valuable when there are a lot of outstanding shares, when the corporate philosophy changes, or when the company is bought out or . merged with another company.

**round lot:** Stocks purchased or traded in a unit or "lot" of 100 shares; the basic trading unit of stock; opposite of an *odd lot*.

**sales:** The amount of business a company transacts. Generally, the more sales a company has, the more its profit and the more its stock price increases.

**Securities and Exchange Commission (SEC):** The federal regulatory agency that oversees the securities markets and administers the securities laws.

**shareholder:** A part owner who owns stock or shares in a company.

**shares outstanding:** The number of shares that a company has available for purchase or investment.

**Standard & Poor's 500 Stock Index (S&P 500):** A capitalization-weighted index of 500 major U.S. companies used to measure the stock performance of the entire domestic stock market. Standard & Poor's specializes in stock indexes; the S&P 500 is the second most closely followed and widely quoted of the major indexes, next to the *Dow Jones Industrial Average*.

**stock:** Represents an ownership position in a company and a claim on a proportionate share of a company's *earnings* or *assets*.

**stock appreciation:** The amount the price of a stock has gone up since the stock was first purchased.

**stockbroker:** A person who buys and sells securities and stock for a fee.

**stock certificate:** A paper document issued by a company that shows the number of shares owned by the purchaser.

**stock split:** A type of dividend where the company increases the number of shares of stock but not the value per share. A two-for-one stock split results in twice as many shares, but the price of each share is cut in half. A company sometimes divides or splits shares to reduce the price needed for the formation of round lots or to make the price more attractive.

**stock symbol:** A system of letter abbreviations used to identify a stock in exchange listings in financial publications or on a *ticker.*

**ticker:** A scrolling, computerized display of current stock prices and trading volume.

**trend analysis:** A comparative analysis or examination of a company's financial ratios over time.

**valuation:** The process of determining the total value of stock or other assets.

**value:** The price of a stock multiplied by the number of shares owned.

**volatility:** The rate at which a stock price moves up and down. It may also be applied to an entire exchange or the stock market in general.

**volume:** The number of shares a stock traded in a given period. It may also refer to the number of shares traded in a given period on an entire exchange.

**yield:** The annual dividend per share divided by the price of the stock.

**T**hese are activities your child should be able to complete on his or her own anytime.

# Word Game

See how many words of two or more letters you can find in the word below. There are at least 60.

## INVESTMENT

**Possible answers:**

em, en, even, in, inn, inset, intent, invent, invest, item, it, its, me, meet, men, met, mete, mien, mine, mint, mist, mite, mitt, nest, net, nine, nit, see, seem, seen, seine, semi, sene, sent, set, seven, sin, sit, site, smite, stem, stint, tee, teem, teen, ten, tenet, tent, test, tie, time, tin, tine, tint, tit, vein, vent, vest, vim, vine, vise.

# Beyond the Broker

*Answers are up, down, across, diagonal, and backward.*

| M | S | S | U | A | P | T | U | E | W | E |
|---|---|---|---|---|---|---|---|---|---|---|
| O | N | A | T | W | O | D | U | A | A | S |
| K | S | B | M | O | N | E | Y | R | L | R |
| R | A | V | I | R | A | Z | I | N | L | O |
| G | I | Q | O | T | E | K | E | E | S | O |
| N | B | E | H | H | C | F | L | P | T | P |
| I | A | A | N | Y | S | E | D | S | R | D |
| T | D | I | R | S | D | I | K | N | E | N |
| S | C | O | C | R | N | C | M | A | E | A |
| E | A | R | K | B | O | N | D | S | T | D |
| V | E | N | P | T | A | N | K | D | J | R |
| N | C | O | S | E | L | I | S | A | O | A |
| I | N | T | E | R | N | E | T | Q | U | D |
| G | A | I | N | O | K | O | J | A | R | N |
| R | N | A | T | N | C | L | U | B | N | A |
| K | I | P | L | I | N | G | E | R | A | T |
| S | F | U | M | R | S | I | E | P | L | S |

NASDAQ  INTERNET  KIDS  BONDS
WORTH  YIELD  BARRONS  FINANCE
GAIN  CLUB  NAIC  STOCKS
MONEY  EARN  NYSE  WALL STREET JOURNAL
INVESTING

*Answer key on page 264.*

# Find the CEO

*Answers are down, across, diagonal, and backward.*

| S | C | H | A | R | L | E | S | S | C | H | W | A | B | W | E |
|---|---|---|---|---|---|---|---|---|---|---|---|---|---|---|---|
| M | S | X | R | E | N | S | I | E | L | E | A | H | C | I | M |
| O | O | W | E | R | T | D | S | C | X | V | B | N | J | L | F |
| P | R | I | C | H | A | R | D | G | R | A | S | S | O | L | T |
| Q | N | S | R | E | B | M | A | H | C | N | H | O | J | I | P |
| R | E | D | E | F | R | G | T | C | D | U | N | R | A | A | O |
| V | R | S | K | L | N | X | V | B | T | R | E | E | C | M | I |
| E | S | U | L | I | A | E | F | D | B | N | L | L | K | G | D |
| T | T | E | F | F | U | B | N | E | R | R | A | W | W | A | A |
| M | N | A | E | R | S | U | T | U | N | M | L | O | E | T | E |
| O | E | E | S | D | F | G | T | Y | U | I | O | P | L | E | G |
| A | R | W | E | E | R | D | C | V | B | E | A | O | C | S | O |
| B | I | J | G | R | E | E | N | B | E | R | G | X | H | X | W |
| C | A | V | E | T | T | I | O | P | B | S | T | R | N | M | E |
| R | C | A | R | L | E | T | O | N | F | I | O | R | I | N | A |
| E | E | N | O | T | S | D | E | R | R | E | N | M | U | S | X |

WARREN BUFFETT (Berkshire Hathaway)
MICHAEL EISNER (Disney)
CARLETON FIORINA (Hewlett-Packard)
WILLIAM GATES (Microsoft)
RICHARD GRASSO (NYSE)
J. GREENBERG (McDonald's)
SUMNER REDSTONE (Viacom)
CHARLES SCHWAB (Charles Schwab)
TED TURNER (Time Warner)
JACK WELCH (General Electric)

*Answer key on page 265.*

## Answer:

| | | | | | | | | E | W | |
|---|---|---|---|---|---|---|---|---|---|---|
| | | | W | | | | | A | A | S |
| | | M | O | N | E | Y | | R | L | R |
| | | | R | | | I | | N | L | O |
| G | | | T | | | E | | | S | O |
| N | B | | H | | | L | | | T | P |
| I | A | A | N | Y | S | E | D | S | R | D |
| T | | I | R | S | D | I | K | N | E | N |
| S | | | C | R | | C | | A | E | A |
| E | | | B | O | N | D | S | | T | D |
| V | E | | T | | N | | | D | J | R |
| N | C | | S | | | | S | A | O | A |
| I | N | T | E | R | N | E | T | Q | U | D |
| G | A | I | N | | | | | | R | N |
| | N | | | | C | L | U | B | N | A |
| | I | | | | | | | | A | T |
| | F | | | | | | | | L | S |

**Answer:**

| | | | | | | | | | | | |
|---|---|---|---|---|---|---|---|---|---|---|---|
| | C | H | A | R | L | E | S | S | C | H | W | A | B | W | |
| | | | R | E | N | S | I | E | L | E | A | H | C | I | M |
| | | | | | | | | | | | | | | L | |
| | R | I | C | H | A | R | D | G | R | A | S | S | O | L | |
| | | | | | | | | | | | J | | I | |
| | | | | | | | | R | | A | | A | |
| | | | | | | E | | | C | | M | |
| | | | | | | N | | | K | | G | |
| | T | E | F | F | U | B | N | E | R | R | A | W | W | A | |
| | | | | | | U | | | | | W | | E | | T | |
| | | | | | T | | | | | L | | E | |
| | | | | D | | | | | C | | S | |
| | | J | G | R | E | E | N | B | E | R | G | | H | |
| | | T | | | | | | | | | |
| | C | A | R | L | E | T | O | N | F | I | O | R | I | N | A |
| | E | N | O | T | S | D | E | R | R | E | N | M | U | S | |

# Ask Stock MarKids

Read the following letters to Stock MarKids and then write your answer to each question. Compare your answers to the ones from Stock MarKids and see if you agree with the advice. If not, write a letter to Stock MarKids and tell them why you disagree with their advice.

## Letter #1

*Dear Stock MarKids:*
My name is Joe, and I just inherited $5,000 from my uncle John. I want to start buying stock, and my parents think it is a good idea. My mom wants me to set up an account with her full-service broker, but I want to go online and use E*trade. My parents think it is too risky, but I know what I am doing and think I can make a lot of money. Oh, by the way, I am sixteen years old.
Desperate to Invest in Delaware

*Dear Desperate in Delaware:*
Your mom may not realize that an online account is just a variation of a discount broker and just another way to buy and sell shares for a lower commission. If your mother still thinks online trading is risky, then there are other options for investing your money. Have you considered these:

1. You can trade stocks at a discount at a discount brokerage firm.
2. If you join NAIC, you can participate in their low-cost investment programs.

Oh, make sure your mom registers stocks in your name using the Uniform Gifts to Minors Act form of registration, as required in

Delaware. And remember that investing is a long-term commitment and that most people don't make money overnight. It is better to choose good companies and stick with them.

Good luck.

Stock MarKids

## Letter #2

*Dear Stock MarKids:*

I am a fifty-eight-year-old-grandmother, and I want to start teaching my thirteen- and fifteen-year-old granddaughters how to invest in stocks. I don't have a lot of money, but I can spare about $200 a month for the girls. I have been in a stock club for several years and am a member of NAIC, so I know that I can use their low-cost programs. But I don't want to just put money in an account for the girls because I really want my granddaughters to learn about investing. What should I do?

Conscientious About Investing in Connecticut

*Dear Conscientious in Connecticut:*

First, let me say that we applaud your efforts to get your granddaughters interested in investing, and think this will create a lasting bond between the generations. It sounds as if you have some great ideas already, but have you considered these:

1. Let your granddaughters pick a company that offers a direct-purchase program.
2. Take your granddaughters to a discount brokerage firm so they can make trades themselves.

As we are sure you are aware, you need to register stocks for your granddaughters in custodial accounts. Since you live in Connecticut, you need to use the Uniform Gifts to Minors Act.

Happy investing.

Stock MarKids

## Letter #3

*Dear Stock MarKids:*

How can I buy stocks? I am fifteen years old and have saved about $1,000 from my baby-sitting job. My mom opened a savings account for me at her credit union at work. I baby-sit for two little girls after school every day and get paid on Fridays. I give half of the money to my mom so she can put it in my savings account the following Monday. I'm making only 3 percent interest in the account and have heard that I can make a lot more in stocks, but I need help. My parents don't think I'm old enough to invest, but I think I am.

*Interested in Investing in Idaho*

*Dear Interested in Investing:*

You sound like a very levelheaded girl who should be commended for having such good work and savings ethics. You sound as though you are ready to start investing, and we hope your mom will work with you to do one of the following:

1. Open an account with a discount broker
2. Open an account with an online broker
3. Establish an account with a company that offers a direct-purchase program

Tell your mom that the accounts should be established with her as the custodian for you, using the Uniform Transfer to Minors Act form of registration.

Have fun.

*Stock MarKids*

## Letter #4

*Dear Stock MarKids:*

I want you to resolve a dispute with my dad. He likes to tell me about the stocks he is buying and selling, and the other day he said that he put in an order to buy 100 shares of Dell at 35. He told the broker to make a "good-until-canceled order," which means it could take him months to buy Dell because it is currently trading above 40, plus it recently received an analyst upgrade. I told my dad that I think he should buy it "at market," but he says he likes to buy stocks when they are on sale.

Wondering About Stocks in Wyoming

*Dear Wondering in Wyoming:*

We think you are both correct. Your dad is correct to try to buy Dell at the cheapest price possible even if it takes a while. We assume he has done some research and thinks the price will dip to his purchase price sometime in the future, and he's willing to wait until then. On the other hand, you are correct that since Dell is already trading 5 points above your Dad's purchase price, it may be a long time before the stock dips down to 35. Also, with an analyst upgrade, the price of the stock is more likely to increase than decrease. Investing is a matter of personal taste, and your letter shows two different but valid viewpoints. We are often reminded that there are no right or wrong answers in investing—just different viewpoints.

By the way, it sounds as though you have learned a lot about stocks from listening to your dad, and we hope he will open an account for you using one of the following methods:

1. Full-service broker
2. Discount broker
3. Online broker
4. Low-cost purchase program, such as the type currently offered by NAIC
5. Direct-purchase program

When your dad opens an account for you, remind him that Wyoming requires custodial accounts to be registered in the Uniform Transfer to Minors Act form of registration.

Many happy returns.

Stock MarKids

# CEO Trading Cards

Photocopy this page and create your own trading cards by filling in the information for each of your favorite investment leaders.

**NAME**

**TITLE**

**COMPANY:**

**$$$:**

**BIRTH DATE AND LOCATION:**

**EDUCATION:**

**HOME:**

**TIDBIT:**

**FIRST JOB:**

**QUOTE:**

# Wordfind

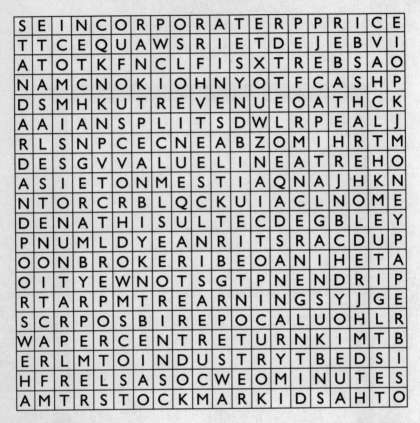

| S | E | I | N | C | O | R | P | O | R | A | T | E | R | P | P | R | I | C | E |
|---|---|---|---|---|---|---|---|---|---|---|---|---|---|---|---|---|---|---|---|
| T | T | C | E | Q | U | A | W | S | R | I | E | T | D | E | J | E | B | V | I |
| A | T | O | T | K | F | N | C | L | F | I | S | X | T | R | E | B | S | A | O |
| N | A | M | C | N | O | K | I | O | H | N | Y | O | T | F | C | A | S | H | P |
| D | S | M | H | K | U | T | R | E | V | E | N | U | E | O | A | T | H | C | K |
| A | A | I | A | N | S | P | L | I | T | S | D | W | L | R | P | E | A | L | J |
| R | L | S | N | P | C | E | C | N | E | A | B | Z | O | M | I | H | R | T | M |
| D | E | S | G | V | V | A | L | U | E | L | I | N | E | A | T | R | E | H | O |
| A | S | I | E | T | O | N | M | E | S | T | I | A | Q | N | A | J | H | K | N |
| N | T | O | R | C | R | B | L | Q | C | K | U | I | A | C | L | N | O | M | E |
| D | E | N | A | T | H | I | S | U | L | T | E | C | D | E | G | B | L | E | Y |
| P | N | U | M | L | D | Y | E | A | N | R | I | T | S | R | A | C | D | U | P |
| O | O | N | B | R | O | K | E | R | I | B | E | O | A | N | I | H | E | T | A |
| O | I | T | Y | E | W | N | O | T | S | G | T | P | N | E | N | D | R | I | P |
| R | T | A | R | P | M | T | R | E | A | R | N | I | N | G | S | Y | J | G | E |
| S | C | R | P | O | S | B | I | R | E | P | O | C | A | L | U | O | H | L | R |
| W | A | P | E | R | C | E | N | T | R | E | T | U | R | N | K | I | M | T | B |
| E | R | L | M | T | O | I | N | D | U | S | T | R | Y | T | B | E | D | S | I |
| H | F | R | E | L | S | A | S | O | C | W | E | O | M | I | N | U | T | E | S |
| A | M | T | R | S | T | O | C | K | M | A | R | K | I | D | S | A | H | T | O |

| | | |
|---|---|---|
| STANDARD AND POOR'S | RANK | QUARTER |
| COMMISSION | REBATE | EARNINGS |
| FRACTION | CASH | NASDAQ |
| PERCENT RETURN | SPLIT | DRIP |
| VALUE LINE | PERFORMANCE | DOW |
| INCORPORATE | PROFIT | DEBT |
| STOCK SELECTION GUIDE | REVENUE | PRICE |
| MINUTES | CAPITAL GAINS | NAIC |
| MONEY PAPER | SHAREHOLDER | INDUSTRY |
| STOCK APPRECIATION | BROKER | SEC |
| NET CHANGE | SALES | NYSE |

*Answer key on page 274.*

# Matching Columns

Match the words in the left column with their definitions in the right column.

Bull market
Going public
Bear market
Hot stock
Portfolio
Dow Jones Industrial
   Average
Standard & Poor's
Full-service broker
NYSE
Discount broker

Place in New York City where stocks are traded

When the market is doing poorly

Most expensive trading service in which a broker advises you on your investments

An index of 30 representative companies

A personal collection of stocks or mutual funds

When a company starts to sell shares of stock

When the market is doing well

An index of 500 stocks

A stock whose price skyrockets on its market debut

A brokerage service in which advice is not expected

**Answer:**

| S |   | I | N | C | O | R | P | O | R | A | T | E |   | P | P | R | I | C | E |
|---|---|---|---|---|---|---|---|---|---|---|---|---|---|---|---|---|---|---|---|
| T | T | C | E |   | A |   |   |   | I | E |   | E |   | E |   |   |   |   |   |
| A |   | O | T |   | N |   |   | F |   | S |   |   | R |   | B |   |   |   |   |
| N |   | M | C |   | K |   | O |   | Y |   |   | F | C | A | S | H |   |   |   |
| D | S | M | H | K |   | R | E | V | E | N | U | E | O | A | T | H |   |   |   |
| A | A | I | A |   | S | P | L | I | T |   |   | R | P | E | A |   |   |   |   |
| R | L | S | N |   | E |   |   |   |   | M | I |   | R |   | M |   |   |   |   |
| D | E | S | G |   | V | A | L | U | E | L | I | N | E | A | T |   | E |   | O |
| A | S | I | E |   |   | E |   |   | A | Q | N | A |   | H |   | N |   |   |   |
| N |   | O |   | C |   | Q | C |   | I | A | C | L |   | O |   | E |   |   |   |
| D |   | N |   |   | U |   | T |   | C | D | E | G |   | L |   | Y |   |   |   |
| P | N |   |   | D |   | A |   | I |   | S |   | A |   | D |   | P |   |   |   |
| O | O |   | B | R | O | K | E | R |   | O | A |   | I |   | E |   | A |   |   |
| O | I |   |   | W |   | T |   |   | N |   | N | D | R | I | P |   |   |   |   |
| R | T |   |   |   | E | A | R | N | I | N | G | S |   |   |   | E | R |   |   |
| S | C |   |   |   | R |   |   |   |   |   | U |   |   |   |   | R |   |   |   |
|   | A | P | E | R | C | E | N | T | R | E | T | U | R | N |   | I |   |   |   |
|   | R | L |   |   | I | N | D | U | S | T | R | Y | T | B | E | D |   |   |   |
|   | F |   | E |   |   |   |   |   |   | M | I | N | U | T | E | S |   |   |   |
|   |   |   | S | T | O | C | K | M | A | R | K | I | D | S |   |   |   |   |   |

# Birthday Check

Danielle has $500 she received as a birthday gift from Uncle Raymond and Aunt Ruth. What will Danielle have after investing in stock? Cross out the letters M, G, Q, and P to find the answer.

```
M  A  G  Q  M  P  G  S
Q  P  G  T  Q  O  M  P
C  Q  G  K  M  A  G  G
C  G  C  O  U  G  N  Q
T  G  G  Q  M  N  D  Q
M  C  G  E  G  R  M  P
T  I  G  F  I  M  P  C
A  M  G  T  P  Q  E  M
```

# Quadruple Cross

What is a stock called when it is first traded? Cross out the letters Q Y D Z for the answer.

```
Y  Z  Q  I  D  N  Z  I  D  D  Z
T  Q  I  Y  A  Q  D  D  D  Z  Y
L  Z  P  U  D  Z  D  B  Z  D  L
Q  Z  Z  U  Y  Z  D  C  Z  O  D
F  Z  D  Q  F  Y  E  R  Q  Q  Y
D  I  D  Q  N  Y  Z  Q  Y  Q  G
```

# Crossword Puzzle

*(Note: there is one non-letter symbol used in this puzzle.)*

**ACROSS:**
1. A Dow company that sells hamburgers
6. Symbol for Marshall Industries
9. Creator of the Dow Jones Industrial Average
11. Symbol for Teekay Shipping Corporation
12. Where the trading all takes place
13. Symbol for the National Westminster Bank
14. What happens when the market does very well
15. Symbol for Aetna, Inc.
17. Symbol for Harley-Davidson, Inc.
18. Symbol for Berry Petroleum Company
19. Symbol for Home Depot, Inc.
21. Symbol for Green Point Financial Corp.
24. Question
26. Symbol for Aquapenn Spring Water Company
28. What you do with your money in the stock market
32. A technology and TV union
35. Every trade has a _____
36. A Dow company that makes movies such as *The Little Mermaid*
38. When you owe money you are in _____
39. Symbol for the ING Group
40. Symbol for the Sherwin-Williams Company
42. The term for the market that goes up and up
45. A word for watching your stocks go up or down
46. Symbol for SunAmerica, Inc.
47. Term given to high-quality stocks such as the Dow stocks
48. The money you have earned
49. A Dow company that makes soft drinks

**DOWN:**
1. What you hope to do with money
2. Symbol for the Dana Corporation
3. A major marketplace known for its high number of technology stocks
4. Symbol for Sterling Software, Inc.
5. What investing could become for you, like bike riding or reading
7. A company eliminated from and then readded to the Dow in 1979
8. An index of 500 stocks that is the most widely used after the Dow
10. Investing money won't seem like _____
16. A national holiday and a day when the New York Stock Exchange is closed
20. Symbol for Dow Jones and Company
21. Initials of a Dow company that makes lightbulbs
22. Amount you pay for a stock
23. An event that causes a change in the number of shares you own
25. Symbol for Universal Communications, Inc.
27. A marketplace where you can use the Internet website for a live look at the trading floor
29. Symbol for Executive Risk
30. Symbol for Smith International, Inc.
31. Symbol for Tyson Foods Corporation
33. A shorthand way to locate a stock
34. Symbol for Budget Group, Inc.
37. Symbol for the New York Times Company
41. Symbol for Western Resources
43. You can reinvest the money that you _____
44. Something a broker gives clients to help them invest
45. Symbol for MBIA Insurance Corporation

Answer:

| | M | C | D | O | N | A | L | D | S | | H | | M | I |
|---|---|---|---|---|---|---|---|---|---|---|---|---|---|---|
| S | A | | C | H | A | R | L | E | S | D | O | W | | B |
| T | K | | N | Y | S | E | | N | W | | B | O | O | M |
| A | E | T | | H | D | I | | | | | B | R | Y | |
| N | | H | D | | A | | G | P | T | | Y | K | | |
| D | S | A | J | | Q | U | E | R | Y | | | | | |
| A | P | N | | A | | V | | I | N | V | E | S | T | |
| R | L | K | | M | S | N | B | C | | | R | I | S | K |
| D | I | S | N | E | Y | | D | E | B | T | | I | N | G |
| & | T | G | Y | X | M | | | S | H | W | | | | |
| P | S | I | T | | B | U | L | L | M | A | R | K | E | T |
| O | T | V | | M | O | N | I | T | O | R | | S | A | I |
| O | O | I | | B | L | U | E | C | H | I | P | | R | P |
| R | C | N | | I | | N | E | T | G | A | I | N | | |
| S | K | G | | C | O | C | A | C | O | L | A | | | |

# Stock Market Scramble

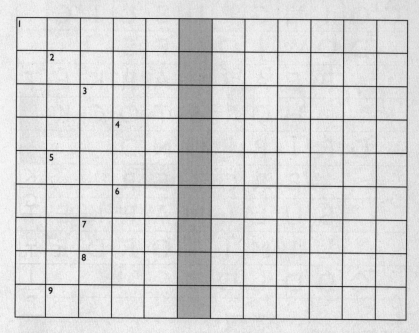

Unscramble the following words. Write the letters in the corresponding spaces, leaving no spaces between words.

1. GGNIO CPLIBU = _____ _____
2. ODW EOSNJ = _____ _____
3. AERB KAMTER = _____ _____
4. OHT KTCOS = _____ _____
5. RDPI DNUF = _____ _____
6. KRBEOR = _____
7. ULBL RTMKEA = _____ _____
8. MITIL RORDE = _____ _____
9. DOD TLO = _____ _____

The shaded vertical spaces should spell out a word with the following definition: a collection of stocks that is owned by an investor. Start writing answers in the spaces here.

___ ___ ___ ___ ___ ___ ___ ___ ___

## Answer:

| | | | | | | | | | |
|---|---|---|---|---|---|---|---|---|---|
| ¹G | O | I | N | G | P | U | B | L | I | C |
| | ²D | O | W | J | O | N | E | S | |
| | | ³B | E | A | R | M | A | R | K | E | T |
| | | | ⁴H | O | T | S | T | O | C | K |
| | ⁵D | R | I | P | F | U | N | D | |
| | | ⁶B | R | O | K | E | R | | |
| | ⁷B | U | L | L | M | A | R | K | E | T |
| | ⁸L | I | M | I | T | O | R | D | E | R |
| ⁹O | D | D | L | O | T | | | | |

Unscramble the following words. Write the letters in the corresponding spaces, leaving no spaces between words.

1. GGNIO CPLIBU = <u>GOING</u> <u>PUBLIC</u>
2. ODW EOSNJ = <u>DOW</u> <u>JONES</u>
3. AERB KAMTER = <u>BEAR</u> <u>MARKET</u>
4. OHT KCTOS = <u>HOT</u> <u>STOCK</u>
5. RDPI DNUF = <u>DRIP</u> <u>FUND</u>
6. KRBEOR = <u>BROKER</u>
7. ULBL RTMKEA = <u>BULL</u> <u>MARKET</u>
8. MITIL RORDE = <u>LIMIT</u> <u>ORDER</u>
9. DOD TLO = <u>ODD</u> <u>LOT</u>

The shaded, vertical spaces should spell out a word with the following definition: a collection of stocks that is owned by an investor.

<u>P</u>   <u>O</u>   <u>R</u>   <u>T</u>   <u>F</u>   <u>O</u>   <u>L</u>   <u>I</u>   <u>O</u>

# Wordfind

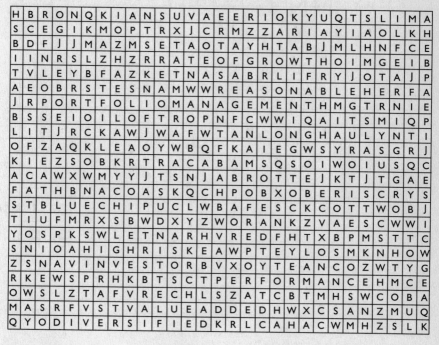

| | | | | | | | | | | | | | | | | | | | | | | |
|---|---|---|---|---|---|---|---|---|---|---|---|---|---|---|---|---|---|---|---|---|---|---|
| H | B | R | O | N | Q | K | I | A | N | S | U | V | A | E | E | R | I | O | K | Y | U | Q | T | S | L | I | M | A |
| S | C | E | G | I | K | M | O | P | T | R | X | J | C | R | M | Z | Z | A | R | I | A | Y | I | A | O | L | K | H |
| B | D | F | J | J | M | A | Z | M | S | E | T | A | O | T | A | Y | H | T | A | B | J | M | L | H | N | F | C | E |
| I | I | N | R | S | L | Z | H | Z | R | R | A | T | E | O | F | G | R | O | W | T | H | O | I | M | G | E | I | B |
| T | V | L | E | Y | B | F | A | Z | K | E | T | N | A | S | A | B | R | L | I | F | R | Y | J | O | T | A | J | P |
| A | E | O | B | R | S | T | E | S | N | A | M | W | W | R | E | A | S | O | N | A | B | L | E | H | E | R | F | A |
| J | R | P | O | R | T | F | O | L | I | O | M | A | N | A | G | E | M | E | N | T | H | M | G | T | R | N | I | E |
| B | S | S | E | I | O | I | L | O | F | T | R | O | P | N | F | C | W | W | I | Q | A | I | T | S | M | I | Q | P |
| L | I | T | J | R | C | K | A | W | J | W | A | F | W | T | A | N | L | O | N | G | H | A | U | L | Y | N | T | I |
| O | F | Z | A | Q | K | L | E | A | O | Y | W | B | Q | F | K | A | I | E | G | W | S | Y | R | A | S | G | R | J |
| K | I | E | Z | S | O | B | K | R | T | R | A | C | A | B | A | M | S | Q | S | O | I | W | O | I | U | S | Q | C |
| A | C | A | W | X | W | M | Y | Y | J | T | S | N | J | A | B | R | O | T | T | E | J | K | T | J | T | G | A | E |
| F | A | T | H | B | N | A | C | O | A | S | K | Q | C | H | P | O | B | X | O | B | E | R | I | S | C | R | Y | S |
| S | T | B | L | U | E | C | H | I | P | U | C | L | W | B | A | F | E | S | C | K | C | O | T | T | W | O | B | J |
| T | I | U | F | M | R | X | S | B | W | D | X | Y | Z | W | O | R | A | N | K | Z | V | A | E | S | C | W | W | I |
| Y | O | S | P | K | S | W | L | E | T | N | A | R | H | V | R | E | D | F | H | T | X | B | P | M | S | T | T | C |
| S | N | I | O | A | H | I | G | H | R | I | S | K | E | A | W | P | T | E | Y | L | O | S | M | K | N | H | O | W |
| Z | S | N | A | V | I | N | V | E | S | T | O | R | B | V | X | O | Y | T | E | A | N | C | O | Z | W | T | Y | G |
| R | K | E | W | S | P | R | H | K | B | T | S | C | T | P | E | R | F | O | R | M | A | N | C | E | H | M | C | E |
| O | W | S | L | Z | T | A | F | V | R | E | C | H | L | S | Z | A | T | C | B | T | M | H | S | W | C | O | B | A |
| M | A | S | R | F | V | S | T | V | A | L | U | E | A | D | D | E | D | H | W | X | C | S | A | N | Z | M | U | Q |
| Q | Y | O | D | I | V | E | R | S | I | F | I | E | D | K | R | L | C | A | H | A | C | W | M | H | Z | S | L | K |

| | | |
|---|---|---|
| BLUE CHIP | HIGH TECH | PORTFOLIO MANAGEMENT |
| BROKER | INDUSTRY | RANK |
| BUSINESS | INVESTOR | RATE OF GROWTH |
| COMPETITOR | LONG HAUL | REASONABLE |
| DIVERSIFICATION | LONG TERM | STOCK OWNERSHIP |
| DIVERSIFIED | OVERSEAS | TRENDS |
| EARNINGS GROWTH | PERFORMANCE | VALUE ADDED |
| HIGH RISK | PORTFOLIO | WINNING STOCK |

## Answer:

```
                                            L
S                                           O         H
  D                                         N     C
  I N           R A T E O F G R O W T H     G E
  V   E                             I       T A
  E   B R S             R E A S O N A B L E H E R     G R
  R P O R T F O L I O M A N A G E M E N T       G   R
  S     O I L O F T R O P     C       I     I     M
  I     C K               N L O N G H A U L       N
  F     K   E     Y       A     G       R         G
  I     O     R     R     M     S       O         S
  C     W     T     R     T     T       G
  A     N     S     O     O       I       R
  T B L U E C H I P U     F     C       T         O
  I   U     D       O R A N K   E               W
  O S   R     N       V   E     P               T
  N I   H I G H R I S K E     P   M           H
    N   I N V E S T O R       O
    E   P       S     P E R F O R M A N C E
    S       E
    S       V A L U E A D D E D
    D I V E R S I F I E D
```

# INDEX